BLAKE MORRISON

The Movement

ENGLISH POETRY AND FICTION
OF THE 1950s

Methuen
LONDON and NEW YORK

First published in 1980 by
Oxford University Press

t published as a University Paperback in 1986 by
Methuen & Co. Ltd
11 New Fetter Lane, London EC4P 4EE

Published in the USA by
Methuen & Co.
in association with Methuen, Inc.
29 West 35th Street, New York NY 10001

© 1980 Blake Morrison

Printed in Great Britain at the
University Press, Cambridge

British Library Cataloguing in Publication Data
Morrison, Blake
The Movement: English poetry and fiction of
the 1950s.
1. English fiction—20th century—History
and criticism
I. Title
821'.914'09   PR 601
ISBN 0-426-30250-5

Library of Congress Cataloging in Publication Data
Morrison, Blake.
The movement: English poetry and fiction of the
1950s.
(University paperback; 917)
Bibliography: p.
Includes index.
1. English—poetry—20th century—History and
criticism—Addresses, essays, lectures. 2. English
fiction—20th century—History and criticism—
Addresses, essays, lectures. I. Title.
PR610.M67   1986   821'.914'09   85-29798
ISBN 0-416-30250-5

Contents

Preface

The work of the writers under consideration here is, by common consent, an important feature of post-war literary history. We would expect an account of English poetry in the 1950s to discuss the work of Philip Larkin, Donald Davie and Thom Gunn; we would expect an account of the fiction to discuss Kingsley Amis and John Wain. What is less well known is the extent of the collaboration and interaction between these writers. This book is an attempt to examine them as a group: I have tried to identify certain beliefs, attitudes, tones, forms and techniques which are common to their work.

This is not, however, a comprehensive history of the English (let alone British) poetry and fiction of the 1950s. Any account that omits, or makes only passing reference to writers such as Ted Hughes, Geoffrey Hill, Jon Silkin, R.S. Thomas, William Golding, Iris Murdoch, Muriel Spark and Angus Wilson (to mention but a few) is clearly not functioning as a general survey of the decade. The ground I have covered is therefore limited; but it is, as I hope to show, richly interesting ground.

A number of Movement writers have been good enough to answer queries: I would like to thank Donald Davie, John Holloway, Elizabeth Jennings, John Wain and, in particular, Robert Conquest for their help. Others who have kindly helped provide information of various sorts are B. Bergonzi, B.C. Bloomfield, Alan Brownjohn, G.S. Fraser, Allan Rodway, J.D. Scott, David Timms and Charles Tomlinson. I am grateful, also, to the staff of the British Museum; of the George Arents Research Library, Syracuse, for allowing me to consult letters written by the Movement poets to the American critic William Van O'Connor; of the BBC Script library at The Langham, where I looked at transcripts of John Wain's radio series *First Reading*; and of the Senate House Library Periodicals Section, London, where I spent many hours reading through copies of the *Spectator, New Statesman, Times Literary Supplement, Listener, Encounter* and several other magazines of the 1950s and 1960s. My chief debt, though, is to Karl Miller, who supervised this study when it was in Ph.D. thesis form, and whose encouragement, informed criticism and editorial skill were of incalculable help.

Blake Morrison
London, 1979

Acknowledgements

The author gratefully acknowledges permission to reproduce the following copyright material:

Kingsley Amis: Extracts from 'Beowulf', 'A Bookshop Idyll', 'Against Romanticism', 'Here Is Where', 'Ode to the East-North-East-by-East Wind', 'On Staying Still', 'Sonnet from Orpheus', 'After Goliath' and 'Nothing to Fear' from *Collected Poems*. Reprinted by permission of the Hutchinson Publishing Group Ltd.

Donald Davie: Extracts from 'Pushkin: A Didactic Poem', 'England', 'Via Portello', 'Creon's Mouse', 'Eight Years After', 'Remembering the Thirties', 'Rejoinder to a Critic', 'Revulsion', 'Hypochondriac Logic', 'Among Artisans' Houses', 'The Evangelist', 'July 1964', and 'Time Passing Beloved' from *Collected Poems 1950–1970* (© Donald Davie 1972). Reprinted by permission of Routledge and Kegan Paul and Oxford University Press Inc. Extract from 'House Martin' from *Events and Wisdoms* (Copyright © 1965 by Donald Davie). Reprinted by permission of Wesleyan University Press.

William Empson: 'Let It Go' from *Collected Poems*. Reprinted by permission of Chatto & Windus Ltd.

D. J. Enright: Extracts from 'The Cure' and 'Class' from *The Terrible Shears*. Reprinted by permission of Bolt & Watson Ltd and Wesleyan University Press. Extracts from 'On the Death of a Child' from *The Laughing Hyena*, 'The Interpreters' and 'Standards' from *Bread Rather Than Blossoms*, 'No Offence', 'A Polished Performance' and 'Saying No' from *Some Men Are Brothers*, and 'After the Gods, After the Heroes' from *Un-*

lawful Assembly. Reprinted by permission of Bolt & Watson Ltd.

Thom Gunn: Extracts from 'Lerici', 'Lofty in the Palais de Danse', and 'The Secret Sharer' from *Fighting Terms*, extracts from *The Sense of Movement*, and 'Touch' from *Touch*. Reprinted by permission of Faber and Faber Ltd. Extract from 'Considering the Snail' from *My Sad Captains* and also from *Moly and My Sad Captains* (copyright © 1961, 1971, 1973 by Thom Gunn). Reprinted by permission of Faber and Faber Ltd and Farrar, Straus and Giroux, Inc.

Elizabeth Jennings: 'Delay' from *Collected Poems*. Reprinted by permission of Macmillan, London and Basingstoke. 'Pain' from 'Sequence in Hospital', first published in *Recoveries* (Deutsch), and also from *Collected Poems* (Macmillan). Reprinted by permission of David Higham Associates Ltd.

Philip Larkin: Extracts from 'At Grass', 'Toads', 'Reasons for Attendance', 'Next, Please', 'Lines on A Young Lady's Photograph Album', 'I Remember, I Remember', 'Born Yesterday', 'Dry-Point', 'Poetry of Departures', and 'Church Going' from *The Less Deceived*. Reprinted by permission of The Marvell Press. Extracts from 'The Importance of Elsewhere', 'Ignorance', 'Reference Back', 'Dockery and Son', 'MCMXIV', 'Mr Bleaney', 'Faith Healing', and 'Afternoons' from *The Whitsun Weddings*, and extracts from Poem III and Poem XVI from *The North Ship*. Reprinted by permission of Faber and Faber Ltd. Extracts from 'Going, Going', 'The Old Fools' and 'Homage to a Government' from *High Windows* (Copyright © 1974 by Philip Larkin). Reprinted by permission of Faber and Faber Ltd and Farrar, Straus and Giroux, Inc.

John Wain: Extracts from five poems from *A Word Carved On A Sill* (Routledge). Reprinted by permission of Curtis Brown Ltd.

Introduction

Student: I wanted to ask you, because I see that some
               of the other people in this new movement . . .
Willoughby: There is no movement.
Student: But I thought . . .
Willoughby: Sorry, no movement. All made up by the
               Literary Editor of the *Spectator.*
               Malcolm Bradbury, *Eating People is Wrong* (1959)

On 1 October 1954, an anonymous leading article entitled
'In the Movement' appeared in the London weekly periodical
the *Spectator.* The article drew attention to the emergence
of a group of writers who, it claimed, represented something
new in British literature and society. The 'modern Britain' of
the 1950s was, the article argued, 'a changed place': even its
physical appearance was no longer that of the 1930s and
1940s. Now it was becoming clear that the 'literary scene'
had also been transformed: the 'approved names' of the
previous two decades belonged to an era that was 'all gone,
utterly gone and vanished'. Literary 'Taste' (and here the
article adopted a hectoring tone calculated to alarm those
who value keeping up with changes in fashion) had begun to
move in new directions: 'Who do you take with you on the
long weekends in Sussex cottages? Kafka and Kierkegaard,
Proust and Henry James? Dylan Thomas, *The Confidential
Clerk, The Age of Anxiety* and *The Golden Horizon*? You
belong to an age that is passing.'

The emerging writers, or 'new movement', were presented
by the anonymous leader writer (now known to have been
the literary editor of the *Spectator,* J.D. Scott)[1] as enemies
of the old order, being 'only less hostile to the political

preoccupations of the Thirties than they are to the lush, loose, fashionable writing of the Forties'. Their tough approach was described in a provocative and playfully apocalyptic manner:

Genuflections towards Dr Leavis and Professor Empson, admiration for people whom the Thirties by-passed, Orwell above all (and, for another example, Mr Robert Graves) are indeed signs by which you may recognize the Movement. It is bored by the despair of the Forties, not much interested in suffering, and extremely impatient of poetic sensibility, especially poetic sensibility about 'the writer and society'. So it's goodbye to all those rather sad little discussions about 'how the writer ought to live', and it's goodbye to the Little Magazine and 'experimental writing'. The Movement, as well as being anti-phoney, is anti-wet; sceptical, robust, ironic, prepared to be as comfortable as possible . . .

The article conceded that the Movement was still, in 1954, at a formative stage, but ended with an assertion of its importance as 'part of that tide which is pulling us through the Fifties and towards the Sixties'.

This was not the first time in the 1950s that there had been talk of a new movement in British writing. Already in the poetry anthology *Springtime* (1953), on the BBC Third Programme, and in periodicals like *Encounter,* the *New Statesman* and the *Times Literary Supplement,* tentative references to a new generation of writers had been made. But this was the most striking and comprehensive account so far. It was also the first time that the emerging group had been given the luxury of a definite article and capital letters: henceforth it would be not just 'a movement', but 'the Movement'.

Who were these writers? The article named just two poets, Donald Davie and Thom Gunn, and three novelists, Kingsley Amis, Iris Murdoch and John Wain, while implying that other writers might also be involved. A better indication of the Movement's 'personnel' came with the appearance of two poetry anthologies in 1955 and 1956. *Poets of the 1950's* (1955), edited by D.J. Enright, included poems by Enright himself, Kingsley Amis, Robert Conquest, Donald Davie, John Holloway, Elizabeth Jennings, Philip Larkin and John Wain. *New Lines* (1956), edited by Robert Conquest, contained the same eight poets and added one more: Thom Gunn. In the years since 1956, the term 'the Movement' has come to be taken to mean these nine poets.

What is less generally agreed upon is whether the Movement was really a movement: did the writers properly constitute a group? Such was the sensationalism of J.D. Scott's 'In the Movement' article that commentators, at the time and since, have tended to dismiss the Movement as a journalistic invention. It has been described by Jeff Nuttall as a 'gigantic confidence trick'; by Howard Sergeant as an 'extremely well-organized, not to say well-sustained, publicity campaign'; and by Christopher Logue as a conspiracy in which fame-hungry poets 'promoted themselves by means of a group name'.[2] The *reductio ad absurdum* of this kind of pejorative business terminology can be found in Ian Hamilton's essay 'The Making of the Movement', which talks of a *Spectator* 'P.R. job' securing for a number of minor versifiers a quite unmerited reputation:

When the anthology *New Lines* appeared in 1956, the ground had more than been prepared: it had been practically churned into a quagmire. The advance promotion had in fact been initiated two years earlier, in the *Spectator*, with Anthony Hartley declaring to the world (in an unsigned leading article) that there existed a group of young poets who were ripe to dislodge the old forties gang. 'For better or worse,' he wrote, 'we are now in the presence of the only considerable movement in English poetry since the Thirties' . . .

   The odd thing about Hartley's communiqué (aside from the fact that the poets in question, though assertedly fairly numerous, had published only a few pamphlets and one or two small press hardbacks) was the transparently calculated tone in which it was delivered; the tone, pushing and unblushing, of the hard sell.[3]

Hamilton's is a confident, but in detail inaccurate account. The author of the unsigned leading article was not Anthony Hartley, but J.D. Scott; the sentence which Hamilton quotes

('For better or worse . . .') does not come from the article in question, but from a signed review by Anthony Hartley, 'Poets of the Fifties', which had appeared in the *Spectator* six weeks earlier; the suggestion that the Movement poets were unknown and unread before October 1954 — 'had published only a few pamphlets' — hardly squares with the facts: by this time Wain's *Hurry on Down,* Jennings's *Poems,* Amis's *Lucky Jim,* Davie's *Purity of Diction in English Verse,* and Gunn's *Fighting Terms* had all received considerable attention in the press. Even the basic premise of the conspiracy theory seems dubious, for as Donald Davie has said, 'promotion is of the nature of any artistic movement',[4] and the fact that the Movement poets were 'sold' to the public does not mean that their work was worthless; nor does it mean that a genuine basis for a group identity was lacking.

A more serious problem for anyone writing about the Movement is the fact that the poets themselves have frequently denied the validity of the group label that was affixed to them. Larkin has said that he had 'no sense at all' of belonging to a movement. Amis in a 1960 essay referred to 'the phantom "movement" '. Gunn comments: 'I found I was in it before I knew it existed . . . and I have a certain suspicion that it does *not* exist'. Enright remarks very similarly: 'I don't think there was a movement back in those days, or if there was I didn't know about it'. Jennings argues that 'it is the journalists, not the poets themselves, who have created the poetic movements of the fifties'. Conquest has claimed that, in editing *New Lines,* he 'was not trying to assemble a movement', and since an early draft of his introduction to the anthology contained criticism of the Movement, his claim clearly has some justification. Only Davie has willingly acknowledged both the Movement's existence, and his participation in it, but even he has belittled its artistic importance: his 1959 essay 'Remembering the Movement' contains some of the most informed and incisive criticism which the Movement has so far received.[5]

These disclaimers cannot be lightly dismissed, but they should be treated with scepticism. Some show that same distaste for sensational journalism which can be detected in the Movement's critics. Some, again, take the narrow view that the only *bona fide* movement is one in which all the poets gather together in one place in order to plan strategy. Others seem symptomatic of a dislike of being associated with any group activity — a dislike partly attributable to Romantic ideology concerning the isolated artist, and partly to a typically 'English' repugnance for the notion of literary programmes and manifestos (the tendency for writers to cluster in groups being thought of as an essentially 'Continental' one). Most of the disavowals, moreover, were made in the late 1950s and early 1960s, at a time when the writers were beginning to move in different directions and wanted their 'individual' talents to be recognized. The impugning of the Movement label is an understandable development, but not to be too readily trusted.

Both the writers themselves and their critics have presented the Movement as a collection of separate individuals having in common — as Conquest puts it in *New Lines* — 'little more than a negative determination to avoid bad principles'. What seems to be required now is a broader and more flexible approach, one which, rather than seeking only colourful associations of the literary group — the salon or meeting-place where ideas are feverishly exchanged, the defiant manifesto blasting the old order and ushering in the new — might instead concern itself with a large number of other possible factors which can have a bearing on the formation of movements. Did the writers know each other? Is there any evidence of mutual admiration, mutual influence, or collaboration? Did the writers come from the same social background? Did they have similar political beliefs? Did they intend to write for the same kind of audience? Was there a common belief about the direction which contemporary literature should take?

To ask these questions is not to ignore the existence of tensions and divisions. As we shall see, Movement poets seem sometimes to be writing against their natural impulse, 'against the grain', in order to adhere to group principles to which they have given their conscious assent. There were also certain contradictions inherent, or 'written into', the Movement endeavour. But my main purpose is to show that, for a time at least, there was considerable agreement and interaction, and that out of these was established a Movement consensus. The view that the Movement was a journalistic invention or agreed fiction can no longer be allowed to stand.

The other challenge of this book is to show, not only that the Movement existed, but that it was a literary group of considerable importance — probably the most influential in England since the Imagists. This, again, is to run counter to received opinion, for most previous critical assessments, while allowing the Movement its place in 1950s literary history, have tended to dismiss it as being of small consequence. The attacks began early on. Charles Tomlinson's 'The Middlebrow Muse' (1957) exempted only Donald Davie from a series of strictures against the 'middle-cum-lowbrowism', 'the suburban mental ratio', the 'parochialism', and the 'lack of real poetic talent and ambition' which pervade *New Lines*.[6] A. Alvarez's introduction to the anthology *The New Poetry* (1962) was less severe, but presented the Movement as one of three 'negative feedbacks' from the advances of Modernism, convicting the group — Larkin in particular — of a disabling 'gentility', an outlook unable to deal with the pressures of the modern world.[7] Neither Tomlinson nor Alvarez could claim to be impartial observers (Tomlinson had been rejected as a potential contributor to *New Lines*; Alvarez had been linked with the Movement in the early 1950s), but their essays have a vigour which the two critics to have written most sympathetically about the Movement, William Van O'Connor in *The New University Wits* (1965) and John Press in *Rule and Energy* (1963), are unable to match. Such passing mention as it has received in recent years has tended to assume that the case against the Movement has been decisively proved. Calvin Bedient finds 'the very name' of the Movement suggesting 'an excess of dull plainness'[8] and Geoffrey Thurley sees the Movement poets as academic ironists working against boldness and imagination in poetry, the native hue of resolution sicklied o'er with the pale cast of their thought.[9] The point has been reached where, as Edna Longley summarizes it, 'the Movement may be succeeding the Georgians as everyone's favourite Aunt Sally'.[10]

Part of the reason for this downgrading of the Movement lies, once again, with Romantic individualist ideology. Critics have been happy to accept that individual Movement poets like Larkin, Davie or Gunn are of importance; but in order to establish their reputations it has been felt necessary first to prove their independence from possible confederates. 'Movement', according to this view, is reserved for some minor or reprehensible 'ism' — narrow academicism, second-rate Empsonianism, philistine Little-Englandism, timid conformism, and so on. The vices of an individual poet are held to be Movement vices; his virtues are his own. My emphasis is different. I have tried to rescue the term 'Movement' and to show that it often stands not for what is peripheral and debilitating in these writers but for what is central and enriching. There are many cases, of course, of writers transcending or going beyond the Movement programme; but it is remarkable how many key texts of the post-1945 period — Larkin's 'At Grass', 'Church Going', 'Dockery and Son', Amis's *Lucky Jim* and *That Uncertain Feeling*, Davie's 'The Garden Party', 'Remembering the Thirties' and 'Rejoinder to a Critic', Gunn's 'On the Move' and 'Lines for a Book', Wain's *Hurry on Down*, Enright's 'No Offence' and 'On the Death of a Child' — should have sprung directly from the collaboration and interaction which the Movement represented.

The Movement's main achievement was in the field of

poetry, and most of the texts which I have drawn on can be found in *New Lines* and *Poets of the 1950's* or in the individual collections of the contributors to those anthologies. But Amis and Wain are in fact better known as novelists than as poets, and three others in the group — Larkin, Enright and Conquest — have also published fiction. Amis's *Lucky Jim*, Wain's *Hurry on Down* and Larkin's *Jill* are especially revealing about the Movement identity, and figure prominently here. Critical essays and reviews published by the Movement have been considered as well. The 1950s was a period of buoyant confidence in literary criticism — 'the Age of Criticism' as Randall Jarrell called it — and it is no accident that most of the Movement writers made their living as critics and lecturers in English literature. Their criticism has an intrinsic interest, reflecting the influence of Leavis, Empson, and the Anglo-American 'New Critical' school. It also sheds light on the poetry and fiction.

Not all the texts are drawn from the 1950s. Though the middle of that decade was the period of the group's greatest coherence, the origins of the Movement can be traced back to the 1940s, and many works published in the 1960s and 1970s continue to bear the marks of a Movement sensibility. Larkin's *The Whitsun Weddings*, for example, though published in 1964, might still be considered a Movement collection, not only because several of the poems there were written in the mid-1950s ('Mr Bleaney', 'An Arundel Tomb', 'Reference Back' and 'Days' had all been published by November 1956), but because Larkin has continued to defend and develop principles central to the Movement programme. The criterion for judging certain texts to be Movement texts cannot be purely chronological: the crucial consideration is whether the particular text embodies a sensibility (and this involves questions about subject matter, form, tone and attitude) which is characteristic of the Movement.

This raises a final question: if the Movement is in some

degree a state of sensibility, would it be possible to describe texts by writers outside the group as it is normally defined as being Movement work? My aim here is to establish that the *New Lines* poets are a more unified group, and that the Movement 'membership' is therefore less arbitrary, than has usually been supposed. I have laid emphasis on the three writers — Larkin, Amis and Davie — who seem to me the most central and important of the participants; and I have pointed to Movement elements in the work of other writers — Thom Gunn and Elizabeth Jennings, for example — whose part in the group is sometimes disputed. But it would clearly be wrong to suppose that there are not 'outsiders' who have a sympathy with the group endeavour equal to, and even in some cases greater than, that of the 'official' members. A number of poets (Anthony Thwaite, George Macbeth, Vernon Scannell), novelists (John Braine, William Cooper, Thomas Hinde) and critics (W.W. Robson, Anthony Hartley, Bernard Bergonzi) have at one time or another been said to have links with the group, and there are good grounds for making the connections. There has also been a tendency, increased of late, to use the term 'Movement' as an adjective as well as noun: critics not only speak of 'the Movement', a specific 1950s group, but identify a 'Movement tone' or 'Movement manner' in texts not necessarily produced from within the group and not necessarily written in the 1950s. The identity of the Movement has, it seems, transcended both the group and the decade, coming to stand for certain characteristics in English writing — rationalism, realism, empiricism — which continue to exert their influence today. It is even possible to talk of a Movement 'ideology' — an identifiable 'line' on sex, religion, politics and other non-literary matters. My main concern is with the literature of the 1950s and with showing that the Movement is as central to that decade as was 'the Auden generation' to the 1930s. But if this study manages to do more than that, to shed light on wider social and cultural issues, I shall not be displeased.

1

The Origins of the Movement

I · OXFORD 1940–51

Life in college was austere. Its pre-war pattern had been
dispersed, in some instances permanently. Everyone paid
the same fees (in our case, 12s. a day) and ate the same
meals. Because of Ministry of Food regulations, the town
could offer little in the way of luxurious eating and drinking, and college festivities, such as commemoration balls,
had been suspended for the duration. Because of petrol
rationing, nobody ran a car. Because of clothes rationing,
it was difficult to dress stylishly . . .

This was not the Oxford of Michael Fane and his fine
bindings, or Charles Ryder and his plovers' eggs. Nevertheless, it had a distinctive quality. A lack of *douceur* was
balanced by a lack of *bêtises*, . . . and I think our perspectives
were truer as a result. At an age when self-importance
would have been normal, events cut us ruthlessly down
to size.

Philip Larkin, *Jill*

The origins of the Movement can be traced back to Oxford in
the early 1940s, when a number of key friendships were
made. The first and most important of these was that between
Larkin and Amis. Both were undergraduates at St John's
College, Larkin beginning his studies in the Autumn of 1940,
Amis coming up two terms later. Larkin's description of their
first meeting, in the 1963 introduction to his novel *Jill*,
suggests that it was Amis's 'genius for imaginative mimicry'
which attracted him: 'For the first time I felt myself in the
presence of a talent greater than my own'.[1] He recalls how
Amis's imitations could make him 'incapable with laughter',
and he pays further tribute to Amis's mimicry by way of an

oblique allusion in the Willow Gables section of the novel, where John Kemp's imagined sister, Jill, befriends a girl called Patsy who 'could make Jill sick with laughing. She could imitate almost anybody. Together they had formed an alliance against the rest of the world'.

This shared sense of humour was perhaps the most important part of the Larkin-Amis friendship, for it influenced their notions of what they should attempt in their writing. Some favourite jokes were even reproduced in their work. Larkin has said that *Lucky Jim* 'commemorates a period of intensive joke-swapping' between them, and there are two known examples of Amis drawing on Larkin's jokes for the novel. Dixon's 'philistine' outburst against 'Filthy Mozart' expressed Larkin's views, not Amis's,[2] and the 'graveyard gag' — 'Lecturers were fond of lauding to their students the comparative receptivity to facts of "the Honours class over the road" . . .' — was based on the location of Leicester University library, at which Larkin took up employment in 1946 (it is situated directly opposite a cemetery). A joke which Larkin shared with a tutorial partner called Norman also had a later bearing on Movement work: between them they 'invented "the Yorkshire scholar", a character embodying many of our prejudices'. 'The Yorkshire scholar' was a parody of the dour but ambitious scholarship boy; as well as providing the basis for Whitbread in *Jill*, he lies behind later variations of the type, such as Amis's Dixon in *Lucky Jim* and Wain's George Hutchins in *Hurry on Down*. Even the Movement poets were themselves sometimes depicted as 'Yorkshire scholars' by their critics. The group had several other 'in-jokes', notably Robert Conquest's naming of the spaceships in his science fiction novel *A World of Difference* (1955) — 'Larkin', 'Enright', 'Holloway' and 'Gunn'. But 'the Yorkshire scholar' is perhaps the nearest Movement equivalent to the Mortmere inventions of Isherwood and Upward.

Larkin and Amis also shared an interest in jazz. In his

introduction to *Jill*, Larkin says: 'I suppose we devoted to
some hundred records that early anatomizing passion normally
reserved for the more established arts'. They also had the
same tutor, Gavin Bone, who influenced them in several ways.
Bone was an Anglo-Saxon scholar and believed, so we are
told in the preface to his posthumous *Anglo-Saxon Poetry*
(1943), that 'the importance of the native stock had been
underestimated'. If this encouraged a concern with 'Englishness' in the work of Larkin and Amis, so too Bone may have
helped to develop their respect for clarity and intelligibility:
he made simplicity of expression a priority in his translation
of *Beowulf* (1945). He also seems to have been openly hostile
to Modernist literature: as John Wain noticed[3], Bone in
Anglo-Saxon Poetry had referred disparagingly to T.S. Eliot
as 'an American critic', and it is probable that this anti-
Modernist prejudice communicated itself to Larkin and Amis,
who were also to feel doubts about the worth of Eliot's
poetry. Bone's enthusiasm for Anglo-Saxon and Medieval
texts did not, however, make a favourable impression on
Amis: in *Bright November* (1947) he included a poem
'Beowulf', critical of what he was later to call the 'poverty of
human interest' in that work:[4]

> Consider now what this king had not done:
> Never was human, never lay with women
> (Weak conjugation), never saw quite straight
> Children of men or the bright bowl of heaven.
>
> Someone has told us this man was a hero.
> But what have we to learn in following
> His tedious journey to his ancestors
> (An instance of Old English harking back)?

Bone died in 1942, but even if he had lived Amis would
have had him as a tutor for only a short time: in that same
year he was called up for military service. Larkin also left
Oxford, and, having failed an army medical test, took up
his first library job, in Wellington, Shropshire, in 1943. The
two kept in touch partly by regularly revisiting Oxford

throughout the war, and partly also by correspondence. One of Amis's short stories, 'I Spy Strangers', seems to allude to this correspondence when it mentions a letter from Lieutenant Archer 'to a friend of his in Oxford, one who like most of his contemporaries was medically unfit for military service ... The letter was full of undetailed assertions of hatred and misery, unsolicited news about what Archer's two girlfriends in England had been writing to him, and enquiries about jazz records'.

There were two other Oxford contemporaries who, through their friendship with Larkin and Amis, contributed to the development of a Movement sensibility in the years 1943–7: Bruce Montgomery and John Wain. Larkin met Montgomery, who by this time was already writing detective novels for Gollancz under the pseudonym 'Edmund Crispin', in 1943. In his introduction to *Jill*, Larkin has said that from 1943–5 he saw a lot of Montgomery, and that the friendship may have been 'a curious creative stimulus'. Interestingly the three novels that Montgomery wrote during those years do bear signs of a Movement sensibility. Movement novels like *Hurry on Down*, *Lucky Jim* and *That Uncertain Feeling* were to treat writers as villains rather than heroes, and this is the case in Crispin's *The Case of the Gilded Fly* (1944), which has as its villain a fashion-conscious London dramatist called Robert Warner (Larkin's *Jill*, begun six months after Montgomery's, also has a character called Warner). Crispin's hero, Gervase Fen, concludes that 'the artistic temperament is too often only an alibi for lack of responsibility'. The villain of *Holy Disorders* (1945), in the preface to which Montgomery thanks Larkin for having made 'valuable suggestions', is rather similar, being in Fen's words 'over-clever, incapable of concentration or real thought, affected, arty, with no soul, no morals'. Perhaps the most interesting of Montgomery's early novels is the third, *The Moving Toyshop* (1946). This is dedicated to Larkin, and like *Jill*, which appeared in the same year, has a narrative sequence centred round the search through Oxford for a beautiful girl with blue eyes. There is also in the narrative a typically debunking Movement tone and attitude: one of the characters asserts that 'there's no such thing as a poetic type', and the hero, Fen, in order to pass the time, plays games called 'Unreadable Books' and 'Detestable Characters'. In this combination of intellect and anti-intellectualism, Fen seems a prototype for later Movement heroes like Jim Dixon, a university lecturer who enjoys deriding 'culture', and Patrick Standish in *Take a Girl Like You*, who passes the time one day by inventing a cricket team including such figures as Cicero, Milton and Rimbaud. Montgomery played no later part in the Movement, but his first novels had a wit and humour which Larkin and Amis relished, and which they successfully introduced in their own writing.

John Wain seems to have known Larkin and Amis less well at this stage than did Montgomery, yet it was he whose activities were later to be linked with theirs: the Amis–Larkin–Wain triangle might justifiably be thought of as the nucleus of the Movement. Wain had several things in common with Larkin: he had come from a middle-class family in the Midlands; he had been subsidized by his father rather than going to Oxford as a scholarship boy; he had failed his army medical; he was studying English. But he did not arrive at St John's College until January 1943, by which time Amis had gone into the army and Larkin was studying for his finals. 'Years afterwards,' Larkin writes in the introduction to *Jill*, 'John told me that our acquaintance at this time was limited to a brief bitter exchange at lunch about Albert Ammons's Boogie Woogie Stomp and the poetry of George Crabbe'. Wain's first friendships at Oxford were with older men like his tutor C.S. Lewis and E.H.W. Meyerstein. Though he was exposed to the same climate of ideas at Oxford as were Larkin and Amis — his tutor C.S. Lewis shared Gavin Bone's prejudice against Modernist poetry, fearing Eliot as an anti-Christian and Pound as a 'harmful charlatan' (Lewis even conspired to have Canon Adam Fox elected to the Oxford Chair of Poetry from 1938–43 in order to strike a blow against Modernism) — Wain was not at first on close personal terms with them.

However, Wain did get to know Larkin and Amis rather better in the years 1944–7: during this period they both paid visits to Oxford, Amis returning there for full-time study at the end of the war. Wain's account of these years in his autobiography *Sprightly Running* gives a definite sense of an Oxford group which looked up to Larkin and clustered round him:

It took the trumpet call 'Philip's coming up!' to bring together a motley crew who did not associate at any other time, and who were connected simply by a common admiration for one whom we already considered a Flaubertian saint of letters. Kingsley Amis, appearing on his leaves from active service, was one of this nebulous group, and my first casual meetings with him came about because we were both, so to speak, swimming in the thin fluid that solidified only when Philip Larkin arrived. It was Kingsley who sold me my copy of Philip's first novel, *Jill* . . . We were united in homage to Larkin; we waited eagerly for his successive books . . .

Wain's reminiscences are valuable in clearing up misconceptions about the force of Larkin's personality and about the nature of his interests. Larkin himself has encouraged us to imagine him as being an unimpressive and retiring figure at this time: 'up to the age of twenty-one,' he has said, 'I was still asking for railway tickets by pushing written notes across the counter'.[5] But Wain presents him as a dominant, sociable and much respected figure, a view of Larkin which is shared by other of his acquaintances at this time. Bruce Montgomery, for instance, contrasts him with his bashful protagonist in *Jill*: 'that massive, affable, pipe-smoking undergraduate was no Kemp';[6] and another Oxford contemporary, John Morgan, claims that 'everybody imitated the way he spoke; the kind of jokes he made; even the way he walked'.[7] Larkin also sometimes portrays himself as a person who at that time

lacked an interest in contemporary literature: in his introduction to *The North Ship* he recalls 'coming across John
Heath-Stubbs's "Leporello" and being profoundly bewildered.
I had never heard of Leporello, and what sort of poetry was
this — who was he copying?' Wain makes it clear that Larkin,
far from being a stumbling *naïf* interested only in beer and
jazz, had a wide range of literary interests. He tells, for
instance, how an admiring Larkin lent him and Amis Flann
O'Brien's *At-Swim-Two-Birds*, a novel which did not attract
widespread interest until the 1960s, and which, despite its
qualities of wit, the supposedly 'philistine' and 'anti-Modernist'
Larkin might have been expected to dislike.[8]

By 1947 both Amis and Larkin had a publishing record
sufficient to impress the younger Wain. As well as placing
poems in such disparate Oxford ventures as *Arabesque,* the
Ballet Club magazine, and the *University Labour Club
Bulletin* (the last edited by the then left-wing Amis), Larkin
had ten poems appearing in William Bell's anthology *Poetry
from Oxford in Wartime* (1945). In the same year these were
put together with twenty-one other poems to form his first
collection *The North Ship*. Larkin's publisher was L. Caton,
head of the Fortune Press, which also published poetry by
Dylan Thomas and Roy Fuller (a bogus academic and editor
called L.S. Caton was later to appear in several of Amis's
novels). In 1946 Caton published Larkin's first novel, *Jill,*
and in 1947 Amis's first collection of poems, *Bright
November*. Wain has said that he was encouraged by the
writing of Larkin and Amis: Larkin offered an example of
discipline and quiet self-determination; Amis was also an
example because

when I first knew him, at Oxford, he was writing a novel: of course every
second or third undergraduate one met was 'writing a novel', but Amis
spoke of his with such enjoyment, and seemed to be having so much fun
writing it, that I caught the virus; when, a few years later, I sat down . . .
to 'see if' I could write a novel, Amis's example was certainly one of my
motives . . . I'm quite certain I would never have written *Hurry on Down*
without the example of that first, undergraduate novel of Amis's . . .[9]

Such mutual encouragement was important, but the work of Amis and Larkin was at this time still far from being in a Movement manner. It is true that certain elements in Larkin's novels — the scholarship boy central figure of *Jill,* the provincial setting of *A Girl in Winter* — can be thought of as mature Movement work. But the poems in *The North Ship* and *Bright November* have many features which are alien to Movement poetry of the 1950s. One such feature is Larkin's rather 'precious' habit of addressing and personifying the heart: 'How strange it is/For the heart to be loveless', 'the heart in its own endless silence kneeling', 'the deft/Heart lies impotent', 'If hands could free you, heart'. Larkin has spoken of his youthful susceptibility to Yeats, and it may be that these addresses derive from an early Yeats poem like 'Never Give All the Heart'. Amis also personifies the heart — 'Heart's wealth slides off to zero', 'Heart's injury will not forget us so' — and in his 'La Belle Dame Sans Merci' (its title drawn from Keats, about whom Amis was later to feel reservations) the line 'and who should know some weeping before they pass' echoes Yeats's 'The Man Who Dreamed of Faeryland', which has several similarly constructed refrains.

On other occasions, Larkin and Amis show the influence of earlier Romantic poets. Poem XVI from *The North Ship,* for instance, uses the popular Romantic motif of the underground river (compare 'the sacred river' which 'ran/through caverns measureless to man' in Coleridge's 'Kubla Khan'):

> And I am sick for want of sleep;
> So sick, that I can half-believe
> The soundless river pouring from the cave
> Is neither strong, nor deep.

There is also in that final line an echo of Matthew Arnold's complaint in 'Dover Beach' about the world having 'neither joy, nor love, nor light,/Nor certitude, nor peace, nor help for pain', and it seems clear that Arnold, too, was a poet whom Larkin found it difficult to 'escape'. In Poem III there is a further allusion to 'Dover Beach'. Arnold's poem begins 'The sea is calm tonight./The tide is full, the moon lies fair'. Larkin compresses these lines ('The moon is full tonight') and goes on to share Arnold's lament for the 'certitude' (both use this word) lost from the modern world:

> The moon is full tonight
> And hurts the eyes,
> It is so definite and bright.
> What if it has drawn up
> All quietness and certitude of worth
> Wherewith to fill its cup,
> Or mint a second moon, a paradise? —
> For they are gone from earth.

'And hurts the eyes' is so colloquial as to sound like mockery, and from the point-of-view of Larkin's development this is the most interesting feature of the poem: it briefly hints at a Movement-like impatience with solemn Romantic postures. Similarly, when Larkin writes in Poem XXVII 'In the past/There has been too much moonlight and self-pity:/ Let us have done with it', there is briefly a hint of self-condemnation and a suggestion that new tones and attitudes will have to be adopted.

'Release', the penultimate poem in *Bright November,* suggests that Amis shared Larkin's hopes and ambitions. Written at the end of the Second World War, it pronounces the present 'a time for revision of thought' and gestures towards a future in which the poet will be famous: 'Now I must awake and speak. Now I must cause/Something that will want to remember me'. Such grandiose declarations are common among young poets, but Amis had already shown signs of a valuable change of direction. In his poem 'O Captain! My Captain!' (the title borrowed from Whitman) he had, like Larkin, subverted the pose of the Romantic dreamer. As in Henry Reed's 'Lessons of the War', to which the poem is almost certainly indebted, the voice of an experienced military officer is played off against that of a romantic young recruit:

> Useless to fill the head with pointless abstractions
> About time; time is always expressed in hours;
> And another thing, you; just come away from that window;
> It isn't manly to be always staring at flowers.
>
> I could talk about other things which you must not do,
> Such as staying sober, or hating a dirty picture.
> — What's that? you wish you could fall in love?
> Fetch the M.O., major; this fellow's got a stricture.

Amis has spoken of the army as an experience which toughened and matured him,[10] and the poem seems partly to describe this process: the captain brusquely interrupts the recruit's vague meditations about 'music' and 'flowers' and 'love', insisting on the need to be 'manly'. In the years after 1947 Amis gave increasing attention to this 'second voice' and to the development of a dialogue in which the tough pragmatist would gradually win out.

The promise of a Movement manner is present in *The North Ship* and *Bright November,* then, but Amis and Larkin still required an outlet through which they could consolidate their development and clarify their aims. This purpose was partly served by *Mandrake,* an Oxford-based little magazine, edited from 1945 to 1947 by John Wain and Arthur Boyars (after that Boyars assumed sole control). The third issue (May 1946) contained two poems by Wain and two by Phillip (sic) Larkin. None of these was subsequently collected, but Larkin's 'Plymouth', at least, is revealing about his continuing struggle to find a distinctive manner. The poem betrays the influence of Dylan Thomas ('rivers of Eden, rivers of blood') and of Yeats ('The hands that chose them rust upon a stick'), but in its closing lines looks forward to a poetry that, by implication, would demand the rejection of such influences:

> Let my hands find such symbols, that can be
> Unnoticed in the casual light of day,
> Lying in wait for half a century

> To split chance lives across, that had not dreamed
> Such coasts had echoed, or such seabirds screamed.

Larkin was here beginning to formulate the idea of a self-effacing, unobtrusive, 'modest' poetry. It was an idea to which he gave further thought, and by the time 'Modesties' appeared in *XX Poems* (1951), the ideals of modesty and simplicity were being decisively met:

> Words as plain as hen-birds' wings
> Do not lie,
> Do not over-broider things —
> Are too shy.

The espousal of shyness and readiness to write poems which are about poetry seem typical of mature Movement work. In 'Twilight on the Waste Lands', for example, a text from the mid-1950s, Donald Davie asks his readers to envisage a poem 'With such a nicety of touch/It quite conceals the maker's hand'. It is illuminating, therefore, to see Larkin moving towards such a position in 1946.

Larkin published no further poems in *Mandrake*, but the editorial of the fourth issue (Winter 1946) suggested that his example had been heeded: it announced the magazine's intention 'to oppose sham and cant (not by irritable polemic but by quietly fostering honest workmanship)'. Wain's review of Lawrence Durrell's *Cities, Plains and People* in the same issue also anticipates Movement credo of the 1950s by calling, albeit in simplistic terms, for a return of clarity in poetry: 'The problem of communication is a tangled one, but the underlying truism, one imagines, is that language is like an addition sum: it adds up to a total, and if we do not add it up it remains a mere list of numbers. Mr Durrell follows a good deal of modern, and not so modern, precedent in giving us a list of numbers that apparently wish to exist in their own right, and to resist the process of addition.' By the phrase 'modern, and not so modern' Wain probably means to suggest that 'modern' is not to be confused with 'contemporary'.

This, too, was to be a familiar Movement theme: to follow the Modernist tradition was, they contended, a retrogressive act. As Wain put it earlier in the same review, 'we must not . . . talk about "modern poetry" as if technique and attitude had remained frozen since Pound'.

Mandrake's fifth number (October 1947) contained two poems by Amis and a review by him of Larkin's *A Girl in Winter*: Amis paid tribute to 'the eagerly observant eye, the unswerving attentiveness to the right word, the fondness for the non-sensuous as well as sensuous imagery that denote the poet'. Amis was able to play a more substantial part in promoting Movement work when he edited an anthology called *Oxford Poetry* in 1949. His co-editor was James Michie (when a character called Michie appeared in *Lucky Jim* this would have been recognized as an 'in-joke'), and in a vigorous introduction these two called for toughness and modernity in poetry, complaining about the Georgianism of many of the poems they had received: '. . . most of our poets had looked not to Auden or MacNeice, but back to Alfred Noyes . . . The typical furniture of the mass of the poems was not, as we soon came to wish it would be, the telegraph-pole and the rifle, but the amethyst and the syrup . . . the typical rhyme not of "lackey" and "lucky", but of "bliss" and "kiss"'.[11] The Movement later came to think less highly of Auden and more highly of the Georgians, but in 1949, when the prevailing mode was neo-Romantic, the example of the former was felt to be more valuable.

Amis and Michie were fortunate in finding at least one poet who met their demands for a 1930s-derived diction, a poet whose imagery ('Neither map nor compass tells the heart's decay') and whose beliefs about poetry, evident below in 'Modern Poet', corresponded to their own:

> This is no moment now for the fine phrases,
> The inflated sentence, words cunningly spun,
> For the floreate image or the relaxing pun
> Or the sentimental answer that most pleases.

> We must write down an age of reckless hunger,
> Of iron girders, hearts like plumb-lines hung,
> And the poet's art is to speak and not to be sung
> And sympathy must turn away to anger.

Though 'an age of reckless hunger' sounds melodramatic and the poem as a whole smacks of youthful manifesto-making, the sentiments are Movement ones. The author was Elizabeth Jennings, whose six poems in *Oxford Poetry* made her by far the most favoured of the contributors.

Jennings was one of three other Movement poets who studied at Oxford, but the only one to have any contact with Amis, Larkin or Wain. Robert Conquest attended Magdalen College before the beginning of the Second World War, and it was 1952 before he met any of the other Oxford-educated Movement poets. John Holloway was at Oxford as an undergraduate from 1938–41 and, after military service, returned there for postgraduate work until 1949; but it was 1954 before he met any other Movement poets. Jennings, however, did know Amis: she studied at St Anne's College from 1945–9, and at some point during this period made his acquaintance. Like Larkin, she remembers his mocking sense of humour: 'It was never cruel, however. I can myself remember vividly how Kingsley could cast doubts on one's love of Milton or delight in the theatre, yet never hurt or disillusion one.'[12] Amis has said that he 'knew Liz Jennings quite well at one time, before she or I had really got started on being a poet'.[13] This suggests that they had met by 1947, for they would certainly have been aware of each other's poetry by 1948, when they both appeared in *Oxford Poetry*, edited that year by Arthur Boyars and Barry Harmer.

Jennings's part in the Movement has sometimes been disputed; Conquest notes that 'somebody once described her association with us as comparable to that of a schoolmistress in a non-corridor train with a bunch of drunk marines — a slight slander to both sides'.[14] But it is doubtful whether her work would have developed as it did had it not been for her exposure to the Oxford climate of the late-1940s and early-1950s. Much of her early poetry — 'Unicorn', for example — still adhered to conventions which the Movement wished to disrupt:

> I have ridden the unicorn of my love
> Through angry forests and through glistening meadows
> And I have seen the lissom lovely shadows
> Of his white limbs across the rivers move
> And we have trampled in our restless gallop
> Hard buds of flowers and milky breast-like roses
> And the hard stems of leaves, hairs which envelop
> The shy waterlily as it closes:
> O he has carried me upon his limbs
> His legs of snow but fiery as these roses.[15]

'Unicorn' was not one of the poems included in Amis's *Oxford Poetry*: Amis would have disliked the archaic diction, the inversions of word order, and the lush sexual symbolism. The poems by her which were selected — 'urban' and contemporary in their imagery, tightly controlled in their handling of rhyme and metre — not only indicate Amis's predilections but show that Jennings was developing a poetic style more akin to that of the Movement. The choices were astute: 'Weathercock', 'Winter Love' and 'Time' were found sufficiently accomplished to be reprinted in Jennings's first collection, *Poems,* in 1953.

Another poem from this period, 'Delay', demonstrates the effect that the Oxford climate had on Jennings. She is still writing about love, but the fine manipulation of line endings and stanza break, and the almost slick 'toughness' of the final line, make for a quite different kind of poem:

> The radiance of that star that leans on me
> Was shining years ago. The light that now
> Glitters up there my eye may never see,
> And so the time lag teases me with how
>
> Love that loves now may not reach me until
> Its first desire is spent. The star's impulse
> Must wait for eyes to claim it beautiful
> And love arrived may find us somewhere else.

Jennings liked the last line sufficiently to rework it in 'Black and White' as 'But love is always moving off'.[16] It owes a lot to the last line of Amis's 'Retrospect'—'and love is always moving somewhere else'—which she could have seen either in *Bright November* or in the fifth issue of *Mandrake.* Alternatively, the coincidence might mean only that Amis and Jennings were both indebted to Empson, whose poetry also makes much use of rather offhand and 'throwaway' last lines beginning with the word 'and': 'And stave off suffocation until winter', 'And pump the valley with the tunnel dry', 'And learn a style from a despair'.

If Jennings in the early 1950s was imitating Empson, this would not be wholly surprising: in 1950 John Wain had written an article about Empson for *Penguin New Writing,* and the article was widely read and influential, particularly amongst young poets in Oxford. Wain's piece, reprinted in his *Preliminary Essays*, was far from adulatory (he expressed doubt as to whether it was 'worth trying to decipher' Empson's more obscure poems), but did serve to draw attention to a poet whose wit and erudition young intellectuals could readily admire. The article presented Empson as being at least as important as his more celebrated contemporaries (Auden, Day Lewis, MacNeice), and its final rhetorical flourish—'he has, after all, written at least a dozen poems which pass every known test of greatness: and who has done more?'—overrode all previous reservations. The impact of Wain's article can be seen in little Oxford magazines like *Trio* and *Departure,* and in the early issues of George Hartley's magazine *Listen,* which was founded in 1954: contributors like A. Alvarez, Bernard Bergonzi, George MacBeth, Anthony Hartley, Gordon Wharton, Jonathan Price and James Harrison all write Empsonian verse. One of the refrains from Empson's 'Aubade'—'It seemed the best thing to be up and go'—seems to have had special resonance for this generation of poets, for several of them produced variations on it:

Because these things take time, they had to go
         (John Wain, 'Thoughts on Abandoning . . .')

You could not come, and yet you go
         (Elizabeth Jennings, 'For a Child Born Dead')

A minute holds them, who have come to go
         (Thom Gunn, 'On the Move')

When the alarm clock rang they had to go
         (Gordon Wharton, 'This and That')

It is ourselves that are the first to go
         (James Harrison, 'Villanelle')

Wain's championing of Empson was similar to Amis's championing of Auden in *Oxford Poetry*: both these poets could be held up as examples of writers unaffected by the neo-Romantic modes popular in the 1940s. Amis and Michie printed poems which were indebted to Auden, but excluded those adjudged to show the 'harmful influence' of Dylan Thomas; Wain recommended Empson as an antidote to 'punch-drunk random "romantic" scribblers', and cited his work as evidence that 'it is harder to produce an accurate statement than a careless rapture'.[17] The Movement was now, by 1950, becoming more conscious of its aims, and anti-Romanticism became an increasingly important part of its programme. It began to define the texture of its own poetry by contrasting it with 'the poetry of the 1940s'. By this phrase it meant the poetry not of Roy Fuller, Alun Lewis, Keith Douglas and Henry Reed, poets it admired on the whole, but of Dylan Thomas, David Gascoyne, Edith Sitwell, W. R. Rodgers and of the poets (notably Henry Treece and Tom Scott) who had appeared in the 'New Apocalypse' anthology *The White Horseman* (1941). By taking these figures to be 'the poets of the 1940s' the Movement inevitably produced a distorted picture of the decade, but it was one that allowed their own work to appear to be a radical departure, the 'new poetry'.

Wain's *Mixed Feelings* (1951) is perhaps the first real example of a Movement departure from 'the poetry of the 1940s'. Published by the University of Reading School of Fine Art, it was printed in a limited edition of 120 copies, and subscribers included A. Alvarez, Amis, F. W. Bateson, Arthur Boyars, Anthony Hartley, Frank Kermode, C. S. Lewis and Tolkien. Wain had begun teaching at Reading in 1947, and it was through his friendship with Professor J. A. Betts of the Fine Art department that the publication became possible (Wain subsequently became Betts's adviser in the choice of other young poets to be published, and the next was Kingsley Amis, whose *A Frame of Mind* appeared in 1953). The major influence on Wain's collection was Empson. One poem was called 'Eighth Type of Ambiguity', and contained an image—'When love as germ invades the purple stream'—which resembles a line from Empson's 'Missing Dates': 'Slowly the poison the whole bloodstream fills.' Several other poems had Empsonian last lines—'And language quite a useful kind of noise', 'And underline in red their own disasters', 'And where you love you cannot break away'. Nearly all employed some kind of characteristic Empsonian technique—*terza rima,* heavy endstops, a blend of colloquialism and literary allusion. In *Hurry on Down* Wain's hero Lumley is obsessed by a line from Empson's 'The Beautiful Train'—'And I a twister love what I abhor'—and this seems indicative of Wain's own preoccupation with Empson in the early 1950s.

However, at least one poem in *Mixed Feelings* still exhibits a dependence on the 'poetry of the 1940s' which the Movement claimed to despise. This was 'In Memory of Henry Payne' which, though Movement-like in its localized subject matter—Henry Payne had been the St John's College porter until his death in 1948—used assonance, alliteration and elegiac lament in the manner of Dylan Thomas (in 'grim good man' there is also a touch of Anglo-Saxon):

> Silence? No hint of a chant from the
> bards acknowledged, birds of the college? then
> bear with a tongue untuned, a book-choked brain
> fumbling and faltering, for somehow a word must be said.
> No one was glad when the grim good man lay dead.

Another important book published in 1951, Larkin's *XX Poems,* also shows that Movement poets were continuing to find it difficult to escape Thomas's influence. Larkin had been accused of writing like Thomas when an undergraduate, and his 1944–50 notebook, now in the British Museum manuscript section, shows that he was still labouring to shed Thomas's influence long afterwards. In *XX Poems* Thomas is most evident in 'Oils', the first part of 'Two Portraits of Sex', which opens with a series of elemental and surrealist images:

> Sun. Tree. Beginning. God in a thicket. Crown.
> Never-abdicating constellation. Blood.
> Barn-clutch of Life. Trigger of the future.
> Magic weed the doctor shakes in a dance. . . .

It is indicative of Larkin's development towards a rational Movement manner that this poem should have been dropped from the 1955 collection *The Less Deceived* whereas its more comprehensible companion piece, 'Etching' (now known as 'Dry-Point'), should have been retained. But already by the time of *XX Poems* Larkin had written a number of mature Movement poems—notably 'Deceptions', 'Spring', 'Next, Please', 'Coming', 'No Road', 'Going' and 'At Grass'. All that remained was for him to clarify the direction in which he had begun to move, and this was achieved in the years 1950–5 while he was in Belfast. Larkin has said that his friendship with Amis continued to be a crucial factor during this period: 'I moved to Belfast in 1950 as sub-librarian in the University, which I found very stimulating, and there I wrote the bulk of *The Less Deceived* under no particular influence except Kingsley's. I'd visions of showing him things he would laugh at. It's a formidable experience to be laughed at by Kingsley.'[18] Both the fear of being ridiculed by Amis, and the desire to amuse him, seem to have been in Larkin's mind when writing in the early 1950s.

By the end of 1951 the first stage of the Oxford contribution to the Movement was complete. As well as the appearance of *Mixed Feelings* and *XX Poems,* this was the year in which

Holloway appeared in a *Hudson Review* symposium of 'Five British Poets', Conquest was named as a prizewinner in the Festival of Britain poetry competition, and Jennings met John Lehmann, who was to broadcast her poems on the Third Programme. In this year, too, Amis started to write *Lucky Jim*. The novel was not to appear until 1954, but Amis says that he had it 'clear in mind' in 1949, and that the idea for it had begun even earlier: '*Lucky Jim* really started in 1946. I went to visit Larkin, who was in Leicester at the time. He took me in the Common Room there, and after about a quarter of an hour I said, "Christ, someone ought to do something about this lot". There was a dawning idea about being bored by powerful people.'[19] As well as helping to 'inspire' the novel, Larkin helped its later development. Amis has said: 'The first draft was very feeble, so I showed it to friends, particularly Philip Larkin again, who made very constructive suggestions.'[20]

1951 also saw the founding of *Essays in Criticism*. Edited by F. W. Bateson, and intended to supplement the work of Leavis's *Scrutiny*, *Essays in Criticism* was to serve as a platform for the Movement over the next few years. In 1951 it published articles by Amis, Holloway and Davie, and over the next five years there were poems, reviews and essays by Amis, Holloway, Davie, Wain, Enright, Larkin and Conquest. *Essays in Criticism* was now the only 'Oxford contact' between Movement poets, Amis and Wain having taken University jobs in Swansea and Reading, and Larkin having moved from Leicester to Belfast. This separation was in many ways useful to the poets concerned; in 'The Importance of Elsewhere', Larkin has described his feeling of isolation in Belfast as agreeable:

> Lonely in Ireland, since it was not home,
> Strangeness made sense. The salt rebuff of speech,
> Insisting so on difference, made me welcome:
> Once that was recognized, we were in touch.

Being 'elsewhere' allowed the writers the isolation necessary to produce some of their most important contributions to the

Movement: Amis *Lucky Jim* and *A Case of Samples,* Wain
Hurry on Down and over half the poems from *A Word Carved
on a Sill,* Larkin 'the bulk of' *The Less Deceived.* But it was
the earlier Oxford friendships which laid the foundation for
these achievements; without those friendships neither the
group programme nor the impressive individual works which
emerged out of it would have been possible.

II · CAMBRIDGE 1940-52

> Those Cambridge generations, Russell's, Keynes' . . .
> And mine? Oh mine was Wittgenstein's, no doubt:
> Sweet pastoral, too, when some-one else explains,
> Although my memories leave the eclogues out.
>
> Donald Davie, 'On Bertrand Russell's *Portraits from Memory*'

In a recent essay Donald Davie has examined the connection
between university friendships and the emergence of literary
generations like the 1930s Auden-Spender group, the 1940s
neo-Romantics, the 1950s Movement and the 1960s group
based round Ian Hamilton's *Review.* He observes that 'for the
last fifty years each new generation of English poets . . . was
formed or fomented or dreamed up by lively undergraduates
at Oxford' and that each group 'has picked up its Cambridge
recruits (Christopher Isherwood in one generation, Thom
Gunn in another) only afterwards, and incidentally'.[21] In the
case of the Movement this is a broadly accurate picture, but
it does underestimate the number of 'Cambridge recruits':
apart from Gunn, Davie himself and D. J. Enright were Cambridge graduates who found themselves being linked with the
Movement, and who eventually appeared in *New Lines.* These
three poets did not form a Cambridge group equivalent to that
of Amis, Larkin and Wain because they had little possibility
to become acquainted. Enright was at Downing College from
1938-40, did war service, and then went to teach in Alexandria

in 1947; Davie was briefly at St Catharine's College at the beginning of the 1940s, but had his education interrupted by five years' service in the navy, and his main spell at Cambridge was from 1946–50; Gunn, having completed two years' National Service between 1948–50, was at Trinity College from 1950–3. These Cambridge poets had contact with the Oxford group before they had any contact with each other.

However, at least one of the poets, Thom Gunn, was briefly involved in a group whose sympathies were akin to those of Amis, Larkin and Wain. Through his involvement in the editing and production of the Cambridge undergraduate magazine *Granta,* Gunn not only found an outlet for his early verse but received support and criticism from a group of friends. Amongst these were Karl Miller, John Coleman, Mark Boxer (the cartoonist Marc), and Nicholas Tomalin: 'we promoted each other consistently,' Gunn has said.[22] Miller seems to have been the one to have given Gunn's poetry most attention: 'When I wrote a new poem I would give it to him for criticism, and he would pin it to the wall above his desk for several days before he told me what he thought of it . . . He matured my mind amazingly.'[23] When he later moved on to the staff of the *Spectator* and *New Statesman,* Miller showed a preference for Movement work.

Gunn's early work is renowned for its 'toughness', and toughness seems to have been part of *Granta*'s policy after it had come under new control in November 1952. One issue, for instance, contained a series of 'Cursory Rhymes' by John Coleman: these poked fun at Edith Sitwell, George Barker, Christopher Fry, and, most importantly perhaps, at Stephen Spender, who had recently been involved in a confrontation with the South African poet Roy Campbell:

> Stevie, Stevie Spender, why are you so tender,
> Why do you never go on a bender?
> 'Because in public houses I cannot say my prayers
> And beastly Zulu Campbell keeps kicking me downstairs.'[24]

Spender symbolized for the Cambridge group, and later came

to symbolize for the Movement, the kind of poet whom it was necessary to oppose: effete and upper-middle-class as against tough, heterosexual and beer-drinking. When Gunn came to write his poem in praise of toughness, 'Lines for a Book', it was natural that he should choose Spender as his butt:

> I think of all the toughs through history
> And thank heaven they lived continually.
> I praise the overdogs from Alexander
> To those who would not play with Stephen Spender.

The attack on Spender might be seen as mere undergraduate prankishness, but it should be remembered that Spender had also come in for criticism from F. R. Leavis, who had attacked him as a false metropolitan reputation. Leavis's teaching provided a link between Enright, Davie and Gunn, since all experienced it and all admired him. Enright, as a pupil at Downing College (where Leavis was a Fellow from 1937 onwards), had the most contact with him, and has said that he considers himself 'extremely lucky' to have had Leavis and James Smith (another *Scrutiny* contributor) as tutors: 'Leavis was one of the very few teachers I came across who actively and deeply *wanted* his pupils to follow what he was saying and treated them as something approaching equals, without a hint of condescension'. By 1940, when he was just twenty, Enright had already begun to write for *Scrutiny,* and over the next six years he published over twenty reviews and articles in its pages. Davie also looked up to Leavis: he has described 1946–50 as 'the years when *Scrutiny* was my bible, and F. R. Leavis my prophet'. Gunn says that Leavis helped him to become not only a better critic but a better poet: 'He attracted me as few other teachers at Cambridge did . . . And his discriminations and enthusiasm helped teach me to write, better than any creative writing class could have. His insistence on the realized, being the life of poetry, was exactly what I needed'.[25]

Leavis, like T. S. Eliot and I. A. Richards before him, approached poetry with rigour and scepticism, and was quick to condemn preciosity or vagueness. He looked sternly upon the great Romantic poets, and his stance was an implicit rebuke to the efforts of 1940s neo-Romantics. In this way, Leavis, though not a poet himself, was able to influence the poetry of the Movement. Gunn has said that Leavis's famous *Scrutiny* essay on Shelley was instrumental in '[helping one] to hold in leash, or to a certain extent transform, one's own self-pity.'[26] Davie also owed much to Leavis's example. The five poems which he had published in an anthology in 1946, were immature, making archaic overtures to the heart in the way that the early Larkin and Amis had done:

> Turn, two-faced heart,
> By mind caught out.
> So heart and heart, and heart
> That mind doth flout,
> A keener compound smart
> Will breed, and deeper doubt.[27]

By the early 1950s, however, Davie had decided that, as he puts it in 'At Knaresborough', 'the heart is not to be solicited'. Poems like 'Among Artisans' Houses', 'Hypochondriac Logic' and 'Pushkin: A Didactic Poem' (all of them completed by October 1951) show Davie abandoning lyricism and feeling for a poetry of reason and statement. The poems show a general indebtedness to Leavis's rigour, and the last of them also has a specific debt to Leavisian ideas about the 'Line of Wit' and lost 'organic community':

> Self-consciousness is not at fault
> In itself. It can be kept
> Other than morbid, under laws
> Of disciplined sensibility, such
> As the seventeenth-century Wit.
> But all such disciplines depend
> On disciplines of social use,
> Now widely lost.

It is a feature of Davie's early poems that they read at times like critical essays: he seems to be attempting to incorporate into poetry certain qualities (fastidiousness, scepticism, carefully constructed argument) which, though not usually thought of as 'poetic' qualities, can be found in Leavis's criticism.

The impact of Leavis on Enright was made much earlier: by 1942 Enright was already expressing opinions which bore the mark of Leavis's influence and which looked forward to the Movement. His review 'Ruins and Warnings' took exception to the latest collections of Spender and of the neo-Apocalyptic poet Henry Treece:

Mr Spender has given us plenty of evidence from which to deduce his inability to use his imagination in a truly poetic way. Like those of so many of our contemporary poets, his imaginative faculties alternate spasmodically between the bathetic 'plain statement' kind of thing and that ghastly modern Homeric metaphor which fills one with regressive yearnings for the good old Georgians of yesteryear . . . Mr Henry Treece, on the other hand, has Imagination by the ton. But Treece (a member of the not-so-new and not-so-apocalyptic New Apocalypse) is a semi-surrealist poet and that kind of Imagination has always been quite un-rationed. It strikes me that the semi-surrealist poet occupies a highly privileged position on Parnassus: when he can't go on meaning any longer he can always slip into a stanza or two of non-meaning (which relieves him of the strain genuine poets must occasionally suffer under).[28]

The insistence on the effort demanded by poetry; the com-mitment to moderation implicit in the pejorative 'unrationed'; the suggestion that 'Imagination' is not self-evidently desir-able; and the esteem for clarity of meaning (if not of 'bathetic "plain statement"'); these at once betray the influence of Leavis and anticipate the Movement. Enright's capacity to put together such a comprehensive statement of Movement belief as early as 1942 may suggest that he was precociously certain of the direction which contemporary poetry should take; more probably, though, it simply confirms the compa-tibility of orthodox Leavisite judgment with what was even-tually to be the Movement programme.

Enright's first serious attempts to write poetry seem to have begun when he went to Egypt in 1947. His little-known *Season Ticket* was published in Alexandria in 1948 and was well received by the *Times Literary Supplement* on 19 August

1949. Eight of these poems were retained in *The Laughing Hyena* (1953), and what is striking about them is Enright's vigorous, debunking and familiarizing treatment of nature. A wave 'tosses the nervous yellow crabs/And hurries away. Then returns a little later/To reclaim its busy passengers'; the palm tree is 'volatile' and 'young dates hang from her cheeks like beads of sweat'; the willow tree has 'long hair' which 'trails/Across the earth's relaxed and hairy chest'. The rather jaunty images seem intended as a reaction against what Enright had called 'modern Homeric metaphor', and they prefigure the kind of imagery to be used by Enright himself, and by Amis, when the Movement was more firmly established.

Enright's preoccupation with metaphor around this time is also evident in an attack, in 1947, on what he saw as the undiscriminating editorial policy of *Poetry London,* which was regarded in some quarters as the leading poetry magazine in England.[29] 'I have written this article,' Enright claimed, 'not merely because I consider *Poetry London* a rather uninspired collection of verse, but because I believe it has a positively harmful influence on contemporary writing.' Enright exempted from his criticisms only one *Poetry London* contributor, Henry Reed, whose 'Lessons of the War' he admired because 'too modest, or too wise, to attempt to deal directly with War' (this approval of a modest and oblique approach to 'big subjects' is again indicative of an emerging Movement aesthetic). Otherwise Enright is unremittingly hostile to *Poetry London,* developing his earlier *Scrutiny* criticisms of the metaphorical excess of neo-Romanticism: 'There really ought to be a society for the prevention of cruelty to metaphors. These *Poetry London* poets flog their overworked metaphors mercilessly, force them into the most unnatural postures, pour gallon upon gallon of obscure pathos into them, until they burst—into bathos.' Enright was equally critical of an alternative school of social realists, arguing that the editor of *Poetry London,* Tambimuttu, had 'confused intellect with the "I Spy" game of the Reporter poets'. This deploring of political reportage ('1930s poetry'), on the one hand, and metaphorical lavishness ('1940s poetry') on the other, later became a common Movement theme. It was in very similar terms in the introduction to *New Lines* in 1956 that Conquest dismissed both 'residual nuisances like the Social Realists' and 'the debilitating theory that poetry *must* be metaphorical'.

Enright's disparaging view of *Poetry London* was shared by the Oxford contingent of the Movement: *Mandrake* in October 1947 called its special Tenth issue 'disastrous'. *Poetry London* was identified as the chief purveyor of the '1940s poetry' which the Movement wished to oppose. Apart from Keith Douglas and Henry Reed, the only *Poetry London* contributor to have earned respect seems to have been Allan Rodway, who published under the pseudonym Edwin Allan: when Amis met Rodway in 1954, he told him that he had been influenced by the example of Edwin Allan's light verse. Otherwise, the Movement felt hostile to *Poetry London*: its title and its flamboyant editor Tambimuttu, nicknamed 'Tamby-Pamby' by Conquest,[30] had Bohemian and metropolitan associations for which the Movement felt a Leavisite mistrust. There may also have been personal grievances against *Poetry London*: Tambimuttu has said that some of the Movement poets sent him their work, but were among those whom '*Poetry London* rejected from 1939–51 as not very interesting'.[31] For those Movement poets who saw it, Enright's attack must have sharpened and dignified their animosity.

There was, however, one Movement poet who appeared in *Poetry London,* and who helped destroy its values from within. Having had three poems accepted by the magazine in the previous couple of years, Donald Davie published one of his first critical articles there, 'The Spoken Word', in November 1950. This followed up a suggestion by S. L. Bethell in the previous issue that Anglo-American poetry was moving into a new but conservative phase. Davie found evidence to support Bethell's suggestion in an American anthology, *Poets of the Pacific,* edited by Yvor Winters. The anthology, he said, would satisfy poets looking for 'a new perspective and a new departure', for Winter's Stanford group were of the view

> that a poem is none the worse for being built around a structure of rational discourse, and that a poet's intelligence can be brought into play as effectively when he follows a rational argument as when he has recourse to witty metaphor or juxtaposition . . . They recognize the achievements of French symbolists, and of post-symbolists and experimentalists such as Eliot, Pound, Wallace Stevens and Hart Crane; but they think that this vein is now worked out and that healthy poetry today must find again a basis in rational philosophy. In general they eschew free verse and write in strict metre and in rhyme. . . .
>
> For the young English poet resentful of the tyranny of the 'image' in the restricted sense of 'metaphor' (whether inflated into symbols, worried into conceits, or compressed into 'striking' epithets), this American anthology points in a direction which may provide a wholesome alternative; i.e. it points to a renewed poetry of statement, openly didactic but saved by a sedulously noble diction, from prosiness.[32]

This is one of the earliest examples of a Movement manifesto, for while purporting to describe an American anthology, Davie is giving expression to a number of ideas central to the Movement programme. He addresses himself specifically to 'the young English poet', confident that like-minded contemporaries do exist.

Davie's confidence was justified. Some of the virtues which he found in the Winters anthology—'intelligence', rational argument, severity of design—John Wain had also been finding in contemporary American poetry. Ironically, as Wain explains, he owed his introduction to such poetry to the leading neo-Romantic of the day—a writer whom, as the result of the re-discovery of clarity and argument, the Movement would displace:

> I well remember, in 1947, the excitement of a reading by Dylan Thomas in Oxford; as well as poems of his own, he read us American poems from an anthology some friend had sent him. . . . Whoever it was who had the kind thought of sending Thomas that book, he started a great many budding poets reading John Crowe Ransom, Allen Tate, Wallace Stevens,

Karl Shapiro, Richard Wilbur, Robert Lowell, Randall Jarrell and a dozen more . . .

One result of this study of American verse by younger English poets was to help them back to an understanding of, and respect for, poetic form. The American poets, however much they differed from one another in style and outlook, were united in being conscious craftsmen.[33]

That the Movement were able in the late 1940s and early 1950s to discover an increasing number of poets whose 'conscious craftmanship' lent support to their own aesthetic would seem to indicate a growing sureness of purpose. In 1949, Davie even managed to include Eliot in his design, arguing, in another manifesto-like essay, that Eliot's turning away from Corbière and revaluation of Milton signified a conviction that contemporary poetry must 'be re-organized, by an emphasis not upon wealth and experiment, but upon order, severity, and correctness'.[34] He also spoke of 'a new movement of spirit in society', and it was this idea—that of a new society or *zeitgeist* requiring a new poetry—that was to prove most crucial to the establishment of Movement poetry over the next few years.

In the late 1940s, then, Cambridge poets like Davie and Enright were reaching much the same conclusions about contemporary poetry as were their Oxford counterparts. There may indeed have been mutual influence, for it seems likely that Amis and Wain, for example, would have seen at least some of the work published by Davie and Enright in *Scrutiny, The Critic, Poetry London, Cambridge Writing* and *Prospect,* just as Davie and Enright might have seen Wain's contributions to *Mandrake* and *Penguin New Writing.* J. W. Saunders has pointed out that periodicals and magazines can often 'compensate the poet for lack of centres in which he can meet his colleagues',[35] and around 1950—with Amis in Swansea, Davie in Dublin, Enright in Birmingham, Holloway in Aberdeen, Larkin in Belfast and Wain in Reading—such 'compensation' was undoubtedly essential to the formation of a Movement aesthetic. What is certain is that Davie's critical study, *Purity of Diction in English Verse,* when it appeared in 1952, was noticed by Wain, Enright and Amis. Wain reviewed it in *Mandrake,* finding in it a 'solid merit' which he believed other 'grumbling' reviewers had ignored; and Enright in a 1953 article 'The Poet, the Professor and the Public' used terms and made distinctions which clearly derive from a reading of the book.[36] Amis, too, was able to tell Davie how much he had enjoyed reading the book when they met at a university teachers' conference in 1954; the meeting, and the book's relation to the development of the Movement, are described by Davie in a 1966 postscript:

One of my pleasant memories is of Kingsley Amis, when we met for the first time, telling me how he had come across *Purity of Diction in English Verse* in Swansea Public Library, and had read it with enthusiasm. What pleased me was that Amis had liked the book, not in his capacity of university teacher (as he then was), but from the point of view of himself as poet . . .

All this was at a time when Amis and I and one or two others discovered that we had been moving, each by his own route, upon a common point of view as regards the writing of poems. That point of intersection, or an area of agreement around it, came to be called the Movement . . . I like to think that if the group of us had ever cohered enough to subscribe to a common manifesto, it might have been *Purity of Diction in English Verse.*

Davie's description of the book as a 'manifesto' for the Movement is not merely hindsight: he said at the time, in his conclusion to its first part, that it was 'to the would-be poet of today that I should like to address myself . . . I should like to think that this study might help some practising poet to a poetry of urbane and momentous statement'. Davie sought to revivify the concept of 'poetic diction' (he believed that it lent dignity to 'ordinary things') and to defend poems commonly accused of being metaphorically impoverished as having, rather, 'economy of metaphor'. He drew attention to the value of poets interested, not in experimenting with language, but in 'purifying' it and in revitalizing old usages. There was a suggestion that at certain points of literary history retrenchment was more valuable than innovation. Thus while Pope and Eliot were right to be innovative, Johnson and the Augustans were equally justified in being conservative: all were acting correctly in the context of the times. It was clear that Davie regarded the present as a time best suited to 'conservation', and at least one reviewer picked up the hint: William Empson in the *New Statesman,* though finding the prospect 'a bit flat' conceded that 'a recovery from "experimental" and "transitional" work does seem overdue, and many poets seem to be recognizing it'. A month previously, G. S. Fraser had also detected a spirit of retrenchment, and spoke of a 'new smoothness' in contemporary poetry.[37]

By the end of 1952, then, London reviewers had begun to talk of a new poetry and had taken note of the defence of it in Davie's *Purity of Diction in English Verse.* Within the Movement, further links and friendships were being made. Conquest and Amis met in the summer of 1952 at a party for contributors to the first of the annual P.E.N. anthologies, *New Poems 1952*, and discovered they shared a taste for bawdy verse (Amis listened respectfully as Conquest recited 'Eskimo Nell'). The friendship seems to have developed quickly; when a correspondent to the *Listener* criticized one of Conquest's poems in November 1952, Amis defended the poem and ridiculed the criticism.[38] Throughout the 1950s Conquest accommodated Amis for weekend visits (Conquest was the only London-based Movement poet), and they later collaborated on several ventures, including a novel, *The Egyptologists* (1965).

Conquest also had his first contact with Enright in the summer of 1952. Both had been regular contributors of poetry to the *Listener* since 1947 and to the *New Statesman* since 1950. When the special Penguin collection of prizewinning Festival of Britain poems, *Poems 1951,* appeared, Enright picked out Conquest's 'Reflections on Landscapes' as the poem which 'most interested' him, and praised it as 'cold, intelligent and self-contained'.[39] Enright wrote to Conquest in June 1952, sending him a copy of the review, and the two

met during the next few months when Enright visited London.
They were in correspondence after Enright departed for Japan
in 1953, and exchanged advice when they came to edit the
two Movement anthologies, *Poets of the 1950's* and *New
Lines*. Though slightly older than the other Movement poets
(Conquest was born in 1917, Enright in 1920), they shared
with them a sense of being up against the literary 'Establishment'. Enright's poem 'Frankenstein', dedicated to 'R.C.',
communicates a feeling of two young poets clubbing up
against a common enemy of elders:

> The public complain that young writers are tongue-tied
> — perhaps struck dumb by listening to their elders?

Outside the Amis-Larkin-Wain circle this was the closest friendship within the Movement, and each lent support to the other.
When G. S. Fraser gave Enright's *The Laughing Hyena* only a
lukewarm review in 1953, Conquest wrote to protest, describing Enright's as a 'mind of enormous intellectual and emotional capacity'.[40]

Another Movement poet to whom Enright wrote around
this time was Larkin. When *XX Poems,* Larkin's privately
printed edition of 100 copies, was sent to editors and leading
literary figures in 1951, none of them paid it any attention.
But Enright did review it for *The Month* in November 1951,
finding in Larkin a 'respect for language which is beginning to
look old-fashioned these days; he persuades words into being
poetry, he does not bully them. This little pamphlet whets
the appetite: it is to be hoped that some publisher will take
the hint.'[41] It was four years before any publisher took the
hint, but Enright and Larkin did become acquainted, exchang-.
ing letters shortly after the review appeared.

Thom Gunn had also begun to have contact with other
Movement poets. He admired the poetry of Elizabeth Jennings,
and travelled over to Oxford to meet her in 1953. He also
met John Wain around this time, though his description of
the meeting seems intended to show that it made no deep

impression on him:

I'd never heard of John Wain; he was coming to speak to some club in Cambridge, and I met him afterwards. He was extremely nice to me and had read some of my poems in a Cambridge magazine. He said, There are some other chaps up in London who are writing like you, we must all get together. Or something of the sort. It wasn't as bad as that because we didn't really get together. I wasn't quite sure who these other chaps were . . . The big joke about the Movement was that none of the people had ever met each other and certainly never subscribed to anything like a programme. There were a few chance resemblances, but they were pretty chance.[42]

The disclaimer is typical of the kind that Movement poets have made when confronted with the suggestion that theirs was an organized programme. Davie has said that 'we were all morbidly anxious not to seem to be acting in concert',[43] and though Gunn has more justification than most for denying his part in the Movement, his statement does fly in the face of most of the evidence we have. By the end of 1952, something approximating to a movement had certainly developed: contacts had been made, friendships formed, correspondences begun. More importantly, statements and poems contributing to the formation of a group aesthetic had appeared in various small press and little magazine outlets; few of the poets consciously 'subscribed' to a programme, but all helped to further it in one way or another. What was required, now that much of the Movement work (*Lucky Jim, Hurry on Down, The Less Deceived, Brides of Reason, Fighting Terms*) was in progress, was for the group identity to be more sharply defined, and for that identity to be brought to public notice. It was in the years 1953-5, in London rather than in Oxford or Cambridge, that this was achieved.

III · LONDON 1953-5

I thought of London spread out in the sun,
Its postal districts packed like squares of wheat:

There we were aimed.

> Larkin, 'The Whitsun Weddings'

So poetry, which is in Oxford made
An art, in London only is a trade.

> Dryden, 'Prologue to the University of Oxford'

Between 5 March 1952 and 6 March 1953, John Lehmann
edited on the BBC Third Programme a series of twelve radio
broadcasts featuring contemporary writing. During the Second
World War George Orwell and others had speculated about
the long-term possibilities of radio as a means of popularizing
poetry, and Lehmann's programmes, given the title *New
Soundings* and broadcast at monthly intervals, partly fulfilled
such hopes. They achieved audiences estimated at 100,000
and provided the opportunity for several new writers to have
their poems read on the air. Amongst these poets were
Donald Davie, Thom Gunn, John Holloway, Elizabeth Jennings
and John Wain. Though *New Soundings* was regarded by the
BBC and by radio reviewers to have been a successful venture,
Lehmann learnt before the end of the series that his contract
was not to be renewed, and that he was to be replaced as
editor by John Wain. Wain was asked, initially, to prepare six
programmes. These were broadcast under the new title *First
Reading*—a title which, since Wain was teaching at Reading at
the time, was in some quarters taken to be a pun. The six
programmes went out between 26 April and 24 September
1953.

First Reading has been seen as a crucial breakthrough for
the Movement writers. Larkin claims that 'the Movement, if
you want to call it that, really began when John Wain succeeded

John Lehmann on that BBC programme', and Wain himself
has said that *First Reading* 'was a chance to move a few of the
established reputations gently to one side and allow new
people their turn . . . The result was the birth of what later
became known as the Movement'. In a 1956 retrospect of the
programme Wain went even further, suggesting that *First
Reading* was a unique event in English literary history:

> . . . the present literary generation is the first one in the history of
> English literature, and quite possibly the last, to have made its *début*
> by means of broadcasting . . . Some representative names would be:
> A. Alvarez, Kingsley Amis, Anthony Hartley, Philip Larkin, Mairi
> MacInnes, Philip Oakes, Burns Singer. Every one of these writers, all
> of whom are squarely before the public eye today, was introduced to
> a wider public on the Third Programme; it doesn't behove me to talk
> about it, because I edited the series, called *First Reading*, in which they
> all appeared . . . However, it is a fact that the very people who are now
> dominant were unknown before they became the centre of controversy
> in these six programmes, and that the reviewers laughed at me for
> bringing foward exactly those writers whose boots they are now licking.[44]

Wain's boasts must be treated with caution, for most Movement writers had already made their '*débuts*' in the 1940s.
Moreover John Lehmann has claimed with some justification
that it was he, not Wain, who 'introduced' the Movement to
a wider public. His *New Soundings* had not only preceded
First Reading in the featuring of Movement work, but had
included more of it: fifteen Movement poems were read, while
Wain offered only nine. Lehmann had also tried to define the
characteristics of the 'new poetry': on 24 September 1952, in
a programme which included poems by Wain, Jennings and
Gunn, he observed that the Romanticism of recent poetry was
being offset by 'a very different mood and impulse, not precisely satirical but of a dry anti-romantic flavour, and using
the contrast or conflict of a conversational tone and an exact-
ing technical pattern.' *First Reading* was less of a revolution
than Wain pretends: Lehmann had got in there before.

However, it would be true to say that Wain's broadcasts
were more partisan than Lehmann's: they not only drew

attention to the new poetry, but actively promoted it. Wain had prepared the ground in a broadcast about Wallace Stevens on 29 March 1953, one month before the opening of the series, when he contended that in contemporary poetry 'those poets and critics claiming to represent the Romantic attitude have been driven from the field. I must try not to pronounce this too sadly. In my opinion what happened was right.' This provocative tone and attitude were present again in *First Reading*'s opening broadcast on 26 April 1953. Lehmann had prided himself on his receptivity to material of all kinds, but Wain announced at once that he was 'biased', and said that he would interpret 'good' poetry as being 'what is good for the present moment; what needs to be encouraged, brought out and stressed, so as to develop the most healthy shoots that we can find in the tangled literary scene'. He characterized the 'present moment' as one of retrenchment: 'a period of expansion has to be followed by a period of consolidation'. The terms here sounded very much like those used in Davie's *Purity of Diction in English Verse,* and this may help to explain why Wain's word 'consolidation' should immediately have become something of a catch-phrase, one that was to be associated with the Movement throughout the 1950s; by 1955 at any rate, Davie was noting that the word 'consolidation' had 'achieved such general currency as a literary talking point that it has become, what perhaps Mr Wain never intended, a sort of manifesto'.[45] Wain also supplied on his first programme a striking image of the new writers whom he wished to promote: 'they are suspicious of anything that suggests sprawling or lack of discipline. They are keenly aware of belonging to a tradition; not only the tradition of the last thirty years, but the longer tradition that stretches away behind, and with which the more recent discoveries will have to be put in perspective.' These editorial pronouncements were followed by a vivid opening example of new but tradition-conscious writing: an extract (the bed-burning episode) from Amis's then unpublished *Lucky Jim.*

Promotion of the Movement continued throughout the series. In the second programme (24 May 1953), A. Alvarez, later to be hostile to the Movement but at this point a friend of Wain and admirer of Empson, called for 'a revival in poetry of what Donne called "masculine persuasive force" and intellectual objectivity'. In the next programme (1 July 1953), a poem by A. J. Bull made similar pleas, wishing to see 'the hard, unyielding sculptor's line' and 'the sacred square established again': 'Order must come: for surely we are sick/Seeing rococo writhe about the dome.' This programme also included an investigation by Davie into the 'difference between English and Irish poetry'; Larkin's 'If My Darling' was read, and the point made that he was often mistaken for an Irish poet.[46] Poems by Davie and Holloway were read on the penultimate programme (23 August), and in the final one (24 September) there was a special feature on Thom Gunn, whose work was deemed to satisfy Wain's taste for 'the spare and athletic rather than the lush and proliferating'.

It was not surprising when *First Reading* aroused a certain amount of controversy. Wain's editorial statements had been calculated to alarm the literary 'Establishment' by suggesting that a disgruntled new generation of writers was emerging. In the second broadcast he said that he 'should like to see the younger men do some grumbling . . . and every now and then I shall incite one of them to say what he would like to see altered or done away with'; in the third he noted 'a quite widespread feeling among younger writers, and particularly poets, that the decks are going to be cleared'. These declarations, and the inclusion in the series of a number of writers of questionable merit, finally incited the *New Statesman* radio reviewer, Hugh Massingham, to pour scorn on Wain's editorial policy: 'Our brave new world is over at last and the old fogies can be led off to the slaughter-house after being festooned with the usual sacrificial garlands. After that Mr Wain and his fledgelings can move in and establish the new dispensation.' Massingham went on to ask whether there was 'not something faintly ridiculous in treating young men, whom some of us have never heard of, with the solemnity that should be reserved for Mr Eliot or Mr Empson?'[47]

Massingham's attack brought protests not only from Wain but from G. S. Fraser, at that time perhaps the principal poetry reviewer in London. Fraser held weekly poetry evenings at his Chelsea home, and through these had become acquainted with Wain and other young poets; despite his previous 'New Apocalypse' affiliation he was sympathetic to the Movement. In his reply to Massingham, he drew the most detailed picture to date of the new generation:

First Reading does not really purport to be a bird's eye view of recent English writing in general; it purports, I think, to be a platform for a new generation of writers — the under-thirties — who have really today no other platform of this sort. We shall not be fair to this new generation, unless we realize how differently situated they are from ourselves They were children during the struggle against Fascism in the 1930s. They were mostly too young to be uprooted and cast into a wider society during the last World War . . . They are most typically (Mr Amis, Mr Corke, Mr Davie, Mr Alvarez, Mr Wain himself) young dons, and often young dons in provincial universities. The centre, moreover, of their intellectual universe lies not in London, but in Oxford or Cambridge. In that sense, *we* perhaps look provincial to them. They discuss passionately not what Mr Toynbee said about Mr Connolly but what Dr Leavis said about Mr Bateson. They think metropolitan urbanity rather hollow and metropolitan smartness rather vulgar. Possibly, in fact, their attitude towards us is a little like that of D. H. Lawrence towards Bloomsbury. Again, they are not ashamed of being dons.[48]

In so far as the future of *First Reading* went, Fraser's defence served little purpose. The criticisms of Massingham and other listeners had been noted at the BBC, and after only six programmes Wain was replaced as editor by Ludovic Kennedy. But the row over the programme was far from damaging to the Movement; it brought the writers attention and, as Larkin says, forced the public to look upon them as a new group: '[we] got attacked in a very convenient way, and consequently we became lumped together'.[49] Fraser's letter also described the group as having a distinctive identity: that of a generation of provincial dons who were suspicious of the metropolis. This provided the Movement with an 'image' which reviewers found useful; more importantly, it provided them with a 'self-image' at a time when they were still struggling to assert themselves. Davie, for example, was to return to Fraser's metropolitan/provincial distinction, and to mull over its implications, on no less than five occasions over the next year.

G. S. Fraser's other service at this time was his editing of an anthology, *Springtime*, which included among its fifty contributors six Movement poets: Amis, Davie, Gunn, Jennings, Larkin and Wain. Davie has said that it was *Springtime* which first revealed to him that there were others who shared his 'indignant distaste for the Dylan Thomas or George Barker sort of poetry which had been *de rigueur* in London for a decade'.[50] As important as the inclusion of Movement poems were Fraser's introductory remarks, which reiterated the claims of Davie and Wain, depicting the present as 'a period of consolidation'. Fraser divided his poets into various categories, the Movement being said to consist of Empsonians and Academics. Groupings were also made in the 1953 P.E.N. anthology edited by Conquest, Michael Hamburger and Howard Sergeant: Conquest himself, Amis, Enright and Jennings were placed together.

Such groupings were not without their effect on the poets themselves. 'When a few reviewers and columnists noted the same connections I had seen for myself,' Davie writes, 'I exerted myself bit by bit to get to know the other members of the group.'[51] He met Wain as a result of *First Reading,* and then Larkin, whom he invited to read and put up in Dublin. Conquest first corresponded with Jennings while he was editing the P.E.N. anthology, and later wrote a poem about her, 'A Woman Poet'. He also provided London accommodation for several Movement poets: 'From early 1953 until mid-1956 I had a small house up in Hampstead with room to put people up, and Amis and his wife, Enright and his wife and daughter, Davie, Wain and Larkin, stayed with me for the odd night or nights at one time or another—the Amises quite frequently.'[52]

But one of the most important friendships during this period had begun much earlier. Anthony Hartley, whose reviewing for the *Spectator* was to play an important part in the establishing of the Movement, had been friendly with Wain (and also knew Amis and Larkin) while an undergraduate at St John's College, Oxford, in the 1940s. Wain had featured a short story of Hartley's on the fifth of his *First Reading* programmes, and Hartley's poems, which were much indebted to Wain's (one of them, for instance, was called 'And Where You Love You Cannot Break Away', a title taken from the last line of Wain's 'Reasons for Not Writing Orthodox Nature Poetry'), had begun to appear in the *Spectator* in 1952. Like Wain, Hartley was a devotee of Empson, and made much use of Empson's favourite *terza rima* form. On 10 July 1953 Hartley's first review appeared in the *Spectator*. It praised Amis's and Wain's contributions to the 1953 P.E.N. anthology, criticized what it saw as the pseudo-religiosity of contemporary neo-Romanticism, and called for a new rationalism in poetry. Over the next three years Hartley continued to attack Romantic poets, reviewed Movement work at every opportunity, and helped a large amount of Movement poetry to appear in the *Spectator*'s pages. It was through his efforts that the *Spectator* became the Movement's principal platform.

Until the appearance of Hartley's first review, the *Spectator* could hardly have been less likely to become a platform for new writing. It published poems by Davie and Holloway in May and June of 1953, but before this its only publication of Movement poetry had been four years previously, when it printed poems by Conquest and Jennings. During the same period, its principal competitors among the London weeklies, the *Listener* and *New Statesman*, had in comparison been lavish in their acceptance of Movement work. The *Listener* had published over fifty Movement poems (Conquest, Enright,

Holloway, Wain) and the *New Statesman* over forty (Conquest. Enright, Holloway, Jennings, Wain and Davie—the last of these beginning a spell as poetry reviewer in April 1953). The turning point for the *Spectator* was not only Hartley's arrival on the paper in 1953 (he was to be, in effect, the Poetry Editor), but the arrival of J. D. Scott as Literary Editor in the same year. Between June 1953 and July 1956 (the month in which the Movement anthology *New Lines* appeared) there were over 240 Movement contributions to the *Spectator*—poems predominantly, but also articles, reviews, letters and one short story, 'Samuel Deronda', by John Wain (appropriately, the story described a young man's infiltration of the 'London literary world'). Wain and Amis were under contract to write the chief book reviews, and of the nine *New Lines* poets only Enright was not a regular contributor of poetry.

These weekly periodical appearances had a large part to play in the development of the Movement. They allowed the writers to clarify their ideas, to disseminate their views, and to create the taste by which their own work was to be enjoyed. Davie has described the way in which reviewing can abet a literary programme:

Precisely because the positions that matter are so few, it is entirely feasible for a group to secure one or two sub-editorial chairs and a few reviewing 'spots', so as to impose their shared proclivities and opinions as the reigning orthodoxy for a decade. It is altogether fatuous to cry out at this as scandalous; it is inevitable, given the smallness of England, and the economic advantages of metropolitan centralization. Quite simply, these are the facts to be borne in mind . . .[53]

Two of Anthony Hartley's reviews were of particular importance in the imposition of a Movement 'orthodoxy'. In 'Critic Between the Lines' on 8 January 1954, he distinguished between two tendencies in English poetry: the 'academic', present in the work of 'our young academic poets, the University Wits (Kingsley Amis and Donald Davie, for example)', and the 'symbolist', present in the work of Kathleen Raine and Edith Sitwell. Hartley was critical of Sitwell, admitting his preference for the 'more-or-less metaphysicals' who belonged to the Movement. Sitwell's reputation was at its peak in the early 1950s, and Hartley's criticisms brought an indignant reply from her. Over the next few weeks a lively correspondence ensued in which Wain and Jennings came to Hartley's defence, and there was a pseudonymous attack on Sitwell signed 'Little Mr Tomkins'. In the course of the correspondence Sitwell praised Amis's recently published *Lucky Jim*, but the compliment rebounded when Amis revealed that it was he who had been 'Little Mr Tomkins'. Sitwell-baiting was no less popular with the Movement than it had been with Geoffrey Grigson in the 1930s: Amis had already attacked her in 1952, and Davie was later to call her 'no poet at all'.[54] Trivial though such literary squabbling might appear, it did have the effect of bolstering the group: 'friends' and 'enemies' were identified, and the nature of Movement taste became clearer.

Hartley's other important review was 'Poets of the Fifties', published on 27 August 1954 and devoted to recent publications by the Fantasy Press. The Fantasy Press had been founded by Oscar Mellor at Eynsham, Oxford, in 1952, and ran a series of poetry 'pamphlets', slim volumes with about half-a-dozen poems by a single author. The Movement poets represented were Jennings (no.1, 1952), Gunn (no. 16, 1953), Davie (no. 19, 1954), Larkin (no. 21, 1954), Amis (no. 22, 1954) and Holloway (no. 26, 1954). The Press also published the first full-length collections by three Movement poets, Jennings's *Poems* (1953), Gunn's *Fighting Terms* (1954) and Davie's *Brides of Reason* (1955). Hartley recognized the Fantasy Press as being an important outlet for new developments in English poetry, and tried to put these into perspective in his leading article. He covered much ground, noting a reaction against 1940s neo-Romanticism, tracing a heritage of Leavis, Empson and Logical Positivism, describing the stance of the poets as 'a liberalism distrustful of too much richness or too much fanaticism', and introducing the idea that a 'new movement'

was about to overthrow a 'twenty-year-old domination' of
the literary 'Establishment'.

Hartley's review might have had little impact had it not
coincided with economic difficulties which were then being
experienced by the *Spectator*. The coincidence, and its major
part in the naming and establishing of the Movement, have
been described by J. D. Scott:

> In 1954, I was literary editor of the *Spectator*. The circulation was not
> behaving as it should, and one day in the autumn the editor, Walter
> Taplin, gave the staff a pep-talk. What could we do to liven things up,
> get ourselves talked about, be more influential, more sensational, and so
> more circulation-building, more money-making? . . .
>
> . . . I had an idea for a box of fireworks . . . The idea that had occurred
> to me was to take the movement in poetry and see how far it extended
> beyond poetry, and specifically into the novel, and to consider the
> extent to which it represented some historic change in society. Two of
> the poets named in 'Poets of the Fifties' had then recently published
> first novels; Kingsley Amis's *Lucky Jim* and John Wain's *Hurry on Down*.
> Not very much, but I used it as the basis for my attempt.
>
> And so there appeared, on 1 October 1954, an article entitled 'In the
> Movement'. It was dignified as a Leading Literary Article, and was there-
> fore anonymous. It was designed to grab the attention of any casual
> reader who . . . might happen on it. It was written in a tone brisk, challeng-
> ing and dismissive.[55]

The part which journalism had to play in the development
of the Movement must therefore be admitted: had Walter
Taplin not needed a 'circulation-building' article the transformation of 'a movement' into 'the Movement' might never have
occurred. Nor would the writers have been the subject of a
lively and reputation-making correspondence which involved,
among others, Evelyn Waugh, Anthony Thwaite, Alan Brownjohn, Denis Donoghue, G. S Fraser and Malcolm Bradbury.

But it should be realized that the idea that there was a new
movement in writing had already been aired not only by
Anthony Hartley, on whose review Scott based his article, but
by a number of other writers as well. Reviews in the *Times
Literary Supplement* on 2 April and 28 May 1954 had spoken
of a 'set of young university poets' with a 'common style or

at least common tone', and just one week before the 'In the Movement' article, on 24 September 1954, a commentary page in the TLS provided a portrait of the new 'tough-minded rather than tender-minded' young poet. Much earlier, in November 1953, Stephen Spender had published an article in *Encounter* called 'On Literary Movements' which identified a 'movement' of 'teachers who, coming from the "red brick" universities, resent being called "dons"'. There was also a foreword to the newly founded *London Magazine,* in March 1954, in which John Lehmann expressed his misgivings about the new breed of poets with their policy of 'consolidation': 'This seems to me the most lamentable slogan ever invented for a generation of writers at the outset of their careers.' Even when hostile, such mentions of a movement in writing had their effect: by the time of Scott's article the idea of a movement had been put forward often enough for a certain amount of curiosity already to have been aroused. The literary public, as it had been in the late 1920s, was 'waiting for someone'.

Scott was also able to exploit the curiosity aroused by the publication of Wain's *Hurry on Down* in October 1953 and Amis's *Lucky Jim* in January 1954. On the whole well received, and read by those who knew the authors as *romans à clef* (some of the characters were thought to be based on Oxford contemporaries like Iris Murdoch, Wallace Robson and Monica Jones), these novels were discussed together as examples of a new fiction hostile to 'experimentalism'. C. P. Snow, J. B. Priestley and Walter Allen were among the critics to note the emergence of this fiction, and it was Allen who in his review of *Lucky Jim* provided a much-quoted sketch of the 'new hero' created by Amis and Wain:

A new hero has risen among us. Is he the intellectual tough, or the tough intellectual? He is consciously, even conscientiously, graceless. His face, when not dead-pan, is set in a snarl of exasperation. He has one skin too few, but his is not the sensitiveness of the young man in earlier twentieth-century fiction: it is the phoney to which his nerve-ends are tremblingly exposed, and at the least suspicion of the phoney he goes tough. He is at odds with his conventional university education, though he comes generally from a famous university: he has seen through the academic racket as he sees through all the others. A racket is phoneyness organized, and in contact with phoneyness he turns red just as litmus paper does in contact with acid. In life he has been among us for some little time. One may speculate whence he derives. The Services, certainly, helped to make him; but George Orwell, Dr Leavis and the Logical Positivists – or, rather, the attitudes these represent – all contributed to his genesis. In fiction I think he first arrived last year, as the central character of Mr John Wain's novel *Hurry on Down*. He turns up again in Mr Amis's *Lucky Jim.* [56]

When Allen mentions the influence of the Services, Orwell, Leavis and Logical Positivism he might equally well be discussing the authors of the novels as their characters. Such conflations of the ficitional and real are a common feature of the large amount of contemporary journalism about the Movement and, a few years later, about the 'Angry Young Men'. Amis's Dixon and Larkin's church-going bicyclist are often discussed as if they were real people, epitomes of the post-war Welfare State Englishman. This tendency suggests that much of the impact of Movement literature was caused by what was felt to be the pertinence of its fictional types to contemporary social concerns. Even before J. D. Scott calculatedly presented the Movement's work as relevant, reviewers like Walter Allen were linking it to the *zeitgeist*.

By the beginning of 1955, sufficient Movement work had appeared for some reviewers to be sure that it represented the 'literature of the 1950s'. 'Let no-one doubt,' the TLS announced on 7 January 'that the characteristic poetry of the mid-century is now established'. That a group of 'provincial dons' supposedly hostile to the metropolis should make use of London-based magazines in order to establish itself was an irony that at least one magazine noticed: the *New Statesman* commented drily that it was 'a pity that they cannot get together and produce a literary magazine of their own to counter the wicked influence of London'.[57] Arguably George Hartley did this on behalf of the Movement in 1954 when he founded the Marvell Press and *Listen* magazine, in Hessle, near Hull: *Listen,* 'that institution of the movement' as Davie has called it,[58] was predisposed towards the new poetry (the second issue, for instance, in Summer 1954, carried three poems by Davie, three by Larkin, two by Amis and one by Wain) and the Marvell Press published Larkin's *The Less Deceived* (1955), Holloway's *The Minute and Longer Poems* (1956) and Davie's *The Forests of Lithuania* (1959). But this provincially-based outlet was not the Movement's main one: it was in London that most of its work, and most of the comment on it, appeared. In June 1954 Davie was still enough of an 'outsider' to be asking, in a Leavis-like essay of that title, 'Is There a London Literary Racket?'; by October his own reputation had been made there.

Such access to the London 'publicity machine' was not something which fellow poets and fellow academics could easily forgive, and this helps to account for the intemperate tone of much of the early critical comment on the Movement. By now it should be possible to see that the Movement had a long and gradual development before the final *putsch*. But the question of why the Movement should have been received so eagerly by London journalists, and why it should have been thought so relevant to post-war preoccupations, is one that needs to be considered in more detail in the next chapter.

2

Class and Culture

The poetry of the 1930s may have been left-wing, but it was profoundly upper-class. It reads 'you' not 'we' . . . Its chief poets learnt at public (i.e. great upper-class private) schools and taught at preparatory schools. Behind it, at varying degrees of only half-discredited remoteness, stood literary Bohemia or Bloomsbury or the literary country-house week-end . . . The recent social revolution, gentle though real, in England, has changed this. The typical 'Movement' writer's childhood background appears to be lower-middle-class and suburban (often staunchly non-conformist, often in the industrial or semi-industrial Midlands or North of England). The crucial point is, that he is on the whole staying there. If he is teaching, it is not in an upper-class preparatory school, but in a 'red-brick' provincial university. The automatic decanting process into upper-class England has been interrupted. Perhaps it is no longer wanted. If true, this is important: we are witnessing the end of something which has been established ever since the death of Keats and Hazlitt.

John Holloway, 'New Lines in English Poetry' (1956)

From the moment that critics began to take note of it, the Movement was depicted as having not only a distinctive literary identity but a distinctive social identity as well. G. S. Fraser's suggestion, in his defence of *First Reading* in 1953, that there existed a new generation of 'young dons in provincial universities' was the first of many references to the social basis of the Movement. Drawing partly upon factual information about the social backgrounds of the Movement writers and partly upon literary sources such as 'Church Going' and *Lucky Jim,* critics began to construct vivid images of a new post-war 'type'. Martin Green defined this type as 'the decent man—as opposed to the gentleman' and visualized him as 'a grammar school teacher . . . with leather-patched elbows'. A. Alvarez drew a rather similar picture of 'the post-war Welfare State Englishman: shabby and not concerned with his appearance; poor—he has a bike not a car; . . . underfed, underpaid, overtaxed, hopeless, bored, wry'. Philip Oakes supplied a detailed 'identikit':

Born: Coketown 1925. Parents: lower-middle class. Educated: local council school, grammar school and university (after three years' military service). Married. One or two children. Occupation: civil servant/journalist/lecturer/minor executive. Politics: neutralist. Ambition: to live well. Interests: people, money, sex. Worries: money, sex. Enthusiasms: Orwell, jazz, Dr Leavis, old cars. Antipathies: Dylan Thomas, provincial culture, European novels. Future: indefinite.[1]

Though they confirmed that the Movement had a powerful impact upon contemporaries, and was felt to have a significance which extended beyond its literary productions, these sketches were painted in rather broad strokes. They were colourful, even comical, and some of the Movement poets were embarrassed by them.[2] But the Movement poets did not seek to reject or correct this picture; on the contrary, as can be seen from John Holloway's essay 'New Lines in English Poetry', they too suggested that it was possible to talk of 'a typical Movement writer' with a series of characteristic features. By the middle of the 1950s the image of the typical Movement writer as a provincial, lower-middle-class, scholarship-winning, Oxbridge-educated university lecturer was firmly established, though it was apparent even then that there were certain incompatibilities between this image and the kind of work which the Movement produced.

This image was accepted and even promoted by the Movement because most of its poets do fulfil at least two or three of the conditions of 'membership'. Amis, Davie and Holloway consider their backgrounds to be lower-middle-class. Davie, Enright, Larkin and Wain grew up in industrial towns in the North or Midlands. Amis, Davie and Enright had a Nonconformist religious upbringing. Davie, Enright, Holloway, Jennings, Larkin and Wain attended local grammar schools. Amis, Davie, Enright and Holloway went to university as scholarship boys, and all the group attended either Oxford or Cambridge. Amis, Davie, Enright, Holloway and Wain have taught in British provincial universities, and only Jennings has not at some stage worked full-time for an academic institution. Most importantly, perhaps, the Movement poets are united by their ages: they comprise a generation spanning just over a decade (Conquest, the eldest, was born in 1917, Gunn, the youngest, in 1929) and centred on the year 1922, in which Amis, Davie and Larkin were born. The differences in the group (particularly the differences in age and social background) should not be forgotten; in his poem 'England' Davie writes how at the time he was doing wartime service in the navy

> Thom Gunn
> played in the overgrown
> gardens of Hampstead.

In Gunn's case, age and upbringing eventually contributed to a sense of not 'belonging' to the Movement. But for the most part the similar backgrounds and experience of the poets helped foster a sense of group solidarity.

This social cohesion is in itself an interesting feature of the Movement, since not all literary groups are united on a social as well as aesthetic basis. What was especially significant, though, was that the Movement writers were assigned an identity which presented them as the 'coming' class. They were identified with a spirit of change in post-war British society, and were felt to be representative of shifts in power and social structure. When Holloway refers to the 'recent social revolution' in his account of the Movement he means to draw attention to the relation between the emergence of a 'lower-middle-class' literary group and the re-distribution of income and status, 'gentle though real', in the newly-created

Welfare State. Davie, too, has ascribed to the Movement great 'sociological importance':

I'm like Wain and Larkin and others in being a product of the provinces, and not of the rural provinces known to the tourist, but of the industrial Midlands, in my case the South Yorkshire coalfield; and, like nearly everyone else in the group I'm a product of the lower-middle class . . . Accordingly, my history is the history of my education and duplicates that of all the rest — a winning of the way to one of the ancient universities by competitive examinations, rather than the going there as a matter of course as in the case of products of more privileged classes, such as Spender, Auden, Lehmann and Connolly and almost every writer of previous generations that you can think of . . .

[The Movement's] sociological importance is very great, and it consists in this — that for the first time a challenge is thrown down, not by individuals like Lawrence, Arnold Bennett, Dylan Thomas, but by a more or less coherent group, to the monopoly of British culture sustained for generations by the London haut-bourgeois.[3]

The identification of the Movement with a wider class-struggle was one reason why the group established itself so quickly in the years 1953–5: it gave them the advantage of seeming to represent a newly empowered class, and it helped them to define themselves in opposition to the 'haut-bourgeois' 1930s generation which Davie mentions. Not surprisingly this generation reacted aggressively to the emergence of the Movement, acknowledging in peevish and often snobbish outbursts the relation between Movement literature and recent social change. Spender labelled them 'Lower Middle Brows'. Edith Sitwell compared their 'lifeless quatrains' to 'the cramped dimensions of prefabricated houses'. Evelyn Waugh saw them as beneficiaries of the 1944 Butler Education Act (which he described as 'one of the things that politicians did when no-one was looking, towards the end of the war'), and spoke of a 'new wave of philistinism with which we are threatened by these grim young people coming off the assembly lines in their hundreds every year and finding employment as critics, even as poets and novelists'. Waugh was mistaken—the Movement poets were too old to be beneficiaries of the Butler

Act—but the mistake was a common one, and formed the basis for Somerset Maugham's infamous attack on the 'ominous significance' of *Lucky Jim*. In his view the novel symbolized the arrival of a generation of young people best described as 'scum':

They do not go to university to acquire culture, but to get a job, and when they have got one, scamp it. They have no manners, and are woefully unable to deal with any social predicament. Their idea of a celebration is to go to a public house and drink six beers. They are mean, malicious, and envious. They will write anonymous letters to harrass a fellow undergraduate and listen in to a telephone conversation that is no business of theirs. Charity, kindliness, generosity are qualities which they hold in contempt. They are scum. They will in due course leave the university. Some will doubtless sink back, perhaps with relief, into the modest class from which they emerged; some will take to drink, some to crime, and go to prison. Others will become schoolmasters and form the young, or journalists and mould public opinion. A few will go into Parliament, become Cabinet Ministers and rule the country. I look upon myself as fortunate that I shall not live to see it.[4]

Maugham's attack, with its combination of fictional details (mostly inaccurate) from *Lucky Jim* and paranoid impressions of current social change, is one of the most striking inventions of a class 'type' based on Amis's Dixon, and confirms how threatened by the Movement the older generation felt.

What elements in the work of the Movement caused this insecurity? There was, first of all, what was spoken of as its 'philistinism'. Movement texts often included obscene or deprecating references to 'culture'—Amis's 'Filthy Mozart', Larkin's 'a Grecian statue kicked in the privates'—which gave the impression that it had no feeling for artistic achievement. The respect felt by the 1930s generation for a broad or cosmo- politan culture was unsettled by the seeming 'little Englandism' of the Movement. Dixon in *Lucky Jim* finds the cultural evening at the Welches especially unbearable because there is a reading of Anouilh—'Why couldn't they have chosen an English play?'—and 'a violin sonata by some teutonic bore'. Wain in an early review made jokes about 'Turks' and 'Croats', and Larkin, asked in an interview if he read foreign poetry, replied 'Foreign Poetry? No!'[5] This flaunting of insular prejudice extended into a more general attack on 'abroad'. In Evelyn Waugh's *Decline and Fall* a character reflects that marriage and love are 'like abroad: no-one would want to go there if they hadn't been told it existed', and this is very much the attitude of Garnett Bowen in *I Like It Here,* who dislikes his holiday in Portugal because 'the place is located abroad and the people are foreigners, . . . so we can't understand each other or get to know each other as well as chaps from the same nation can'.

The Movement's prejudice against 'abroad' and the culture of 'abroad' can partly be explained in terms of the post-war socio-political climate. With Britain's decline as a world power particularly apparent in the years just after the war, and the government's emphasis upon 'buckling to' and getting things right at home, a period of comparative insularity ensued. The imposition of a £50 travel allowance discouraged foreign travel and few British intellectuals elected to live abroad. As Anthony Hartley has argued, the work of the Movement transmitted the norms of this society by making 'a sort of mythical virtue out of necessity, [by] pretending that Birmingham is as interesting a place to inhabit as Berlin, or that the amenities of Manchester compare with those of Milan.'[6] According to this view, the poems of Larkin might be seen as serving the needs of post-war Britain: when in 'Poetry of Departures' he depicts escape from everyday routine to 'swagger the nut-strewn roads' as an impossibly romantic dream, or in 'I Remember, I Remember' shows the emptiness of a Coventry childhood to be 'not the place's fault' since 'nothing, like something, happens anywhere', he is (despite the seemingly bleak outlook) being consolatory: he reassures readers that, as Holloway also reassured them in his article 'A Writer's Prospect' in 1957, 'nothing is likely to be gained by packing off hastily to Rapallo, the Isles of Greece, or any other hot favourite'.[7]

The Movement's insularity may have this historical foundation, but it also reflects a class viewpoint, and it was this element which most disturbed the 'Establishment' (the term 'Establishment' itself belongs to the 1950s, having been coined by Henry Fairlie in the *Spectator* in 1955). Garnett Bowen in *I Like It Here* is aware of being influenced by 'a long history of lower-middle-class envy directed against the upper-middle-class traveller', and it is this, not 'abroad' itself, which motivates his criticisms of Portugal; as Amis later explained, 'in *I Like It Here* people thought I was attacking Europe. But I was attacking the people who like it.'[8] Amis's famous claim, in the introduction to the first Movement anthology *Poets of the 1950's*, that 'nobody wants any more poems about philosophers or paintings or novelists or art galleries or mythology or foreign cities' is an expression of social as well as artistic prejudice—a fact which Davie acknowledges in his poem 'Via Portello':

> Yes, my friend,
> I know you have decided for your part,
> That poems of foreign cities and their art
> Are the privileged classes' shorthand.

When he wrote *Lucky Jim* Amis knew that there would be readers who would understand Dixon's desire to torture Professor Welch 'until he disclosed why, without being French himself, he'd given his sons French names': two contemporary prejudices are simultaneously enlisted—one against abroad, the other against upper-middle-class pretentiousness.

The philistinism and little Englandism which alarmed and angered many older readers also bear a relation to the Movement's 'provincialism'. This provincialism is not to be confused with 'regionalism', a mode of writing which the Movement saw as consisting of sentimental, and usually Celtic, celebrations of one's 'roots' (a word which Larkin puts in inverted commas in 'I Remember, I Remember'). Amis once criticized Sean O'Casey for having promoted vulgar notions about the 'Oirish',[9] and in *That Uncertain Feeling* John Lewis is similarly scornful of local Welsh poets like Gareth Probert who 'pretend to be wild valley blabbers, woaded with pit-dirt and sheep-shit, thinking in Welsh the whole time and obsessed by terrible beauty':

> What a disgrace it was, what a reproach to all Welshmen, that so many of the articulate parts of their culture should be invalidated by awful sentimental lying. All those phoney novels and stories about the wry rhetorical wisdom of poetical miners, all those boring myths about the wonder and the glory and the terror of life in the valley towns, all those canonizations of literary dead-beats, charlatans and flops . . .

The Movement's is an emphatically English provincialism, and does not glamorise backwaters. Far from being vital or picturesque, the provinces of Movement texts are ugly and boring. In Wain's *The Contenders* (1958) Joe Shaw, in a passage reminiscent of Larkin's 'I Remember, I Remember', describes his home town in the Midlands as 'that place you stop at on the way to Manchester—the one where you look out of the train window when it's slowing down and think "Well, at least I don't live here"'. The dominant features are fire and smoke: in his 'Black Country Women' Enright describes the 'flames' from factories and this word recurs in Davie's 'An English Revenant':

> You that went north for geysers or for grouse,
> While Pullman sleepers lulled your sleeping head,
> You never saw my mutilated house
> Flame in the north by Sheffield as you fled.

Movement landscapes usually bear the marks of industry, and they also bear the marks of the class divisions which the industrialization process exacerbated. Davie in 'An English Revenant' is resentful of the privileged traveller from the 'opulent' South for whom the industrialized North is merely a place to pass through en route to business or leisure.

The Movement is 'provincial', then, not because it idealizes the North but because it resents the South—London especially. In *Lucky Jim* Bertrand Welch's crime is to have not only a French name, but a London flat: 'why', Dixon asks, 'hadn't he himself had parents whose money so far exceeded their sense as to install their son in London?'. London is responsible for Bertrand's overdressing and for his patronizing suggestion that he has come home to see whether 'the torch of culture is still in a state of combustion in the provinces'. Lumley in *Hurry on Down* shares Dixon's resentment of the London 'type', meeting at a party there people who are very similar to Bertrand: 'Their appearance, in general, gave the impression of what is usually known as Bohemianism but without its redeeming features; they looked studiedly theatrical instead of harmlessly eccentric, and gave no impression, *en masse,* of intelligence or sensitivity'. London 'types' are dealt with rudely by the Movement's provincial heroes. Propositioned by a homosexual at the party, Lumley threatens to throw him down a lift shaft and to knock out his front teeth; Dixon actually succeeds in giving Bertrand a black eye.

In promulgating the myth of the corrupt metropolis, the Movement writers were able to draw on a long and respectable tradition. Davie found historical sanction for anti-metropolitanism through his study of late-eighteenth-century poetry, arguing in *The Late Augustans* (1958) that the period of Cowper and Wordsworth was characterized by 'the steady alienation of the serious artist from London'.[10] Wain took his bearings from his Potteries forerunner Arnold Bennett, while Amis seems to have been influenced by two more recent manifestations of a 'provincial' tendency: the American novelist J. D. Salinger's *The Catcher in the Rye* (1951), in which Holden Caulfield sees through 'phoney' city talk about culture, and the English novelist William Cooper's *Scenes From Provincial Life* (1950). But in this as in many other respects the Movement's most important authority was Leavis, who had argued throughout his career, but most importantly in the 1951 *Scrutiny* essay 'Keynes, Spender and Currency Values' that the 'London literary world' had been corrupted by a web of 'social-personal' relations. Wain has said that as a result of Leavis's writings 'the smartness of London weekly journalism . . . came to be felt, by a whole generation, as manifestations of one and the same sinister power working for the suppression of everything genuine in life and literature'.[11] Davie in particular made use of Leavis's ideas when trying to define, and sometimes to promote, the Movement's work. In a series of reviews and essays written in 1953-4, he argued that the power-base of cultural achievement was shifting from London coteries to provincial universities—'not just to Oxford and Cambridge, but to Leeds and Liverpool and Manchester. Even the poet nowadays is likely to be a don; at any rate his centre of operations is less and less London, more and more one or other of the university towns.'[12]

This picture of an exodus from London is, however, a belying of what happens in Movement texts. Several of these—*Lucky Jim, Hurry on Down*, 'The Whitsun Weddings', Holloway's 'Journey to a Capital'—trace not a movement out of and away from London but into and towards it. Movement texts 'aspire to the south', as Davie's poem 'An English Revenant' puts it. Just as the Movement itself relied heavily on London publishers for the promotion of its provincial identity, so Movement fictions depict protagonists who, though provincial in origin and seemingly hostile to the city, measure success in terms of graduation to the capital. Lumley's success, after working in several different parts of England, is to be awarded a three-year contract as a London scriptwriter; and Dixon gains a 'five-hundred a year' job in London as Gore-Urquhart's private secretary. Admittedly in *Lucky Jim* certain qualifications are made as to where Dixon will live, and these have the effect of underplaying the graduation and making it more acceptable: 'he pronounced the names to himself: Bayswater, Knightsbridge, Notting Hill Gate, Pimlico, Belgrave Square, Wapping, Chelsea. No, not Chelsea'. For Dixon Chelsea smacks too much of Bertrand Welch and Bohemia. Nevertheless it is in London that Dixon and Lumley end up.

The Movement's provincial identity is therefore characterized by interesting tensions. Provincial values do underlie the group's aesthetic, but their work in no sense romanticizes provincial life; metropolitan and Bohemian values seem to be under challenge, but London finally retains its appeal. Had the 1930s generation which the Movement saw as largely constituting the London literary world taken note of these tensions, it might well have felt that the Movement represented less of a challenge to established values than had at first been imagined. But the 1930s generation noticed only texts like Gunn's 'Lines for a Book', which by its praise of 'those who would not play with Stephen Spender'—a reference to Spender's poem 'Rough', which describes how as a child he was kept from playing with rough children—contributed to the image of the typical Movement person as a tough insensitive 'stone-thrower' rather than as a soft-hearted and soft-minded Spenderian. As Anthony Hartley says, 'after the war it seemed essential to a new generation to be unfair to the thirties',[13] and the Movement tended to exaggerate its opposition. But even before both Davie and Wain had, in the early 1960s, recounted experiences which showed them to have shared Spender's vulnerability in the face of roughness (Wain in his autobiography *Sprightly Running* and Davie in his poem 'Barnsley and District'), it should have been clear that the Movement's appearance of being 'cultural teddy boys' was largely a tactical move.

The existence of tensions in the Movement—tensions point-ing to a spirit of compromise at the heart of its work—becomes even clearer when we look at its handling of class. The large number of contemporary articles dealing with sociological aspects of Movement work show that readers of the time believed the Movement's emergence to be intimately bound up with what Holloway called 'the recent social revolution'. Such articles frequently overstate the degree to which the Movement's fiction can be considered working-class (only Enright in the Movement came from a working-class back-ground, and his novels were not counted as important as Amis's, Larkin's or Wain's), but they are useful in relating the theme of 'mobility' in Movement fiction to current social change. Upward social mobility is not only a theme of Movement work, but a determinant of narrative structure. The plots of Larkin's *Jill,* Wain's *Hurry on Down,* and Amis's *Lucky Jim* and *That Uncertain Feeling* are all concerned with the struggle of a male protagonist to adjust to the values of another class. In each novel, a hero from the working or lower-middle class (the exception is Wain's middle-middle-class Lumley—but he too 'ascends') is thrust into an upper-middle-class milieu by virtue of acquaintance with someone of higher social status than himself. He meets there a physically attractive woman from the middle or upper-middle class, desires her, but is initially prevented from attaining her by the intervention of a spouse, guardian or rival. After a drunken social gathering at which the hero makes his feelings plain, the action reaches a climax either with the hero's attainment of his woman (*Lucky Jim, Hurry on Down*) or with his withdrawal after a brief sexual encounter (*Jill, That Uncertain Feeling*). The novels end with the successful heroes also gaining better jobs and with the unsuccessful ones reverting to their original social status (Lewis gives up his library job to join his father at the mine, Kemp also is re-united with his working-class parents).

In his attempt to adjust to the norms of another class, the hero is subject to two kinds of pressure. On one side, he is likely to incur the disapproval of members of his own class who feel that he should 'know his place'; on the other, he is likely to incur the disapproval of those who resent his 'climbing': both sides discourage his 'ascent'. In *Jill* John Kemp is warned by Whitbread, a fellow working-class scholarship boy, that it's 'no good going about with millionaires', a reference to Kemp's friendship with the public school-educated Christopher Warner: 'if you take my advice, you'll let him know where he stands, pretty sharp. Can't have him mucking up your work'. The dogged Ieuan Jenkins in *That Uncertain Feeling* also makes an appeal to class solidarity, though in his case it is a rationalization of his fear that Lewis's friendship with the

Gruffyd-Williams family will lead to Lewis and not himself being promoted:

'To tell you the truth, John, I'm rather surprised that you have any acquaintance of any sort with people like that.'
'You disapprove, do you?'
'I have no right either to approve or disapprove, as you know. It merely seems to me that they are not your sort, or you are not their sort, whichever you prefer . . . Who can be relied upon? Where is there any loyalty left, any . . . any trust?'

Margaret Peel in *Lucky Jim* has a rather different role to that of Jenkins. But just as Jenkins stands to lose if Lewis 'moves up', so Margaret is threatened by the possibility of losing Dixon to the upper-middle-class Christine Callaghan, and at the crucial moment rationalizes her fear of rejection into a reminder to Dixon to know his place: 'You don't think she'd have you, do you? a shabby little provincial bore like you'. Margaret's words might easily be Bertrand's who calls Dixon 'a lousy little philistine': the resentment of the class equal is identical with that of the snob. In a recent autobiographical poem called 'Class' D. J. Enright, himself 'a poor boy who won a scholarship', makes this very point:

> The wife of a teacher at school (she was
> Mother of one of my classmates) was
> Genuinely enraged when I won a scholarship.
> She stopped me in the street, to tell me
> (With a loudness I supposed was upper-class)
> That Cambridge was not for the likes of me, nor was
> Long hair, nor the verse I wrote for the school mag.
>
> Her sentiments were precisely those of the
> Working class. Unanimity on basic questions
> Accounts for why we never had the revolution.

The Movement's concern with, and insights into, class questions make it understandable that readers in the 1950s should have seen its work to be the literature of the age— 'the only *zeitgeist* literature we have' as one Oxford undergraduate put it.[14] With the passing of legislation like the Butler

Education Act and promise of equal opportunity in the Welfare State, the issue of social mobility was a topical one, and to find the theme of moving and marrying upward in contemporary literature (it was present, also, in Osborne's *Look Back in Anger* and Braine's *Room at the Top*) seemed to reflect the possibility that the social hierarchy was less rigid than it had been before the war.

The Movement writers have nevertheless tried to discourage critics from thinking of their work as class-conscious and responsive to social change. Amis has claimed that 'the social element in what I write has largely been invented by reviewers,'[15] and Larkin is not impressed by readings of *Jill* as a precursor of the Northern working-class fiction of John Braine, Alan Sillitoe, David Storey and others. As he says in the introduction, 'In 1940 our impulse was still to minimize social differences rather than to exaggerate them. My hero's background, though an integral part of the story, was not what the story was about'. At one level these disclaimers simply express an aversion to fashionable interpretations and groupings: the Movement writers dislike the thought of their work being judged on sociological grounds. But when Larkin says that the Movement writers were, as undergraduates, encouraged to 'minimize social differences', he betrays a deeper and more interesting reason for the disclaimers of class-consciousness.

Most of the Movement poets were, as scholarship boys in centres of learning still largely dominated by the upper-middle class, subject to pressures to understate social difference. Amis admits that this was a pressure which he experienced when a scholarship boy at the City of London school: 'My fellows, I saw dimly, were drawn from a wide variety of social strata: accents varied from those that discomforted me to those that made me feel superior. But example at once taught me to put such attitudes to one side'. Gunn, though himself from a fairly affluent middle-class background, also notes that during his education it was common for accents to be suppressed in order to conceal regional and class difference: 'One of my contem-

poraries arrived at Cambridge with a broad Yorkshire accent.
But this was 1950, and he made it his business to reform it.'
Wain, using a metaphor which implies that it is as important
to conceal one's class origins as it is to cover an unsightly
wound, has said that he and his Movement contemporaries
'were inclined to approach the question of social class as, say,
George Orwell approached it, rather than as a piece of Elasto-
plast that must, with delighted masochism, be pulled off every
twenty-four hours'.[16] Implicit in these statements is the belief
that since the late-1950s, as a result of the development of
Northern working-class fiction and the cultural explorations
of Richard Hoggart, Raymond Williams and others, there has
been a tendency for intellectuals to 'play up' rather than
'play down' their class origins. This is not a development of
which the Movement approves.

The Movement writers were, then, in a difficult position—
on the one hand, acutely conscious of social differences and
on the other encouraged to minimize them. The result is a
literature resourceful in managing to play down class differences while at the same time making class one of its central
concerns. Such Movement novels as *Jill, Hurry on Down,
Lucky Jim* and *That Uncertain Feeling* effect this compromise
by confusing social status with sexual status. The pursued
heroines—Jill, Veronica, Christine, Elizabeth—are attractive
as well as being from a higher social rank. 'Class' is a word
that has ambiguities—literally it means social status, collo-
quially it can mean physical attractiveness—and these ambiguities are exploited by the Movement so that the social and
sexual desirability of their heroines become synonymous. This
is particularly apparent in *Lucky Jim*: when Dixon complains
that Christine is 'a bit out of my class', just as when Larkin
complains to the woman in 'Lines on a Young Lady's Photograph Album' that the young men photographed with her are
'not quite your class, I'd say, dear, on the whole', we cannot
be sure whether superior social status or superior physical
status is at issue. From the very first description of Christine,

with its ambiguous use of the words 'class', 'standards', 'ambitions', 'property' and 'place', the distinction between beauty and breeding is blurred:

The sight of her seemed an irresistible attack on his own habits, standards, and ambitions: something designed to put him in his place for good. The notion that women like this were never on view except as the property of men like Bertrand was so familiar to him that it had long since ceased to appear an injustice. The huge class that contained Margaret was destined to provide his womenfolk . . .

When Dixon's social and sexual infiltration begins, he is surprised that barriers can be so easily crossed. As he first dances with Christine he finds it 'hard to believe that she was really going to let him touch her, or that men near them wouldn't spontaneously intervene to prevent him'. This sense of being 'lucky' is also experienced by Lumley in *Hurry on Down*: he is amazed by his 'good fortune' and 'could never have believed that such a girl as Veronica could . . . allow herself to be taken about by him (she usually found him at least one evening a week), and to give the appearance of enjoying these occasions, and looking forward to them with pleasure'. As the heroes move up a peg, the heroines move down one to meet them. Veronica is found to have been the mistress, not niece, of Mr Roderick, and Lumley realizes that he has won her from Roderick only because he is now 'rich': '"At one time it just looked as if our," she hesitated, "our thing hadn't got a chance . . . But things have altered, altered so strangely." Mentally he translated this into: *You're rich now, you're doing as well as Roderick. And you're fifteen years younger . . .'.* Lumley nevertheless decides to 'accept her'. Dixon in *Lucky Jim* not only accepts Christine, but finds her more desirable the less she approximates to an ideal. He is excited to find that 'her front teeth were slightly irregular. For some reason this was more disturbing to his equanimity than regularity could ever have been'. He had thought her at first 'excessively "dignant" in demeanour', but is pleased to see her hearty appetite and use of sauce with her breakfast:

'she didn't seem such a bad sort after all'. As she begins to look and behave in ways he can understand, Dixon sees that Christine is less 'above' him than he had at first imagined, and by the end of the novel she is in league with him against the Welches, having attained Dixon's view of their offensiveness: 'I wanted to get away as quickly as I could from the whole bunch of them. I couldn't bear any of them for another moment'.

The handling of Christine is important, for by means of it Amis makes Dixon's 'ascent' more tolerable, and thereby achieves a partial solution to one of the novel's problems: the problem of retaining our admiration for the hero while moving him upward into a class which he seems, and which we have been encouraged, to dislike. Such admiration as we might feel for Dixon has been based on his losing the battle to be accepted by the Welches (we can believe that he wants, subconsciously, to fail) and to see him finally 'winning' is potentially disquieting. Amis overcomes this problem by laying increasing emphasis upon the differences between Christine and the Welches: it is not the 'phoney' world of the Welches that Dixon has infiltrated but the morally legitimate world of Christine and her uncle, both of whom secretly admire Dixon's failure to adjust to the values of the Welches.

In devising this ending, however, Amis also creates further tensions in the novel. He makes it possible to interpret *Lucky Jim* not as an attack upon upper-middle-class metropolitan values (this was how it was usually interpreted at the time) but as an attack upon the imitation or vulgarization of such values by the provincial middle classes. This, indeed, was how the novel was seen by John Wain: 'It is sometimes said . . . that there is currently an attempt by some writers to reaffirm the vitality and vigour of provincial life. I cannot say that I agree. The most successful product of that 'movement', so far, has been a satirical novel whose main butt is the aping of upper-class culture by the provincial bourgeoisie . . .'[17] According to this reading, the Welches become 'country cousins', a provincial middle-class family with only dim notions of what upper-class culture is like; Gore-Urquhart, rich, aristocratic and London-based, represents genuine culture, and Dixon has no compunction about entering the Gore-Urquhart world.

It is not necessary to accept this reading in its entirety to see that *Lucky Jim* is characterized by an ambivalence which allows 'old' values—social inequality, 'élitist' culture, metropolitan patronizing of the provinces—to be preserved while seeming to be under attack. This kind of ambivalence is noticeable again in Amis's second novel *That Uncertain Feeling*. The hero, John Lewis, on hearing the double-barrelled name Gruffyd-Williams reflects that it is his 'political duty to seem unimpressed'. Yet, just as Dixon wishes to be accepted by the Welch set, so Lewis is drawn into the Welsh set, or Aberdarcy high society, while having an affair with Elizabeth and being offered a promotion by her husband. The beauty of the heroine again softens the hard edges of class difference: Lewis feels a 'familiar embarrassed defensiveness at talking to a member of the anglicized upper classes' but 'quite liked the look of this particular member of those classes'. The novel ends with Lewis resisting the temptation to 'sell out': as if to compensate for the ending of *Lucky Jim*, Amis has Lewis move away to a colliery job and revert to his working or lower-middle-class origins. But it is an ending that carries little conviction. Larkin's poem 'Poetry of Departures' describes the impulse to 'chuck up everything/And just clear off' as artificial and retrogressive, 'a deliberate step backwards', and Lewis's action seems an empty gesture of this kind.

The ending of *That Uncertain Feeling* is not just unconvincing, it is the only moment in Movement fiction where the refusal of the hero to 'sell out' to the values of a higher class is offered as a matter for congratulation. Part of the humour of *Lucky Jim* comes from its implicit 'gap'—its failure to acknowledge the existence of a literary tradition in which fictional heroes are often seen anguishing over whether or not to compromise themselves. In the area of employment, for instance, Dixon is totally oblivious to questions of conscience and integrity, so desperate is he to remain in a job. In this sense, because it does have a hero with a conscience about employ- ment and class, *That Uncertain Feeling* is more akin to fiction such as Alan Sillitoe's *The Loneliness of the Long Distance Runner*: both Amis's Lewis and Sillitoe's Smith 'lose' when in a position to 'win'. But Lewis's defiance is considerably more muted than Smith's, and to make too much of the similarity would be misleading. Comparison of the treatment of social class in the work of the Movement with its treatment in the fiction and non-fiction of later writers such as Storey, Sillitoe and Hoggart reveals the high priority which the Move- ment placed upon 'adjustment' and 'compromise'. Though conscious and at times resentful of class distinction and privilege, the work of the Movement never seriously challenges their right to exist. There is little sense that the social structure could be altered; the more common enquiry is whether indi- viduals can succeed in 'fitting in'. Wain described *Hurry on Down* as a 'young man's problem of how to adapt himself to "life"',[18] a description which echoes something said by his hero Lumley: 'I never rebelled against ordinary life; it just never admitted me, that's all'.

There was not much twentieth-century fiction to which the Movement could turn in order to discover models for the compromising hero. But George Orwell's novels did provide the precedent which they required. The heroes of Orwell's novels tend to be lower-middle-class in origin; they have 'healthy' and 'normal' appetites for food, drink and sex; they are quite well-informed about politics, but do not get too involved; they are passive, having little control over their own lives or the processes of history: in all these respects, they anticipate the heroes of Movement fiction. Gordon Comstock in *Keep the Aspidistra Flying* (1936) was especially influential. Though in one sense quite unlike Dixon and Lumley (he is a poet and wishes to hold a poorly-paid job that will enable him to write), his plight is very much theirs. He hates his boss and job but is desperate to remain employed, lives in dismal lodgings presided over by a malevolent landlady, likes but gets bored by his girlfriend, goes on a drunken spree which he regrets next morning, and, most importantly, regards 'culture' with suspicion, equating it (as Dixon does) with the upper-middle class; 'it was the snooty "cultured" kind of books that he hated the worst. Books of criticism and belles-lettres. The kind of thing that those moneyed young beasts from Cambridge write almost in their sleep . . . Money and culture! In a country like England you can no more be cultured without money than you can join the Cavalry Club'. For much of the novel Comstock, like Wain's Lumley, goes 'slumming' in order to avoid conventional middle-class employment, but at the end, with his girlfriend pregnant, Comstock decides to 'sell out', taking a respectable copy-writing job. His final defence of 'the money-code' is one that prefigures and sanctions the Movement tendency to adjust and conform: 'It occurred to him that he was merely repeating the destiny of every human being. Everyone rebels against the money-code, and everyone sooner or later surrenders. He had kept up his rebellion a little longer than most, that was all . . . Now that he had acknowledged his desire and surrendered to it, he was at peace'. Comstock and Lumley discover this belatedly; Dixon takes it for granted from the beginning.

What emerges in the work of the Movement, then, is an uneasy combination of class-consciousness and acceptance of class division; an acute awareness of privilege, but an eventual submission to the structure which makes it possible. On the one hand, the Movement writers were identified with a viewpoint hostile to the 'old order'. They resented social inequality, and were not so credulous as to suppose that it had been eliminated as the result of wartime Coalition and post-war Labour government reform. Oxford and Cambridge—as Amis explains—still seemed to them to be riddled with class prejudice: 'A few provincials might have got in because of the vulgar recency of their subjects, or as egalitarian window-dressing, but the main outline fitted with my early picture—which I have since had to modify only in detail—of British culture as the property of some sort of exclusive club.'[19] On the other hand, the 'club' which the Movement writers resented was one which they had succeeded in joining. For the scholarship boys, in particular, a feeling of pride in, and gratitude for, having achieved Oxbridge places necessarily qualified feelings of hostility; there was a tendency to see in their own 'success' evidence of the basic justice and openness of British society. Historians analyzing what they take to be the political apathy shown by intellectuals during the 1950s have on occasions argued that the scholarship boy system was responsible for creating an unusually meek intelligentsia. Peter Laslett, for instance, suggests: 'If you relentlessly search out the best brains from every social and geographical area of the community, search them out and satisfy them early with the delights of a carefully preserved and ingeniously improvised social superiority, you have instilled self-satisfaction good and early. That is the secret of the angry young men of Britain. They have nothing to rebel against.'[20] As spokesmen for the new self-proclaimed lower-middle-class intelligentsia, the Movement was forced into an ambivalent position: on the one hand opposed to the 'old order'; on the other hand, indebted to, and respectful towards, its institutions.

One way to resolve this problem was for the Movement to criticize the more blatantly unacceptable aspects of the 'old order' while maintaining an underlying respect for many of its values. The Movement's approach to traditional culture, for instance, was to attack the snobbery and exclusiveness surrounding it, but not to demean the notion itself: 'one wants to annoy Mozart lovers, not denigrate Mozart,' as Amis put it.[21] The line is not always clearly drawn. In an essay called 'That Certain Revulsion' (1957), Amis allows his aversion to 'the kind of chaps who make a tremendous business of going to the theatre' (people whose 'clothes, mannerisms and conversation are affected') to lead him into a silly attack on the theatre itself: 'I think I am like many people of my age and upbringing in that I know almost nothing about the theatre, and more or less make a point of not finding anything out . . . Give me a good film any day is what I always say, or even a not-very-good film.'[22] But Amis has over the years also made a serious and constructive effort to enlarge the notion of culture, removing it from the confines of the club by showing that film, science fiction, jazz, Ian Fleming and the detective novel are also worthy of attention. Both the bad and good sides of the Movement's approach to culture show up in a review which Amis wrote in 1955. In opposing what he takes to be the tastes of 1930s intellectuals, Amis is too dismissive of too much; but he also makes some legitimate points, and throws useful light on the cultural stance of the 1950s intellectual, who usually preferred the new and American to the old and European:

His non-literary interests, if he has any, are less liable to be presided over by the shade of Dürer or Monteverdi than by the sinister living figure of Mr Louis Armstrong. Dürer and Monteverdi, together with Bonnard and Prokofiev, first editions, tableware and furniture more than a decade old, meeting foreign intellectuals, even Proust, even Joyce, tend to get lumped together as a waste of time, and – where applicable – of money. To the charge of holding defiant dour scholarship-boy views on culture, he may retort, rather uneasily perhaps, that anyway he is thereby rescued from the 'real' Philistinism of the dilettante. And it might be seriously argued that, for the practitioner if for nobody else, culture made in one's own private still is more potent than that which comes to table in a decanter.[23]

The last sentence throws light on Dixon in *Lucky Jim*, who is often seen as a typically 'philistine' Movement protagonist devoid of any cultural appreciation. On the surface this view appears to be correct, as Dixon himself admits while explaining to Margaret his surprise at being asked to the Welches' 'arty get-together': 'Look, Margaret, you know as well as I do that I can't sing, I can't act, I can hardly read, and thank God I can't read music'. Dixon believes that Welch plans to use culture to measure his (Dixon's) fitness to be a university lecturer, and he feels inadequate and boorish for this reason. But under a broader definition of culture the feelings of inadequacy would be unnecessary. In the course of the novel we see Dixon sing (on the way back from the pub), dance (to jazz music), write fiction (the letter to Johns from 'Joe Higgins'), and act (over the phone with Bertrand and Mrs Welch). He may appear to be 'uncultured' but the culture made in his own 'private still' is more vital, useful and entertaining than the 'decanted' culture of the Welches.

It might well have been expected that the Movement's attack on upper-middle-class cultural snobbery would lead to an attack on upper-middle-class social privilege; but this was not the case. Rather, by focusing resentment on 'phoney' or unacceptable cultural values, the Movement offered only a token rebellion, and did not attempt to change the social structure which made cultural 'élitism' possible. In Amis's work, in particular, attacks on upper-middle-class culture coexist with an almost embarrassing reverence for traditional upper-middle-class 'types'—for Gore-Urquhart in *Lucky Jim,* Gruffyd-Williams in *That Uncertain Feeling,* Strether in *I Like It Here,* Julian Ormerod in *Take a Girl Like You.* To these figures the lower-middle-class heroes of Amis's work gladly defer. Dixon's deference in *Lucky Jim* is especially humble: when Gore-Urquhart first addresses him, Dixon finds himself 'blushing slightly' and is 'pleased that Gore-Urquhart had caught his name'.

Amis's sympathetic treatment of characters like Gore-Urquhart points to the nostalgia which was felt within the Movement for the period before the Labour Party's promised re-distribution of wealth and privilege threatened to eliminate the upper-class 'type'. Consciously identifying with socialist agents of change, Amis and other members of the Movement are nevertheless attracted to the 'old' pre-1945 order. This ambivalence is documented very illuminatingly in 'I Spy Strangers', one of Amis's short stories from *My Enemy's*

Enemy. Set during the weeks between the end of the Second
World War and the 1945 British Election, a time of intense
speculation about the future of Britain, 'I Spy Strangers',
describes the contrasting attitudes of a young private, Archer,
and his superior, Major Raleigh. Archer hopes that the Election will bring to power the Labour Party and thereby create a
new England more to his liking, an England 'full of girls and
drinks and jazz and books and decent houses and decent jobs
and being your own boss'. The reactionary and authoritarian
Major Raleigh, though, regards the forthcoming election with
apprehension, having detected in his men signs of

anarchy mounting, of discipline and seriousness and purpose melting
away. He felt there was some connection here with the chance of a
Labour victory at the polls. Apart from a few negligible wild men like
Hargreaves and Archer, he had never met anyone who confessed to
having cast his proxy vote for Labour. On a recent visit to the Mess at
Hildesfeld he had made a point of questioning his hosts on the matter
and had heard the same story. His wife's letters said that nobody knew
of anybody in the whole town who was a Labour supporter, and that
everybody felt very sorry for poor Mr Jack, the Labour candidate. And
yet the Major was uneasy. Something monstrous and indefinable was
growing in strength, something hostile to his accent and taste in clothes
and modest directorship and ambitions for his sons and redbrick house
at Purley with its back-garden tennis-court.

In an attempt to rescue the situation for the Tory Party,
Major Raleigh intrudes on a mock-parliamentary session
organized by his men, and makes a speech which, like the
speeches of Winston Churchill during the 1945 Electoral campaign, praises the war effort but leaves it in no doubt that the
old pre-war social structure must be maintained. However, the
Major has not been invited to the mock-session, and, in a show
of strength indicative of the growing solidarity of the men, is
asked to leave. Shortly afterwards comes the announcement of
the 'real' Election result: the Labour Party has been voted in.
The story ends with the Major trying to convince himself that
despite his constituency's result—'Labour 28,000, Conservative
9,000'—England will nevertheless 'muddle through somehow'.

There are a number of elements in 'I Spy Strangers' which encourage an identification of the authorial viewpoint with that of the central character, Archer. Archer has been at Oxford before being called up for service and is due to return there; he expresses a liking for 'girls and drink and jazz and books'; he is a Labour Party supporter, whose moderate line is a compromise between the Marxism of his friend Hargreaves and the Toryism of the Major: all these elements suggest that the weight of authorial sympathy is behind Archer, and that he is to be seen as a 'decent' hero in the mould of Dixon or Lewis. But it is noticeable that Major Raleigh is also handled with considerable sympathy and insight: his defence of Empire and of privilege seems quaint rather than offensive, his own position to be pitied rather than despised. The treatment of the Major hints that while Amis and other Movement poets identified themselves with the 'new' (but moderate) values of Archer, they were in sympathy with the 'old' values of the Major to a surprising degree.

Such an interpretation receives additional support from Amis's 1957 statement of his political opinions, *Socialism and the Intellectuals*. He explains in this Fabian pamphlet that he is a Labour voter who once 'went through the callow marxist phase that seemed almost compulsory for my generation' but who has moved towards the view that 'the best and most trustworthy political motive is self-interest'. His position is a moderate one: he carefully situates himself between extremes of 'new' and 'old', Left and Right. Such a stance is also evident in 'Autobiographical Fragment' from the 1956 collection *A Case of Samples*. The speaker of this poem has as regular callers to his cottage 'Constant Angst, the art critic' and 'old Major Courage'. Angst encourages inaction, irresponsibility, anti-authoritarianism. The Major, on the other hand, is part of the old order of authority, responsibility and hard work: he organizes cross-country walks 'up hills, down streams, through briars'. The poem concludes with the speaker making a choice between the 'new' and 'old' values which the two visitors represent:

> What duty's served by pointless, mad
>   Climbing and crawling?
> I tell you, I was thankful when
>   The old bore stopped calling.

One's first impression is that the'old bore' must be the Major, the 'pointless, mad/Climbing and crawling' his demanding country walks. This is the view taken by Donald Davie, who in *Thomas Hardy and British Poetry* reads this poem and several others by Amis and himself as investigations into power and authority. Noting the contradiction between the seeming indictment of the Major and Amis's 'uneasily retrospective admiration for the vanished authoritarian figure', Davie suggests that the way to resolve this contradiction is to take the last stanza to 'refer back discreditably on the speaker'.[24] There is, however, a simpler and more satisfying resolution than that offered by Davie. This is to take the phrase 'pointless, mad/Climbing and crawling' to refer not to the Major's vigorous walks 'up hills, down streams, through briars', but to the sycophancy and vaguely homosexual insidiousness of Angst:

> Angst always brought me something nice
>   To get in my good graces:
> A quilt, a roll of cotton-wool,
>   A pair of dark glasses.

The phrase 'old bore' remains ambiguous, and this points to Amis's divided attitude towards social change: is the disappearance of authority desirable? His answer is not clear, but once the trick in the poem's structure is detected, the balance is tipped to suggest that the Major's authority is preferable to Angst's more covert form of manipulation. In this tipping of the balance, the poem prefigures the openly 'reactionary' postures of Amis's later work.

Amis requires particular attention in any treatment of 1950s English culture because his views, if not at all points representative of the views of the Movement, were certainly found meaningful by a large number of contemporaries. David Lodge has said that they 'focused in a very precise way a number of attitudes which a great many lower-middle-class intellectuals find useful for the purposes of self definition'.[25] These attitudes are often dominated by an uncertainty as to whether the re-distribution of power and privilege in a modern democracy is desirable. On the one hand, the Movement could hardly fail to be influenced by the democratic idealism which followed the end of the Second World War. Several contemporary observers have suggested that these ideals were, if only briefly, extremely powerful, and Amis, for one, has admitted to being affected by them: 'I did share in the general feeling of optimism and liberty abroad at that time'.[26] On the other hand, most of the Movement writers were distrustful of ideals and fearful of radical change: they felt, Davie has said, less 'release and relief' after VE-day than the 'harness' of their careers.[27] They had been trained by teachers, and looked up to writers, who laid emphasis on stability, tradition, continuity, whose influence was to encourage not adjustment *of* society but adjustment *to* it. However much they might lend their support to the 'new', they remained susceptible to the 'old'.

This ambivalence is particularly apparent in the Movement's attitude to Britain's decline as a world power. In his *A State of England* (1963), a work which provides many insights into the Movement and the post-war intelligentsia, Anthony Hartley argues that 'loss of power' has been one of the main facts governing British society since 1939. Dependence on United States support during the war, the granting of independence to several Commonwealth countries from 1947 onwards, the devaluation of the pound in 1949, the Suez crisis of 1956, the application for membership to the European Economic Community in 1961: these are all episodes in the story of Britain's decline as a world force. Hartley suggests that although the inevitability of loss of power was largely accepted by the post-war intelligentsia, it brought with it 'a series of not always conscious frustrations'. There was a public insistence on the inevitability of the dissolution of Empire, and on the 'moral leadership' which Britain would enjoy instead. But there was also nostalgia for the power which the country once enjoyed, and misgivings at a certain 'narrowing of horizons'.

In a country undergoing decline, nostalgia can be expected to be a prevalent emotion, and the Movement and its audience were certainly sensitive to loss, regret, wistfulness, the immediate past: 'Those flowers, that gate,/These misty parks and motors, lacerate/Simply by being over' as Larkin put it in his 'Lines on a Young Lady's Photograph Album'. But an austere post-war Britain was not a place where openly patriotic literature was likely to thrive. The only Movement text frankly to celebrate Britain is Wain's 'Patriotic Poem', and even the self-conscious title cannot prevent the poem from sounding embarrassingly jingoistic:

> This mildewed island,
> Rained on and beaten flat by bombs and water,
> Seems ready now to crack like any other
> Proud organism drugged with praise and torture . . .
>
> Yet from the cauldron
> Where her hard bones are formed by time and anguish
> Rises the living breath of all her children;
> And her deep heart and theirs, who can distinguish?

Other Movement poets may have felt like Wain about Britain, but they understood that to express feelings of this kind it was necessary to transfer them to contexts where they did not seem obtrusive or offensive.

Perhaps this may help to explain why Larkin's 'At Grass' should have become one of the most popular post-war poems. Its subject-matter—racehorses in old age—could hardly be less promising, and looks to be a throwback to the Georgian period (indeed the poem may well have drawn on Georgian sources);[28] yet it is one of Larkin's most widely quoted texts. The reason for its popularity is surely that, by allowing the horses to symbolize loss of power, Larkin manages to tap nostalgia for a past 'glory that was England': it is a poem of post-imperial *tristesse*. The two horses shelter in 'cold shade', and having 'slipped their names' are now 'anonymous'. Their depleted present is measured against a past which may still trouble them with its rich memories of 'faint afternoons' and 'faded, classic Junes': 'Do memories plague their ears?' Larkin wonders, and notes how 'wind distresses tail and mane'. The past is seen as a time of warmth, noise, fame, achievement:

> Silks at the start: against the sky
> Numbers and parasols: outside,
> Squadrons of empty cars, and heat,
> And littered grass: then the long cry
> Hanging unhushed till it subside
> To stop-press columns on the street.

The present, in contrast, is 'dusk', 'shadows' and silence. A wistful sadness is the dominant mood of the first part of the poem. But as it moves into the last stanza, Larkin's poem becomes consolatory: the past will in some degree persist ('Almanacked, their names live'), and the present, now that the demands of competition no longer press, can provide a new kind of 'joy':

> And not a fieldglass sees them home,
> Or curious stopwatch prophesies:
> Only the groom, and the groom's boy,
> With bridles in the evening come.

Anonymous, memory-ridden and powerless, the horses will no longer participate in any race for fame and glory; but Larkin implies that they have new pleasures—peace and quiet— to enjoy. What in another poem, 'Going', he calls the 'evening coming in/Across the fields' is a kindly one.

One must be careful to be clear about what is meant by calling 'At Grass' a post-imperial poem. It would certainly be possible to argue for the presence in the poem of the language of imperial achievement—'squadrons', 'heat', 'littered grass', 'stop-press-columns', 'classic Junes'—and for the language of imperial loss—'cold shade', 'distresses', 'anonymous', 'almanacked', 'memories', 'yet fifteen years ago'. But to see in the poem any intentional allegoric design would be misleading. What can be claimed is that 'At Grass' taps and expresses feelings of loss and regret that might, for a certain section of the British populace at least, have been unusually pronounced around 1950 (when the poem was written), and that it finds for those feelings an acceptable public outlet. The emotion of the poem is in excess of the facts as they appear, is more than an emotion about racehorses in old age.

'At Grass' points to nostalgia and conservatism on the part of the Movement, and to the way in which these moderate participation in a socialist intelligentsia. As a predominantly lower-middle-class group struggling to assert itself, the Movement was expected to offer a socialist perspective, and to some degree did so. Both Dixon in *Lucky Jim* and Lumley in *Hurry on Down* take up attitudes which place them to the Left of those whom they argue with: Lumley is actually accused of 'talking just like a bloody socialist', and Dixon sounds like one when he feuds with Bertrand Welch about taxation of the rich. But Lumley and Dixon have to be harried into making political statements by the provocation of others, and do not of their own accord make active efforts to criticize and change their society. Nor is their political conscience such as to prevent them from taking comfortable jobs higher in the social scale.

Once this tension within the Movement is recognized—and by tension here is meant not that some members of the group disagreed with others, but that most were beset by the same conflict—then it is possible to see why 'failure of nerve' should be such a common Movement theme. A situation frequently arises in Movement texts where the protagonist recognizes that one course of action is desirable or morally correct, but fails (sometimes after much unconvincing rationalization) to act upon his belief. In the title story of Amis's *My Enemy's Enemy*, for example, the central character Thurston resents, but fails to do anything to prevent, the victimization of his friend Dalessio by upper-class military officers. It is left to a comparative outsider, Bentham, to save Dalessio from dismissal. Thurston's failure of nerve in the face of an authority he knows to be unjust is attacked by Bentham in what makes an unsettling conclusion to the story:

I've always understood that you were a great one for pouring scorn on the Adj. and Romney and Cleaver and the rest of that crowd. Yes, you could talk about them till you were black in the face, but when it came to doing something, talking where it would do some good, you kept your mouth shut . . . You know what I think? I don't think you care tuppence. You don't care beyond talking any road. I think you're really quite sold on the Adj's crowd, never mind what you say about them. Chew that over.

'Court of Inquiry', another short story from *My Enemy's Enemy,* contains two studies in failure of nerve. Jock Watson agrees to sit on a court of inquiry even though its anticipated function—to reprimand a young officer for a trivial offence—is one of which he disapproves. The young officer, Archer, is equally ignominious, submitting an abject apology rather than defend himself. Authority is shown to be petty and destructive, but there is a suggestion at the end of the story that it is fruitless to defy it and that to be 'made a man' is to learn cowardice and compromise.

Cowardice and compromise are also central to *Lucky Jim,* where failure to resist a deeply resented authority again dominates the action: Dixon knows that deference to Professor Welch is essential if he is to retain his job. Dixon's only means of maintaining self-respect is to pull faces, make anonymous phone calls and think up violent punishments for his employer: this allows him to express a token resistance that will not endanger his position. Cutting rejoinders are imagined but dare not be spoken:

'There was the most marvellous mix-up in the piece they did just before the interval. The young fellow playing the viola had the misfortune to turn over two pages at once, and the resulting confusion ... my word ...'

Quickly deciding on his own word, Dixon said it to himself and then tried to flail his features into some sort of response to humour. Mentally, however, he was making a different face and promising himself he'd make it actually when next alone . . . Until then he must try to make Welch like him . . .[29]

Dixon's outward deference makes his imagined retaliations unusually savage. He dreams of plunging Welch into 'a lavatory basin, pulling the plug once, twice, and again, stuffing the mouth with toilet-paper'; of 'dashing his fist' into Welch's face; of '[tying] Welch up in his chair and beat[ing] him about the head and shoulders with a bottle'; of 'picking up the spanner he could see in the dashboard pocket and hitting him on the back of the neck with it'. Margaret exasperates him too: 'Dixon wanted to rush at her and tip her backwards in the chair, to make a deafening rude noise in her face, to push a bead up her nose'.

Dixon's plight in *Lucky Jim* is one which Anthony Hartley has compared to the plight of post-war intellectuals:

It is, I think, no accident that such a book should have enjoyed success at the present time . . . The situation is stated in farcical terms, and the solution itself is not particularly heroic, but it is one which is becoming increasingly applicable to the position of the individual in the modern world . . . This is the case of any liberal man who is irritated by certain aspects of the British Welfare State. He cannot reasonably or morally demand its abolition. What is left to him is a limited revolt: the evasion of some of its exactions, irony and (in the case of some intellectuals) outbursts of futile rage over trifles.[30]

Hartley's identification of Dixon's 'limited revolt' as symbolic irritation with the Welfare State demands a reading of Welch as representative of 'Welfare State bureaucracy' which seems inappropriate in view of his association with 'Merrie England' and the 'old' order. More plausibly, Dixon's plight epitomized that of a post-war intelligentsia which to some extent resented the old order, but lacked the nerve openly to oppose it.

Larkin's fiction occasionally prefigures the 'limited revolt' in Amis's. In *Jill* Kemp plays a malicious Dixon-like joke on Whitbread when he smears jam over his books, fills his slippers with butter, and pours sugar and tea in his jacket pockets;

and in *A Girl in Winter* Katherine harbours violent fantasies against her hated employer Anstey: 'Katherine looked at him as if he were an insect she would relish treading on'. The persona of Larkin's poems is also often depicted as someone who lacks the courage to escape or rebel. 'Toads', for example, portrays escape from nine-to-five routine as a fanciful dream:

> Ah, were I courageous enough
> To shout 'Stuff your pension!'
> But I know, all too well, that's the stuff
> That dreams are made on:

In Amis and Larkin 'failure of nerve' is treated sympathetically and humorously, but is not presented as being attractive. In Davie's 'Creon's Mouse' it appears in a slightly different form as a positive humanizing force. Using the characters of Sophocles's *Antigone* Davie explores the origins and aftermath of World War Two, and he upholds 'nerves' (cowardice or timidity) above 'nerve' (courage). The 'colossal nerve' or 'too much daring' which brought about the war (i.e. Hitler and the Nazi party) is contrasted with the 'stubborn loss of nerve' which 'Europe's hero, the humaner king' (i.e. low-profile democracy throughout Western Europe) has brought in its place:

> If too much daring brought (he thought) the war,
> When that was over nothing else would serve
> But no one must be daring any more,
> A self-induced and stubborn loss of nerve.

Davie's use of the word 'stubborn' seeks to make failure of nerve seem not a lamentable condition of passivity but a brave and respectable stance. It is a stance which Davie has continued to defend. In a recent note on the poem, he has confirmed that his recommendation of the policy of Ismene (non-resistance) over that of Creon (authority) and Antigone (revolution) was 'seriously meant', and that as a foreign policy since 1945 'loss of nerve' (i.e. non-intervention by the Western powers in crises like Budapest in 1956 and Prague in 1968) has proved preferable to the 'too much daring' which 'took

Britain into the Suez crisis and America into Vietnam'.[31] That 'no-one must be daring any more'—'How dare we now be anything but numb?' as he asks in 'Rejoinder to a Critic'— is a consistent theme in his work. Davie seems at times to be elevating to a national programme the Movement's own tendency to adjust, compromise and defer: failure of nerve is to be British foreign policy.

Davie's early poetry recommends, also, that poets exhibit a failure of nerve when under pressure to concern themselves with twentieth-century history—the concentration camps, Hiroshima, the Second World War. In 'Eight Years After' he contends that a direct approach to horrific subject-matter diminishes the horror, and that a poet would therefore be irresponsible if he 'squarely faced' the events of recent history. Hiroshima, never actually named in the poem since Davie's premise is that 'to name/is to acknowledge' and thus to diminish, must remain vague, removed, unapproachable if it is to remain horrific:

> If distance lends enchantment to the view,
> Enormities should not be scrutinized.
> What's true of white, holds of black magic too;
> And, indistinct, evil is emphasized . . .
>
> For fearsome issues, being squarely faced,
> Grow fearsomely familiar. To name
> Is to acknowledge. To acquire the taste
> Comes on the heels of honouring the claim.
>
> 'Let nothing human be outside my range.'
> Yet horrors named make exorcisms fail:
> A thought once entertained is never strange,
> But who forgets the face 'beyond the pale'?

Like many Movement texts which set out to defend unpopular ideas ('adjustment', 'compromise', 'failure of nerve', 'neutrality', 'evasion'), 'Eight Years After' is complicated by an underlying doubt as to whether the ideas it upholds are ultimately defensible, and for this reason seems unconvincing and anxiously self-justificatory. Not only are the details of

Davie's argument questionable ('naming' surely *is* a prerequisite of exorcism, as at least one other Movement poet recognized),[32] but the very ingenuity of the poem betrays an over-sensitivity to the charge that, in failing to deal with large subjects like the war and the H-bomb, Movement poets were evading their obligation to engage with the central issues of the time. Like most of their contemporaries, the Movement poets were beset by memories of the war (Amis, Conquest, and Davie had served in the armed forces, Holloway in military intelligence), and recognized that the concentration camps and Hiroshima had a significance which it would be irresponsible to overlook. But several of their works are attempts to persuade themselves that to write about such matters is impossible: 'No, I cannot write the poem of war', as Conquest puts it in his 'Poem in 1944'. They argued that they would be acting more usefully if they looked forward, rather than dwelling on 'the facts of war'; and they assumed (though the assumption would not survive a reading of Second World War poets like Keith Douglas and Alun Lewis) that to write about the war would necessitate a departure from coherence and order. The earlier post-war literary generation—that from which Eliot's *The Waste Land* had emerged—was seen to have reflected the fragmentation of war in its poetry. But the Movement judged that it must counteract fragmentation by constructing what Wain, in an *apologia* for the Movement, calls 'regular and disciplined verse forms':

The earliest modern poets had been formbreakers . . . This breaking of forms was essential, even though it called out the shriek of 'Drunken helots!' But thirty years had rolled by; the world had been drugged by two decades of meaningless peace and then suddenly battered nearly to death by a global war. Worse, that war had ended with the fearful savagery of Hiroshima and Nagasaki . . .

At such a time, when exhaustion and boredom in the foreground are balanced by guilt and fear in the background, it is natural that a poet should feel the impulse to *build*. Writing regular and disciplined verse forms is building in a simple and obvious sense, like bricklaying. Too simple, too obvious? Perhaps. But we were all very young and were doing the best we could to make something amid the ruins.[33]

Wain implies that Movement poetry served the needs of a society preoccupied with post-war reconstruction by expressing through the shape of its own poetry an esteem for 'building'. The Movement slogan 'consolidation' could be adjudged socially useful by its emphasis on order and on the re-establishment of contact with broken traditions.

The Movement's 'counteraction' of the war means that there are only a few texts—the Huddlesford blitz episode in *Jill*, for example, or Wain's poem 'A Song about Major Eatherley'—which attempt a direct treatment of war. More usually references to the war and the bomb are suppressed, and it is left to occasional images to betray the fact that the Movement was a post-war generation. Lumley in *Hurry on Down* is troubled by a 'mushroom-shaped cloud that lived perpetually in a cave at the back of his mind'. In *Lucky Jim* Welch is taken by surprise, 'his attention, like a squadron of slow old battleships, . . . wheeling to face this new phenomenon'. In Enright's 'The Laughing Hyena' one of Hokusai's portraits is described as having ' a face like a bomb burst'. Enright is often more direct in his treatment of recent history than the other Movement poets, but even he seems more assured when approaching it obliquely. In one of his best poems, 'No Offence', what looks to be simply a satire on the clinical efficiency of post-war West Germany exploits the imagery of concentration camps—'disposal services', 'a large cylinder', 'corpse', 'funeral'—to acquire more sinister overtones:

> In no country
> Are the disposal services more efficient.
>
> Standardized dustbins
> Fit precisely into the mouth of a large cylinder
> Slung on a six-wheeled chassis.
> Even the dustbin lid is raised mechanically
> At the very last moment.
>
> You could dispose of a corpse like this
> Without giving the least offence. . . .

> In no country
> Are the disposal services more efficient
> — I reflect —
> As I am sorted out, dressed down, lined up,
> Shepherded through the door,
> Marshalled across the smooth-faced asphalt,
> And fed into the mouth of a large cylinder
> Labelled 'Lufthansa'.

The title hints that 'no offence' is intended: it would not be the wish of a Movement poet to linger on horrific past events. But the invitation to readers to make connections between Nazi inhumanity and post-1945 German efficiency, suggests that, on the contrary, the matter of Auschwitz has not been forgotten. When critics complain that the Movement showed very little awareness of contemporary European history, they are therefore ignoring the presence of oblique historical references in Movement texts.

That the Movement felt obliged to avoid a direct treatment of recent history may be partly explained by their belief that the interpretations of history present in the work of their forerunners (both the Modernists and the generation of Auden and Spender) were so gravely amiss as to discourage any further attempt to be 'relevant' or *engagé*. They believed that the '1914' generation—Pound, Eliot, Wyndham Lewis, Yeats, Lawrence—had openly, or by implication, assisted the development of Fascism. Pound in particular was attacked; Davie claimed that his political misjudgements had caused later poets to turn inward: 'Whatever more long term effect Pound's disastrous career may have on American and British poetry, it seems inevitable that it will rule out (has ruled out already, for serious writers) any idea that poetry can or should operate in the dimension of history . . . History from now on may be transcended in poetry, or it may be evaded there; but poetry is not the place where it may be understood.'[34]

The Movement showed slightly more respect for the historical readings, and political participation, of the 1930s generation of Auden, Isherwood, Day Lewis, Spender and MacNeice.

They acknowledged that the various crises of the 1930s—unemployment, the rise of Nazism, the Spanish Civil War—did demand positive engagement, and that, as Amis puts it, the 'readiness to face death in the pursuit of their principles is obviously much to the credit of the young men of the Thirties . . . It is too easy to laugh at them in retrospect'. Davie's 'Remembering the Thirties' also found a praiseworthy heroism in these young men:

> A neutral tone is nowadays preferred.
> And yet it may be better, if we must,
> To praise a stance impressive and absurd
> Than not to see the hero for the dust.

But these texts make clear that the Movement also found something to 'laugh at' in the 1930s generation: Amis relegated its Marxism to a mere whim of fashion by suggesting that 'it was the "done" thing to be inclined to the left';[35] and Davie found the legends of the 1930s 'not so true/As not to be ridiculous as well', consigning them to a far-off past:

> . . . what for them were agonies, for us
> Are high-brow thrillers, though historical;
> And all their feats quite strictly fabulous.
>
> This novel written fifteen years ago,
> Set in my boyhood and my boyhood home,
> These poems about 'abandoned workings', show
> Worlds more remote than Ithaca or Rome.[36]

Wain, too, emphasized the remoteness of the 1930s, describing it as 'the last age . . . in which people had the feeling that if they only took the trouble to *join* something, get a party card, wear a special shirt, organize meetings and bellow slogans, they could influence the course of events. Since 1946 nobody above the Jehovah's Witness level has taken this attitude.'[37] The Movement thus defined themselves in opposition to the 1930s generation both socially (lower-middle-class as against upper-middle-class) and politically (political neutralists as against political activists).

Common to these various caricatures is the assumption that although the Movement writers are 'sons' reacting against 'fathers', it is they, not their predecessors, who are politically mature: responsible youth reprimands reckless middle age. According to the ideology of the Movement, Marxism is a phase to be passed through in one's adolescence, and to be grown out of as one matures. 'My generation', Davie writes, pointing to the historical event which made the Movement old and wise in comparison to the 1930s generation, 'came up to university in the time of the Molotov-Ribbentrop pact; thus there was no excuse for us if we were starry-eyed about the Stalinist Left'.[38] The Left had little attraction for the British intelligentsia during the 'Cold War' period: it was associated with Stalin, with repression and persecution. The Movement also had the 'maturing' influence of Orwell, whose impact on them can be judged from the large number of their texts—reviews, articles, and even a poem—which are concerned with his work. Amis, who in 1957 was still feeling misgivings about the force of Orwell's example, has best explained what the effect of this influence was:

Of all the writers who appeal to the post-war intelligentsia, he is far and away the most potent . . . No modern writer has his air of passionately believing what he has to say and of being passionately determined to say it as forcefully and simply as possible . . .

But animus remains, and the reason for it is this. He was the man above all others who was qualified to become the candid friend the Labour party needed so much in the years after 1945. But what he did was to become a right-wing propagandist by negation, or at any rate a supremely powerful — though unconscious — advocate of political quietism.[39]

Amis sees Orwell's advocacy of quietism as being 'unconscious', but Orwell had quite explicitly advocated quietism in his 1940 essay 'Inside the Whale', where the works of Henry Miller were preferred to a 1930s literature said to be permeated by 'a sort of Boy Scout atmosphere of bare knees and community singing'. Orwell found Miller's 'passive attitude' to be more appropriate to the contemporary situation than was the old activism, and predicted its resurgence:

> The passive attitude will come back and it will be more consciously passive than before. Progress and reaction have both turned out to be swindles. Seemingly there is nothing left but quietism — robbing reality of its terrors by simply submitting to it. Get inside the whale — or rather, admit that you are inside the whale (for you *are*, of course). Give yourself over to the world-process, stop fighting against it or pretending that you control it; simply accept it, endure it, record it. That seems to be the formula that any sensitive novelist is now likely to adopt.

This was indeed the formula adopted by Amis and Wain, though to learn it they went not to Miller, a writer not generally admired by the Movement, but to the fiction of Orwell himself. George Bowling in *Coming Up For Air* (1939) is a precursor of the quietist heroes of Movement fiction. Lower-middle-class, suburban, bored by but dutiful towards his family, Bowling considers himself to be 'the ordinary middling kind that moves on when the policeman tells him'. He is politically involved to the extent of attending Left Book Club meetings, and he is more politically astute than his friend Porteous, a retired schoolmaster who, in his association with privilege, 'culture', learning without intelligence, and old values, anticipates Amis's Professor Welch: 'I suppose that if the Local Left Book Club branch represents Progress, old Porteous stands for Culture, . . . the classy Oxford feeling of nothing mattering except books and poetry and Greek statues . . .' But Bowling, too, is nostalgic for a world that has passed, revisiting Lower Binfield, the place of his upbringing, and reminiscing about the lost world of 1913. The central tensions of the novel—Bowling's partial identification with the forces of progress co-existing with his fear for the passing of traditional patterns of English life—is one which influenced the Movement writers, and their protagonists are often seen in Bowling-like positions of passivity and neutrality.

Orwell's advocacy of quietism, his disillusion with the Left, his determination to be 'less deceived', his growing fear of totalitarianism: these played a crucial part in shaping the Movement's political identity. In his *A State of England*, Anthony Hartley argues that 'the "no-nonsense" air of an entire generation comes from Orwell', and Hartley's rather genial picture of that generation shows how the Orwellian notions of 'decency' and 'common sense' dominated post-war political aims:

Believing in the necessity of a Labour government, a Welfare State, independence for India, we none the less had few illusions about the possibility of their leading to a new heaven and a new earth. Political acts seemed necessary, and could be supported, even fought for; political programmes were regarded with scepticism. It was a flight from idealism towards an empiricism which was the more welcome in that ideology had visibly proved itself to be the curse of the twentieth century. Between 1945 and 1950 it was all too evident that nothing very ideal was going to happen, but that if a sort of H.C.F. of decent behaviour and tolerable living could be established that would be enough to be going on with. . . . We were a generation of agnostics: neither optimists nor pessimists, but sceptics. Zeal was not at all our line. Humanity, we would have liked to think, was – and also common sense.[40]

This is the kind of image of its political identity which the Movement 'would have liked to think' might survive. They could argue that their 'neutrality' was appropriate to a contemporary situation in which Butskellism (the feeling that Right and Left had achieved a consensus) and 'the end of ideology' were notions attractive to many. They could point to the Beveridge report of 1942, the Butler Education Act of 1944, the election of a Labour government in 1945, and the official inauguration of the Welfare State in 1948, for evidence that the new era was liberal and humane, and that steady social progress had been made. They could reassure themselves that the low tempo of post-war government, typified by Attlee's decision to conduct his 1950 election campaign by travelling round the country in a small car, established a tone of quiet, earnest concern in which political enthusiasm had no part. To be politically astute in the 1950s, the Movement implied, was to be politically inactive.

It might be easier to accept this picture had the Movement's political statements of the 1950s been less complacent. As it is, the Movement's interpretation of Orwell's career as evidence that Communism was the god that had failed looks to have been designed primarily to sanction an already strong conservative impulse in the group. And it seems remarkable that supposedly responsible intellectuals found nothing before Suez to command their political attention. An observant intelligentsia would certainly have noticed that many Welfare State measures were not having their intended impact, and that many of the brave schemes of 1945 had been betrayed since the return of the Conservative Party in 1951. But as late as 1957, in a symposium called 'The Writer in His Age', Thom Gunn was complaining that the 'agony' of post-war intellectuals was in having no cause to support:

. . . many literary commentators seem to think that the trouble with my generation is that it does not have a 'cause' — as if we were wrong for not nosing round after one. But there is no mass unemployment now, the unions are as powerful as they could wish to be, National Health has been around for ten years, and the village squires are all dead . . . The agony of the time is that there is no agony.[41]

Gunn's statement echoes Jimmy Porter's cry in *Look Back in Anger* that 'there aren't any good brave causes left', and this was certainly a dominant post-war myth. It is echoed in Amis's claim that 'when we do shop around for an outlet we find there is nothing in stock: no Spain, no Fascism, no mass unemployment'; and in Enright's comment that 'it is in a sense a tribute to the state of the country that there should be so little political excitement in Britain today'.[42] Having interpreted the contemporary political climate in this way, the Movement presented the notion of 'neutrality' as an attractive and appropriate one: it seemed the only alternative to the dangerous extremes of Right and Left. The Movement's stand became, as Holloway put it, 'a stand against having a political stand'[43], and the idea of a person ingeniously warding off commitment even began to leave its mark on the poetry:

Wain's 'Poem Without a Main Verb', for instance, enacts by its withholding of the main verb the pleasures of resisting action or decision:

> Watching oneself
> being clever, being clever:
> keeping the keen equipoise between *always* and *never* . . .

More interestingly, 'neutrality' can be seen at work in a poem which has some right to be thought the most politically direct of all Movement texts, Davie's 'The Garden Party'. At first sight this seems to be a poem which is severely critical of both class distinction and capitalism. The speaker refers to 'our Black Country'—a phrase which advertises both his provincial background and his deprivation in a countryside despoiled by both the business and leisure interests of 'local magnates'. His background is clearly working or lower-middle-class and he does not attempt to hide that he is 'envious' of the social privilege denied to him but granted to richer children who live nearby; 'I only wish I had my time again', he admits. His attraction to a girl from a higher social class than his own, and awkward dealings with her, heighten this resentment, and at the end of the poem he distinguishes his own radicalism from the 'more submissive' attitude of his father. His father's 'equalizing rule' that money does not bring happiness is replaced by dialectic: 'we' (the underprivileged) have suffered because of 'them' (the rich)—'theirs is all the youth we might have had'. The social analysis, supported by suggestive class detail like 'tennis courts' and 'tango', is sharp and clear-sighted.

Yet this could not be called a committed poem. The strict decasyllabics, heavy end-stops and formal abab rhyme scheme give the impression of emotion all too easily under control. The references to Scott Fitzgerald and jokey word-play ('I shook absurdly as I shook her hand') suggest wit and humour rather than anger. The romantic mood of the fourth stanza, with its vague lyricism 'Faces hung pearls upon a cedar-bough' perhaps intended as another distancing literary reference (there is a faint echo of Pound's comparison of metro faces to 'petals on a wet black bough'), undermines the polemical directness of the rest of the poem. The tone is playful rather than challenging, and though the last lines are unambiguous they are too neat and 'finished' to unsettle the reader. Indeed, one's final impression of 'The Garden Party' is that the speaker has much the same geniality and tolerance as his father, and that his claim to represent a new, tougher approach is not borne out by the operations of the poem itself. Davie amuses himself by seeming to rock the boat but would be disturbed at the thought of overturning it. Like the protagonists of most Movement texts, the speaker of 'The Garden Party' is too attracted to the social structure in which he has eventually prospered to wish to change that structure to any significant extent. He compromises by maintaining neutrality while seeming to offer a critique.

In the early 1950s it was the critique which the contemporary readers and critics noticed, and for this reason the Movement was presented as rebellious and new. It had, after all, a name which suggested possible connections with the Labour Movement, and it did offer a different class perspective. But any close reading of Movement texts would have indicated a marked degree of 'adjustment' and conservatism, a spirit of compromise which would lead it in due course to take up 'Establishment' attitudes.

3

The Sense of an Audience

Father, Mother, and Me,
Sister and Auntie Say
All the people like us are We
And everyone else is They.

Kipling, 'We and They'

In 1959 Donald Davie wrote an essay, called 'Remembering
the Movement', in which he looked back on his involvement
with the *New Lines* poets earlier in the decade. One of the
essay's most interesting contentions is that there is a connection between the Movement's poetic manner and the refusal
of its members to acknowledge the existence of a group
endeavour:

. . . Ours was writing which apologized insistently for its own existence,
which squirmed in agonies of embarrassment at being there in print on
the page at all. In the interstices of our poems — in the metrical places
wasted on inert gestures of social adaptiveness — 'no doubt', 'I suppose',
'of course', 'almost', 'perhaps'—you can see the same craven defensiveness which led us, when we were challenged or flattered or simply inter-
viewed, to pretend that the Movement didn't exist, that it was an
invention of journalists, that we had never noticed how Larkin and
Gunn and Amis had something in common, or that, if we had noticed,
it didn't interest or excite us.'

According to Davie, the denials of participation in a movement are themselves characteristic of the Movement sensibility.
Knowing that English contemporaries were likely to find the
notion of a literary movement distasteful or ridiculous, the
Movement poets made light of their group endeavour. The
fear of being discredited for their association with such a rash
and attention-seeking phenomenon made them speak of the

Movement 'inside invisible quotation marks'; they disarmed enquirers with nudges and winks.

This concern to be on agreeable terms with others can also be found, Davie argues, in a great deal of Movement poetry. He identifies the concern in what he calls the 'gestures of social adaptiveness' which serve to persuade the reader that the poet is modest, friendly, well-mannered and, above all, fair-minded. A glance at *New Lines* is sufficient to confirm the prevalence in Movement poetry of the colloquial, frequently defensive asides to which Davie refers:

> One question, though, it's right to ask,
> Or, at the least, hint tactfully.
>> (Holloway)
>
> Yes, true; but in the end, surely, we cry
> Not only at exclusion, but because
> It leaves us free to cry.
>> (Larkin)
>
> Better of course, if images were plain,
> Warnings clearly said . . .
>> (Amis)
>
> For him, it seems, everything was molten.
>> (Enright)
>
> Yes, some attempt undoubtedly was made
> To lift the composition, and to pierce
> The bald tympana — vainly, I'm afraid;
> The effect remains, as ever, gaunt and fierce.
>> (Davie)

In many such instances, the cautious self-qualification might be seen as evidence of a fear of being committed to any opinion lest ridicule or discredit ensue: statements are made with a tentativeness that amounts, at times, to self-apology. In this sense, what Davie calls the Movement's 'craven defensiveness' might be related to that failure of nerve which was observed in the previous chapter: a scholarship boy's eagerness to please and political neutralist's reluctance to take a stand are manifested in the ingratiating tone of Movement poems. Davie in his 1959 essay is determined to condemn this 'pusillanimity'—though it is noticeable that even he continues to use inverted commas about 'the Movement' and being 'in' it, and that his essay is yet another apology for the group.

Davie's remarks must be seen in the context of his reaction in the late 1950s against his own previous writing methods. In another article appearing in the same month as 'Remembering the Movement' was published, July 1959, Davie called for a poetry that would turn from 'social reality' towards 'spiritual reality'. He applauded Robert Graves for addressing 'the Muse' rather than the reader, and for refusing to write poems 'which have for their sole purpose our getting on terms with one another'.[2] Davie was at this time becoming responsive to a kind of poetry unheard of in the philosophy of the Movement, and for this reason he was particularly eager to castigate his own former methods.

Nevertheless, Davie's hostile view is representative of a considerable body of critical opinion which regards the Movement's poetic socializing as one of its most lamentable features. Before Davie's article appeared, Ronald Gaskell had called the Movement's conversational asides 'sawdust', suggesting that they 'add[ed] nothing to the sense and nothing useful to the tone'. Charles Tomlinson detected in the group's manner 'a sentimentally ingrained habit of mind that knows what the customer wants'. John Press has also condemned the Movement's conversational manner, arguing that 'the practice of scattering here and there such empty phrases as "of course", "I'm afraid", "it seems", insofar as it is not just metrical padding, appears to be a vaguely reassuring gesture intended to show that these highly intellectual poets want their readers to relax and feel at home in a genial atmosphere'.[3] None of these critics regards the Movement's conversational manner as defensible: they suggest that it is wasteful, servile, or patronizing.

The Movement's conversational asides do, however, fulfil other less reprehensible functions. Far from providing the relaxation spoken of by Press, they sometimes alert the reader to difficulties and distinctions which he or she may not previously have recognized. For example, in the opening lines of Elizabeth Jennings's 'Identity'—

> When I decide I shall assemble you
> Or, more precisely, when I decide which thoughts
> Of mine about you fit most easily together

—the poet checks her initial metaphor of 'assembly', which might imply (wrongly) some objective process, and replaces it with a slightly different one, that of 'fitting': the alteration makes clearer that the way we look at others is often slanted to suit our own ends. Minute distinctions of this kind have usually been felt to be the province of prose, and it is true that in poetry they can seem drab and niggling. But to allow hesitations and qualifications into a poem is in a sense more honest than to pretend they do not exist. This is a point made by Larkin's poem 'Ignorance', which suggests that conversational hesitations ensue, not from a desire to hit the right note with others, but because of our deep uncertainty about the world in which we live:

> Strange to know nothing, never to be sure
> Of what is true or right or real,
> But forced to qualify *or so I feel*,
> Or *Well, it does seem so:*
> *Someone must know.*

'Ignorance' is an important defence of Movement poetry, for it implies that since we 'spend all our life on imprecisions', phrases like 'perhaps' and 'it seems' are bound to figure in our speech: they do not require apology, and the poet need not eschew them.

The Movement's emphasis on the fallibility of the poet understandably met with resistance in the 1950s, for received Romantic and Modernist theory grants the poet the more exalted status of prophet or seer—a being who is raised above the common herd. According to such theory the reader is spared the slack and awkward ponderings of the poet, and is presented instead with refined wisdom, an intellectual and emotional complex in an instant of time. But the hesitant and often bewildered persona which appears in much Movement poetry would not have seemed unfamiliar to the Coleridge of 'Frost at Midnight', nor to the Keats who defended 'Negative Capability', the poet's right to be susceptible to 'uncertainties, mysteries, doubts'. Nor would this persona have seemed unfamiliar to the early Eliot, whose speaker in 'Portrait of a Lady' asks 'are these ideas right or wrong?', and whose Prufrock, finding it 'impossible to say just what [he] mean[s]', has

> time yet for a hundred indecisions,
> And for a hundred visions and revisions,
> Before the taking of a toast and tea.

There are similarities, too, between Larkin's 'Ignorance', and the ideas and manner of William Empson's 'Let it Go', where a strangeness of things is also examined. Empson is usually said to have encouraged the Movement's tough intellectual wit, but his fallibility in 'Let it Go', dramatized through his stumbling but haunting imprecisions ('the real thing', 'the whole thing', 'the talk would talk'), anticipates the awkwardness and hesitancy of the Movement persona:

> It is this deep blankness is the real thing strange.
> > The more things happen to you the more you can't
> > Tell or remember even what they were.
>
> The contradictions cover such a range.
> > The talk would talk and go so far aslant.
> > You don't want madhouse and the whole thing there.

The vulnerability of the Empson persona in poems such as 'Ignorance of Death', 'Aubade', 'Missing Dates' and 'Villanelle', with their strong sense of waste and uncertainty, was attractive to the Movement. Even John Wain, the Movement poet most responsive to the 'other', intellectual Empson, could appreciate this vulnerability. In his poem 'The Bad

Thing', he reproduces almost too slavishly the verbal imprecisions of 'Let it Go':

> Then you think: the bad thing inhabits yourself.
> Just being alone is nothing; not pain, not balm.
> Escape, into poem, into pub, wanting a friend
> Is not avoiding the bad thing. The high shelf
> Where you stacked the bad thing, hoping for calm,
> Broke. It rolled down. It follows you to the end.

The hesitations and self-qualification of Movement verse not only express uncertainty but reflect the poet's struggles to find a way out of uncertainty, and to persuade himself that something is the case. Many of Larkin's poems, in particular, are exercizes in self-persuasion. 'Reasons for Attendance' dramatizes the speaker's struggle to convince himself that he is 'right' to stay outside a dance-hall because his true or real interest is not sex but art:

> Why be out here?
> But then, why be in there? Sex, yes, but what
> Is sex? Surely, to think the lion's share
> Of happiness is found by couples — sheer
>
> Inaccuracy, as far as I'm concerned.
> What calls me is that lifted, rough-tongued bell
> (Art, if you like) whose individual sound
> Insists I too am individual.

The asides here — 'But then', 'yes', 'surely', 'as far as I'm concerned', 'if you like' — record the process by which the poet seeks to convince himself that he is on the right side of 'the lighted glass', and that to be deprived of 'the wonderful feel of girls' need not be devastating. But the abundance of such persuader-words is also an indication of the poet's self-distrust: various reasons for attending the Muse are offered, but the poet is not ultimately convinced by them. The last two words of the poem provide a qualification which overturns the carefully elaborated argument:

> Therefore I stay outside,
> Believing this; and they maul to and fro,

> Believing that; and both are satisfied,
> If no one has misjudged himself. Or lied.

Several of Larkin's poems are constructed as this kind of debate between two voices: one voice sober and responsible, the other adventurous and romantic. One consequence of such a construction is that the reader is drawn into the concerns of the poem to a surprising extent: there is an implicit invitation for the reader to 'become' one of the voices, and to participate in an argument with the poet. This is perhaps the most important function of the conversational asides which Larkin and other Movement poets make use of: words and phrases such as 'yes', 'if you like', 'true', and so on, not only record the development of the poet's thought, but keep track of the reader's likely responses, answer or anticipate his comments, and grant him the right to converse and pass judgment. The typical Movement poem can be as much a dialogue as a monologue. Two of Donald Davie's poems, for instance, begin in mid-conversation:

> For such a theme (atrocities) you find
> My style, you say, too neat and self-possessed.
> I ought to show a more disordered mind.
> > ('Method. For Ronald Gaskell')
>
> You call my poems 'contrived': they are indeed.
> Whoever heard of springes raised from seed?
> > ('Rejoinder to a Publisher's Reader')

Both these poems arose out of arguments with particular people, but by publishing them Davie moves beyond the confines of a private dispute, and allows the 'you' of the poems to refer to whoever reads them. Davie's poems resemble Larkin's in that they depend heavily on the reader: it is to the reader that the poet must justify himself. The difference is that while Davie's poems usually end on a triumphant note (self-justification has been achieved), Larkin rarely allows his speakers to present their case convincingly: 'Reasons for Attendance' is not self-vindication but self-inculpation, and in 'Self's the Man' there is a similar final qualification to cast doubt on the bachelor speaker's claim to be happier and saner than the married Arnold:

> . . . I'm a better hand
> At knowing what I can stand
> Without them sending a van —
> Or I suppose I can.

It is not therefore true to say, as Davie does in 'Remembering the Movement', that the Movement conceived of poetry 'as an act of private and public therapy, the poet resolving his conflicts by expressing them and proffering them to the reader so that vicariously he should do the same'. In Larkin's poetry, we are often made to suspect that the poet's conflicts have not been resolved, despite the fact that a process of attempted resolution has been gone through. Davie's critique of the Movement is actually most applicable to his own early work, in which release for the poet depends on the success with which he presents his case to the reader. And if there is 'therapy', it is intellectual rather than emotional: Davie disapproves of mere Plath-like confession, preferring the more cerebral forms of *apologia* and rejoinder.

A good example of Davie's habit of self-defence is 'Rejoinder to a Critic', which seeks to justify the lack of emotion in the author's early work. The poem was written as a reply to Martin Seymour-Smith, who had criticized Davie in the Oxford magazine *Departure* for 'constantly seeking a critico-academic excuse for postponing an attempt to write poetry of a wider range'.[4] In February 1955, Davie wrote to Alan Brownjohn, at that time the editor of *Departure,* explaining that although he partly agreed with Seymour-Smith, and felt that he was writing rather differently in his latest work, he had just for the fun of it composed a reply. Like the two Davie poems quoted earlier, 'Rejoinder to a Critic' begins in mid-argument:

> You may be right: 'How can I dare to feel?'
> May be the only question I can pose . . .

Davie was well aware that other readers of his work might

find its range and depth of feeling limited, and it is to them, not just Seymour-Smith, that the 'you' of the poem is addressed. If self-vindication is to be achieved, these readers must be addressed reasonably and politely: thus the poem begins with Davie half-conceding the point at issue—'You may be right'—and thereby establishing his fair-mindedness. A quotation from Coleridge is used to assist the self-defence, and in the second stanza, Davie reinforces his argument still further by quoting Donne. Before he does so, however, he is careful to forestall any possible objections to this practice of literary allusion. Once again there is a keen awareness of the reader's likely reactions:

> And yet I'll quote again, and gloss it too
> (You know by now my liking for collage):

Davie's subsequent quotation from Donne—'who's injured by my love?'—is intended not to impress the reader, but to make him see the difference between the situation of the contemporary poet and that of earlier ones. English poets of the past could feel confident that 'feeling' in poetry did good rather than harm. But, as Davie puts it in another poem ('At Dachau Yeats and Rilke died'), 'At Dachau man's maturity began'. Intensity of feeling is no longer available to poets since 1945: it has become a dangerous liability. It was intensity of feeling, Davie asks the reader to believe, that led to the dropping of the atom bomb. The contemporary poet must counteract this catastrophic excess of feeling by eschewing emotion and rhetoric. Keith Douglas wrote during World War Two that 'to be sentimental or emotional now is dangerous to oneself and to others', and Davie's view is very similar:

> 'Alas, alas, who's injured by my love?'
> And recent history answers: half Japan!
> Not love, but hate? Well, both are versions of
> The 'feeling' that you dare me to ... Be dumb!
> Appear concerned only to make it scan!
> How dare we now be anything but numb?

At the outset defensive towards his readers, Davie is able by the end of the poem to suggest to them that they also face his problem: in the last line the poet-reader relationship has become sufficiently intimate for the 'I'/'you' antithesis to be dispensed with, and for the pronoun 'we' to take its place. It would have to be admitted that some readers have resisted being inveigled in this way. Charles Tomlinson has disputed Davie's thesis by offering an alternative connection between Hiroshima and poetic style: he argues that the bomb was dropped not through excess of feeling but through 'the death of the faculty of imagination in the leaders of democracy'.[5] Tomlinson thereby affirms the continuing need for a poetry of feeling and imagination. Other readers have dissociated themselves from Davie by taking objection to his penultimate line, which might be seen as a recommendation of indifference: 'appear concerned only if this is an aid to versification'. That an opposite meaning can be inferred—'Don't let your concern show: look as if you only care about versification'—is partly borne out by Davie's own conduct in the poem. The sensitivity shown to readers seems to guarantee the poet's social responsibility.

The impression that the Movement writers were unusually concerned about establishing a close relationship with their readers is reinforced by a number of critical statements which they have made. In introductions to their work provided for Enright's *Poets of the 1950's* anthology, Davie suggested that 'The best thing poetry can do at the present time is to convey a sense of elation and to raise the spirits of its readers'; Larkin said that he wrote in order to 'preserve things I have seen/ thought/felt . . . both for myself and for others'; and Amis claimed to be aware of the reader even at the very early stages of composing a poem: 'When a new poem looks like getting itself written . . . I ask myself: Is this idea likely to interest anyone besides me? and try to forget about it if the answer seems to be No'. To publish one's work, the Movement maintained, indicates a desire to have it read by others, and one must therefore bear the reader in mind. They would have regarded Keats's attitude to audience—'I never wrote a single line of Poetry with the least Shadow of public thought'— as one that required apology rather than self-congratulation.

But to say that the Movement poets were unusually pre-occupied with the matter of an audience is to invite a further question. For what kind of reader was their work intended? In 'Remembering the Movement' Davie says that he 'had hopes of readers from among [the] highbrow élite' and a poem like 'Rejoinder to a Critic', with its learned allusions and preoccu-pation with poetic style, could be said to be aimed at a small, intellectual readership. But 'Rejoinder to a Critic' also gestures towards a wider audience—post-1945 Europeans in general— and so, too, does Larkin's 'Reasons for Attendance', which, though written from the particular standpoint of a poet, dramatizes the by no means remote or unfamiliar problem of the lonely outsider. This desire to reach two seemingly dif-ferent audiences—one a small intellectual circle, the other a large body of 'Common Readers'—is one of the most impor-tant features of the group.

The Movement's interest in poetic audience was at its peak in the years 1952-5, when a series of texts investigated the poet-reader relationship. The first of these was Davie's *Purity of Diction in English Verse,* which argues, among other things, that there had been until the late eighteenth century a close relationship between English poets and their readers, and that its breakdown created important differences between Augus-tans and Romantics. The breakdown is sometimes seen as the source of energy and liberation in Romantic poetry, but Davie insists that it deprived poetry of valuable effects such as urbanity. He is nostalgic for the 'homogeneous society' in which the Augustans and their predecessors wrote:

Wordsworth had no such confidence in his readers as Goldsmith had in his. When he lost confidence in his public, the poet was thrown back upon confidence in himself. When this confidence, too, was shaken, it masked itself as hysterical arrogance. This is one way of describing the

Romantic Revival.

> In the Elizabethan, the Caroline and the Augustan ages, the poet moved in a society more or less stable and more or less in agreement about social propriety . . . Presumably, the violent dislocation of English society at the end of the eighteenth century (the Industrial Revolution) had destroyed the established codes of social behaviour.[6]

Davie made no specific statement to suggest that contemporary poets were in the position of being able to write for a homogeneous audience. But he was clearly recommending Augustan poetry as a model to which 1950s poets should look back, and later acknowledged in a 1966 postscript that the book had been written 'principally so as to understand what I had been doing, or trying to do, in the poems I had been writing'.

One of the Movement writers who most admired *Purity of Diction*, Kingsley Amis, had also considered the poet-reader relationship in a critical essay written in 1952, but not published until two years later. Amis's essay wished to establish that 'a poet who is concerned to communicate with an audience is more likely than one who is not to produce work which will survive the passing of its original readers'. Amis laid special emphasis upon the role played by these 'original readers' or mentors (a role which, as has been suggested, Larkin played for Amis, and Amis for Larkin); the more stringently objective their advice, the more likely the poet was to develop. Amis centred his article on a number of Victorian poets, but, like Davie, saw it not as disinterested literary history but as instruction for the contemporary poet. The various strengths and weaknesses of Victorian poetry were, he concluded,

> traceable in part, sometimes in large part, to the attitudes to communication taken up by those concerned, and/or to their success, or lack of it, in finding a small inner audience suited to its function. If even a slight general connexion could be established between absence of concern to communicate and inability to produce work of lasting interest and value, perhaps the modern practitioners of chap-fallen Romanticism may give up exhibiting themselves before their readers and at last set about telling them something.[7]

Amis and Davie were careful to stress that contemporary poets could not expect a large audience: their readers might be confined to what Amis called 'a circle of intimates' and Davie a 'coterie of personal friends and other poets'. Indeed, Amis suggested that 'concern to communicate with a very large audience is bad for a poet's work'. This conclusion was also reached by D. J. Enright in his introduction to *Poets of the 1950's*—'It is time for a poet to start worrying when his poetry begins to sell half as well as the average nondescript novel'—and, earlier, by John Wain. In an article of 1953, Wain argued that by writing for a small audience the poet was better placed to understand its feelings and prejudices:

In the seventeenth century it was not even necessary for your work to be printed before you became famous as a poet: manuscript copies would reach all the people you wanted to reach ... And the important feature of this small audience was that it was clearly visualised ... Whether or not the poet liked his readers (and Augustan poetry, which enjoyed the tidiest set-up of all, was largely satiric), he knew who they were. He was not shouting into a hole in the wall.

With the beginning of the nineteenth century ... the English poet found himself with the chance of addressing a public so large that its outlines were blurred ... The trouble was that this larger audience could not be known, could not be physically felt as a presence.[8]

Preoccupation with the poet-reader relationship had also been the basis of Wain's sequence of six poems, 'Who Speaks My Language', which appeared in *Mixed Feelings* in 1951. The sequence describes the various 'blocks' which prevent the poet from communicating as he would like. One obstacle, explored in the first section, is the ambiguity of language, which makes 'the simplest words take fright/And shape themselves anew for every ear'. Another obstacle, section two suggests, is the generation gap, which prevents a young poet (as Wain then was) from reaching older readers:

> Both old and middle age are blind
> To read the alphabet I write.
> Their longest journey lies behind ...

> And so my speech must be confined
> To those who taste our epoch's plight.
> Both old and middle age are blind.

In the third section, Wain narrows his conception of audience still further, suggesting that only the middle-class young with a standard of living like that of his own will find his poetry rewarding:

> . . . I could reach
> many who would find my words familiar
> were their and my incomes more similar:
> but those who have money cannot imagine
> what could possibly be the fashion
> of life for those whose daily struggle
> is increased to just about double
> by lack of short cuts: while the rest,
> those whose share is no more than a crust,
> are altogether too deeply
> caught in the mesh of the weekly
> drudge and traipse of existence . . .
>
> And so the pounds, shillings and pence
> have built up a sound-proof fence . . .

The fourth section considers whether 'You can expect the Common Man to share/Your own concern with words'. The answer for Wain seems to be that the Common Man's idea of poetry is extremely crude—'your hearers for their simple needs/Feel that a few crass gestures will do nicely'—and that the poet must therefore either sell out by providing them with a cheap verbal 'rope trick', or confine himself to a small intellectual circle instead. Section five argues that poetry cannot assist 'the maimed, the limping, the half men', whose physical or mental disabilities are nevertheless such as to make the poet 'wish to free them'. The poet's audience is thus severely limited, but the final section of the poem insists 'on you have to go'.

The meeting-point for Wain, Amis and Davie is not simply a renewed interest in the notion of an audience: it is the insistence on the desirability of a small audience. The conditions which are said to have prevailed up until the end of the eighteenth century are resurrected as an ideal. In the mid-1950s, several critics dubbed the Movement poets 'Augustans' or 'New Augustans', and, in relation to this idealizing of the eighteenth-century audience, the description seems apposite.

The wistful longing to re-create Augustan conditions seems to have been in large part due to the Movement's exposure to the teaching of the Leavises. Q. D. Leavis argued in *Fiction and the Reading Public* (1932) that in the seventeenth and eighteenth centuries poetry was 'widely read', and demanded of the reader 'suppleness, concentration and critical awareness'. However, these 'adequate reading habits' were, in her view, lost during the nineteenth century: the Romantics 'yielded a warm sensuous gratification to the most careless perusal', while the Victorians 'appealed to adolescent and childhood sensibility'. Poor reading habits ensued, so that 'as a consequence, the important poets of the twentieth century, like its novelists, are unknown to and hopelessly out of reach of the common reader.'[9] Mrs Leavis's ideas were developed more fully by her husband, who shared the view that there had been a steady deterioration in reading habits since 1800. In *Education and the University* (1943), he wrote, in terms that anticipate Davie's *Purity of Diction in English Verse,* that the eighteenth century 'enjoyed the advantages of a homogeneous—a real—culture. So Johnson could refer to the ultimate authority of the Common Reader . . . But today . . . there is no Common Reader: the tradition is dead.'[10]

Leavis's invocation of the Common Reader might at first seem to contradict the Movement emphasis on the small audience. But it is noticeable that he re-defines Johnson so as to eradicate any suggestion of populism: 'the Common Reader,' Leavis says, 'represented, not the great heart of the people, but the competent, the cultivated, in general'.[11] From as early as *Mass Civilization and Minority Culture* (1930) and *New Bearings in English Poetry* (1932), and with increasing insistence as the years passed, Leavis emphasized that 'competence'

and 'cultivation' could only be expected of an educated
minority. Important poets directed their work towards, and
were part of, this minority:

> Culture has always been in minority keeping . . . In any period it is upon
> a very small minority that the discerning appreciation of art and litera-
> ture depends.

> The minority capable not only of appreciating Dante, Shakespeare,
> Donne, Baudelaire, Conrad (to take major instances), but of recognizing
> their latest successors, constitute the consciousness of the race (or a
> branch of it) at a given time.[12]

> The potentialities of human experience in any age are realized only by
> a tiny minority, and the important poet is important because he belongs
> to this.

> (. . . consciousness being in any case a minority affair).[13]

The influence on the Movement of Leavis's emphasis upon
properly trained, minority audiences can be seen in an essay
like Wain's 'A Stranger and Afraid: Notes on Four Victorian
Poets' (1955). Wain divides the poet's audience into the higher
'mathematicians' who can genuinely appreciate poetry, and
the 'tradesmen' on whom its subtleties will be lost. The metaphor is not one that Leavis would have chosen and the argument is crudely put, but the commitment to specialization
and élites has its source in Leavis's work. Leavis had, for instance, been dismissive of those people who are 'not intended
by Nature for an advanced "education in letters"';[14] his contempt is echoed in Wain's denial of literary sensitivity to those
not 'born with the right kind of brain':

> Obviously a large number of people can enjoy verse, just as any trades-
> man can do simple arithmetic. But the tradesman cannot understand
> higher mathematics; only a few people are able to do that, and they are
> first born with the right kind of brain, and later trained in the right way.
> I should say that the number of people able to read poetry as it should
> be read is about equal to the number of mathematicians; they are usually
> a few thousand. I am not silly enough to think that the others ought
> not to read poetry at all; obviously they will get a lot out of it, and it
> will be good for them. But it is the very small number of able, discrimi-
> nating readers who must constitute the public for new poetry.[15]

Probably none of the other Movement poets would have been so condescending as to suggest that poetry can, in some unspecified way, be 'good for' those too simple-minded properly to appreciate it, but they would not have found Wain's essential argument unreasonable: Leavis's writings on culture and education had familiarized them with the ideal of the university-based and professionally-trained audience. This ideal understandably endeared itself to a group which consisted of Oxbridge products now largely engaged in university teaching. The Movement could feel confident that academic life, far from inhibiting the poet, provided him with a responsive and perhaps stimulating audience. Leavis's teachings, moreover, narrowed the gap between criticism and creation, reinforcing the intimations of Matthew Arnold and T. S. Eliot that good poetry is dependent upon a well-developed 'critical sense'. The editorial to the first number of *Scrutiny* (1932) contends that 'the artist does depend in a large measure on the prevailing standard of taste', and Leavis's essay 'Towards Standards of Criticism' (1933) that where literary criticism degenerates, 'the instruments of thought degenerate too'. Reduced to its crudest, Leavis's argument could be taken to offer an unexpected fillip: as critics and university teachers, the Movement were to participate in the training of an audience which would, eventually, be in a position to appreciate and further stimulate Movement poetry.

Another teacher of the Movement who took up the question of audience was F. W. Bateson, who in his critical study *English Poetry* (1950) suggested that eighteenth-century audiences were the most satisfactory, and that

it is towards the creation and consolidation of a similar class of common readers today that the energies of the friends of English poetry should be directed. The first step, in my opinion, must be the conscious stimulation of a poetry-reading élite, who can be the missionaries of poetry in a world of prose . . . [16]

Bateson's influence on the Movement is clearly of a different order to that of Leavis, but as a friend of Wain's, B. Litt.

supervisor to Amis, and early publisher of Davie's poetry in *Essays in Criticism* (he also helped Davie in the preparation of *The Late Augustans*), he did have a part to play. *English Poetry*, which Bateson described as the 'by-product of the tutorials and weekly seminars I held with that idealistic first post-war generation',[17] contributed indirectly to the Movement programme by reasserting 'the primacy of meaning' in poetry; by attacking Romantic poets for overrating sound at the expense of 'the rule of reason in poetry'; by affirming the importance in poetry of clarity and intelligibility; and, most important of all, by calling for a close partnership between poet and reader: 'Without the reader's co-operation the poem might just as well not exist. A comprehensive definition of the poet's function *must* include a summary of the processes by which he secures that co-operation. The first thing the poet must know is whom he is writing for.'[18]

When Bateson founded *Essays in Criticism* in 1951, he published a number of articles dealing with the idea of the poet and his public, among them J. W. Saunders's excellently researched 'Poetry in the Managerial Age' (later reprinted as a chapter of Saunders's *The Profession of English Letters*), which spelt out very precisely the size and nature of the readership which a contemporary poet could expect to command. But the importance of Bateson and Leavis was not simply that they renewed interest in the question of an audience; through their teaching at Oxford and Cambridge, they actually managed to recreate the eighteenth-century model of the small, homogeneous audience which their work had upheld. Under their guidance, a new literary intelligentsia began to emerge—an intelligentsia whose members were broadly in agreement on cultural and social issues. The Movement poets, united by virtue of age, class, education and professional employment, formed the nucleus of this intelligentsia, and, though they were not all or always conscious of the fact, the poetry which they wrote was deeply influenced by a sense of belonging to it. The point is made by David Timms in his book on

Larkin:

> The Movement poets all 'spoke the same language'. In a sense they were writing poetry for each other, or at least, for people very much like themselves. Their work was first published in limited editions by small private presses, and so was aimed not at the general public, but at the restricted, probably academic, audience which was the only one likely to buy poetry in limited editions. The audience, in fact, was very much like the poets.[19]

Kingsley Amis has put it rather more forthrightly: 'All the people writing it were dons, and all the people who were reviewing it were dons, and all the people who were reading it were dons, and so on. So you've got a kind of donnish poetry.'[20]

In what ways can the poetry of the Movement be said to derive from, and to cater for, an academic élite? In the first place, a large number of Movement poems demand of the reader an interest in poetry equal to that of the poet—an interest that could only reasonably be asked of someone who writes poetry, or who is employed to study and teach it. As many as half the poems in Davie's first collection, *Brides of Reason,* take for granted the reader's interest in the 'dilemma' of the contemporary poet. Discussion of how the poet should, and should not, write recurs throughout the book:

> If poems make a style, a way of walking
> With enterprise, should not a poet's gait
> Be counties-wide, this stride, the pylon's stalking?
>
> ('Poem as Abstract')
>
> Lines should be hoops that, vibrantly at rest,
> Devolve like cables as the switches trip,
> Each syllable entailing all the rest,
> And rhymes that strike, exploding like a whip.
>
> ('Zip!')
>
> Can spells or riddles be articulate?
> We take our stand, to make the music heard.
>
> ('The Owl Minerva')

It is probably inevitable that any aspiring literary group will frequently discuss the question of 'what literature should be doing today'. Other Movement poems to do so are Conquest's 'In the Rhodope', which describes the part that doubt or scepticism can play in poetry, Enright's 'Life and Letters', Wain's 'Reason for Not Writing Orthodox Nature Poetry', Gunn's 'To Yvor Winters, 1955', and Amis's 'Against Romanticism'. There are also several Movement poems about fiction. Both Davie and Conquest have defended the Movement's self-conscious poetry: Davie has argued that 'the reading of a poem, or the seeing of a picture' is 'an experience like any other', and, as such, is worthy of poetic treatment; Conquest goes further, suggesting that 'the nature of art and of the whole problem of communication has in recent years been seen to be the centre of philosophy and of human life, and perhaps no subject is potentially more fruitful'.[21] But Conquest's claim seems grandiose when set alongside poems such as Davie's above, which are little more than poem-manifestos. In Movement poems about poetry there is nothing of the concrete and sensuous immediacy to be found in (say) Ted Hughes's 'The Thought-Fox' and Seamus Heaney's 'Personal Helicon'. Nor is there much interest in looking beyond fellow-experts: certainly only a specialist could be relied on to share Davie's preoccupation with the importance of rhyme, the necessity for a neutral tone, and the dangers of mysticism and rhetoric. Such poems seem to be written, in Davie's own words, 'in the first place for other dons, and only incidentally for that supremely necessary fiction, the common reader'.[22]

Another reason for calling the Movement 'academic' is the fact that its poetry displays the kind of intellectual wit traditionally esteemed by universities. The Movement poets were, in fact, dubbed 'the new University Wits', a name which linked them to Elizabethans like Lodge, Peele, Greene and Nashe. More appropriately, perhaps, they were called 'Empsonian': Empson was the most striking recent example of a successful academic who was, at the same time, an important poet. The wit to which Movement poetry occasionally aspires consists less of ingenious metaphors, than of ambiguities, allusion, or, as can be seen in the following examples, clever-clever word-plays:

> He noticed no-one noticed him at all.   (Gunn)
> Which, when unfailing, fails him most perhaps.   (Davie)
> The lesson is that breaking hearts must break.   (Wain)

This feature of Movement poetry is one of its least attractive. The group had condemned 1940s neo-Romantics for being 'exhibitionist', but a text like Wain's 'Poem in Words of One Syllable', where the poet's only ambition is to demonstrate his versatility in sustaining monosyllabics, is open to the same objection.

The Movement's academicism and rationalism might also be seen to underlie the preference for 'emblem' and 'riddle' rather than 'symbol'. 'One can define the difference,' Davie wrote in a 1960 essay, 'Impersonal and Emblematic', 'by saying that the symbol casts a shadow, where the emblem doesn't; the symbol aims to be suggestive, the emblem to be, even in its guise as riddle, ultimately explicit. Another difference might be that the emblem is made, fabricated, where the symbol is *found*'.[23] Emblem and riddle exercize the ingenuity of the reader by making him guess a missing word, or provide an answer to a question. The pleasure which they provide is thus largely cerebral—they are intellectual puzzles rather than emotional mysteries. Although the riddle form was popular in Old English poetry and traditional ballads, probably only an academic audience could, in the twentieth century, be relied on to recognize, without being forewarned, its presence in a contemporary poem.

The Movement poet to make most use of riddle is Thom Gunn, who seems to have admired Robert Graves's use of it: 'Without a Counterpart', which Gunn has acknowledged to be 'very deliberately a riddle poem',[24] is based closely upon Graves's 'The Terraced Valley', describing various elements of a landscape—'a hillock in the centre', 'two reed-lined ponds', a 'long volcano'—which is eventually revealed to be a lover's body. Several other of Gunn's riddles are also based on love, or a love affair. His 'Wind in the Street' describes a 'shop' (lover) which the speaker briefly frequents before moving off, 'uncommitted', to 'look elsewhere'. 'Looking Glass' describes a garden (love affair) which, for a time, thrived as a kind of 'Eden'; now its 'green towers sweetly go to seed', and it is only in his 'looking-glass' (memory) that the speaker can retain the garden 'Charmed-still for ever at one stage of growing'. A similar metaphor controls Larkin's 'No Road', which compares a finished love affair to a road fallen into 'disuse'. Love is also the answer to Wain's 'Riddle for a Christmas Cracker', but the hackneyed paradoxes diminish the puzzle element so much that it hardly seems worth asking the question:

> Its slime the vapoured dew, its worst the best,
> Its sickness health, its depths the clearest sky:
> 'What is it?' Ah, you never would have guessed . . .

Most readers will have guessed long ago.

Perhaps the most interesting indication of the Movement writers' sense of belonging to a small academic audience is the recurrence of the pronoun 'we' in their poetry: nearly half of the poems in *New Lines* use this form of address. The word 'we' can have a variety of meanings in poems, most of them to do with couples (poet and lover, poet and parent, poet and child, and so on), but in the poetry of the Movement it is used less in these senses than in the sense of 'our generation' or even 'the group of us'. What is revealing about this use of the pronoun is the implied existence of shared feelings and beliefs: the poet presumes to understand his readers sufficiently to be able to speak *for* as well as speak *to* them. This summoning or representing of an audience through the use of the pronoun 'we' helps to create the 'Augustan' quality of Movement poetry: the Movement poet, like the eighteenth-century poet described by the Leavises, by F. W. Bateson, and by Davie in *Purity of Diction,* is confident enough of his readers to suppose that his own experiences will be ones that they also have had. The Movement poet can, as Davie does in 'Remembering the

Thirties', invite his contemporaries to think about their relationship to the previous generation; or he can, as Amis does in 'Wrong Words', address a poetry-reading, and probably poetry-writing, contemporary who is nevertheless likely to feel occasional boredom with, or impatience towards, the poetry of the past:

> Half-shut, our eye dawdles down the page
> Seeing the word love, the word death, the word life,
> Rhyme-words of poets in a silver age:
> Silver of the bauble, not of the knife.

'Wrong Words' made its first appearance in F. W. Bateson's *Essays in Criticism,* and is aimed at that magazine's academic readership.

But need the use of the word 'we' always be so exclusive? Does it not sometimes attain the wider meaning of 'one' or 'everyone'? The question is raised by one of Amis's best-known poems, 'A Bookshop Idyll', (originally called 'Something Nasty in the Bookshop'). This poem develops the comic emphasis implicit in the phrase 'half-shut' above; the speaker both reads and writes poetry, but is not so solemn about this as not to recognize that poetry occupies a minor place in the 'real' world:

> Between the GARDENING and the COOKERY
> Comes the brief POETRY shelf . . .

Amis's is a modest view of poetry: he would not presume, as Davie presumes in poems like 'Creon's House' and 'Rejoinder to a Critic', that events like the Second World War and Hiroshima had anything to do with poetic style: poetry has not that kind of importance. It is only because he has 'nothing else to do' that the speaker of Amis's poem begins to 'scan the Contents page' of a poetry anthology. In doing so, he notices that the authors 'divide by sex': men's poetry has a varied, but often pretentious, subject-matter—'"I travel, you see", "I think" and "I can read"/These titles seem to say'—whereas the women's deals only with love, usually in an excruciatingly frank fashion. The observation leads the speaker to reflect not only on the difference between men and women, but on the proper way to handle emotion in poetry:

> Should poets bicycle-pump the human heart
>   Or squash it flat?
> Man's love is of man's life a thing apart;
>   Girls aren't like that.
>
> We men have got love well weighed up; our stuff
>   Can get by without it.
> Women don't seem to think that's good enough;
>   They write about it.
>
> And the awful way their poems lay them open
>   Just doesn't strike them.
> Women are really much nicer than men:
>   No wonder we like them.

That the poem is primarily a piece of light verse does not prevent there being several interesting tensions at work within it. On the one hand, readers of the poem are surely meant to feel that the speaker's distinction between men and women— 'We men have got love well weighed up'—is simplistic and complacent, and that, as do many of Larkin's speakers, he condemns himself out of his own mouth. This becomes clearer when it is realized that the same phrase also occurs in *Take a Girl Like You*, where Jenny accuses Patrick of having 'everything weighed up', and in *Lucky Jim* not long before Dixon is complacent about the difference between himself and the women, Margaret and Christine, with whom he is involved: 'What messes these women got themselves into over nothing. Men got themselves into messes too, and ones that weren't so easily got out of, but their messes arose from attempts to satisfy real and simple needs'. On the other hand, just as it is difficult not to admire Dixon, despite his complacency, so it is difficult to avoid feeling that the *faux-naïveté* of the male speaker of 'A Bookshop Idyll', finely handled in the line 'no wonder we like them', *is* superior to the female naïvety at which it pokes fun: on the evidence of the speaker's wit, men do have love more successfully 'weighed up' than women. This tension gives the last stanza of the poem greater complexity. It seems to be intended to act as a Larkinesque undermining of the speaker, for it acknowledges that men, too, have attempted to write poetry when 'chockfull of love': they are as vulnerable as women but hypocritically pretend not to be. By putting this stanza in the past tense, however, Amis actually allows the speaker's assertion of male superiority to be upheld: men are as vulnerable as women only in their adolescence, after which (so it might be inferred) they learn maturity and sense:

> Deciding this, we can forget those times
>> We sat up half the night
> Chockfull of love, crammed with bright thoughts, names, rhymes,
>> And couldn't write.

Interestingly, then, a poem seemingly intended to rebound on its speaker finally preserves a male chauvinist view of women. Amis seems to want to oppose complacent sexism, but remains sexist himself.

A more important tension, from the point of view of this chapter, concerns the readership of the poem: for whom is 'A Bookshop Idyll' intended? On the one hand, Amis assumes a reader well-informed enough to recognize an allusion to Byron ('Man's love is of man's life a thing apart/'Tis woman's whole existence' are lines from *Don Juan*), and involved enough in poetry to be concerned whether poets should 'bicycle-pump the human heart/Or squash it flat': this is the specialist reader also addressed by Davie. On the other hand, the poem could certainly not be accused of narrow or arid academicism: much of its vigour comes, in fact, from its repudiation of intellectual pretension and from its awareness of poetry as an emotional outlet. The use of the word 'we' in the final stanza indicates that Amis wishes to speak to and for men who have, at some time in their life, tried to write poetry; but this is hardly the same as speaking to an academic audience. The best way to account for the tension, perhaps, is to suggest that while the confidence which enables Amis to use the pronoun 'we' stems from his sense of belonging to a specific group, the pronoun itself is intended to reach and represent a much wider and more nebulous audience—'we (all of us)' or, at any rate, 'we men'.

This distinction is a useful one to bear in mind when considering the work of Philip Larkin, the Movement poet who most consistently makes use of the pronoun 'we': just over a third of the poems in each of his mature collections—*The Less Deceived, The Whitsun Weddings, High Windows*—profess to speak for their readers. The pronounced awareness of audience in Larkin's poetry may well have derived from his sense of belonging to a small intellectual group which included friends like Amis and Wain. Like their *A Frame of Mind* and *Mixed Feelings,* his *XX Poems* was privately printed in a limited edition for distribution among friends, and in this sense adheres to the 'Augustan' conditions which the Movement admired. But what is remarkable about Larkin's use of the word 'we' is its lack of circumscription: its definition of a possible readership is far broader than Amis's or Davie's, achieving what M. L. Rosenthal has called an 'implication of universal spokesmanship':[25]

> Always too eager for future, we
> Pick up bad habits of expectancy.
> Something is always approaching; every day
> 'Till then' we say . . .
>
> ('Next, Please')
>
> What will survive of us is love.
>
> ('An Arundel Tomb')
>
> . . . Can they never tell
> What is dragging them back, and how it will end? Not at night?
> Not when the strangers come? Never, throughout
> The whole hideous inverted childhood? Well,
> We shall find out.
>
> ('The Old Fools')

In many poets, the habit of attributing to 'us all' particular feelings and beliefs—'We all hate home/And having to be there'—might seem presumptuous. That it never seems so in Larkin is not primarily a matter of his 'common touch' or his superior knowledge of 'what ordinary people think and feel'. Rather, it is a matter of his strategy: he nearly always earns the right to spokesmanship by beginning with a personal experience, and only gradually and tentatively universalizing it. Larkin himself has described this strategy as follows:

I tend to lead the reader in by the hand very gently, saying this is the initial experience or object, and now you see that it makes me think of this, that and the other, and work up to a big finish—I mean, that's the sort of pattern. Other people, I suppose, will just take a flying start several yards off the ground, and hope the reader will ultimately catch up with them.[26]

A Larkin poem in which this process of initial experience, thought, and 'big finish' is most clearly visible is 'Reference Back'. The poem begins by describing a visit which the poet makes to his mother's house. It is a visit which she has 'looked so much forward to', but, rather than spend his time with her, the poet sits playing 'record after record, idly'. In another room, his mother hears one of these records and, when it has finished, calls out: 'That was a pretty one'. The specific details of this 'initial experience' are carefully set down: the record is named—'Oliver's *Riverside Blues*'—and so is the place of its recording, Chicago. The poem then moves into its second phase, what might be termed its 'thought': the incident is significant to the poet because, he imagines, he will 'always remember how' the record which he was playing

> made this sudden bridge
> From your unsatisfactory age
> To my unsatisfactory prime.

Recognition of the 'sudden bridge' between himself and his mother is painful to the son, for it is also a tacit admission that they are normally separated from each other. Not only has the intimacy originally present in the child-parent relationship disappeared, but both parties are haunted by the feeling, however illogical, that 'by acting differently' they might have preserved that intimacy. The 'we' in the poem's last stanza could be taken to refer simply to mother and son, but in a 'big finish' Larkin exploits the possibilities of the pronoun so as to suggest that the dilemma is one which overtakes everybody:

> Truly, though our element is time,
> We are not suited to the long perspectives
> Open at each instant of our lives.
> They link us to our losses: worse,
> They show us what we have as it once was,
> Blindingly undiminished, just as though
> By acting differently we could have kept it so.

The movement of the poem is one that Larkin often reproduces: the poet begins by inviting the reader to listen ('Now this is what happened, and what I thought and felt') and finishes by implicating him in what has been said ('We all experience/think/feel this, don't we?'). Unobtrusively but irresistibly, the reader is drawn into the poem, and made to share its concerns. The assurance with which Larkin's longer poems—'Church Going', 'Dockery and Son', 'The Whitsun Weddings', 'The Old Fools'—are brought to a close greatly depends upon this extension of the word 'we'.

Most of what has been observed so far in this chapter suggests that the Movement writers saw themselves as writing for a small, academic audience. But with Larkin one is confronted with the presence of an opposite tendency in the group: the desire to write pleasurable and 'accessible' poetry that might reach a wide audience. Larkin's feelings on the subject of poetic audiences are set out very clearly in 'The Pleasure Principle', an extended review written for George Hartley's *Listen* magazine in 1957. He argues there that the principal function of poetry—to give pleasure to others—seems to have been forgotten by contemporary poets, and that 'a large-scale revulsion has got to set in against present notions'. His review develops into a warning against the dangers of writing for an 'academic' audience:

It is not sufficient to say that poetry has lost its audience, and so no longer need consider it: lots of people still read and even buy poetry. More accurately, poetry has lost its old audience, and gained a new one. This has been caused by the consequences of a cunning merger between poet, literary critic and academic critic (three classes now notoriously indistinguishable): it is hardly an exaggeration to say that the poet has gained the happy position wherein he can praise his own poetry in the press and explain it in the classroom . . .

In short, the modern poetic audience, when it is not taking in its own washing, is a *student* audience, pure and simple. At first sight this may not seem a bad thing . . . But at bottom poetry, like all art, is inextricably bound up with giving pleasure, and if a poet loses his pleasure-seeking audience he has lost the only audience worth having, for which the dutiful mob that signs on every September is no substitute.[27]

For Larkin, the small academic audience is as bad as no audience at all, for it is an audience which lacks interest in pleasure. He sees an irreconcilable division between pleasure-seeking 'Common Readers' and English departments solemnly preoccupied with the elucidation of texts. He deplores the merging of poet and critic, believing it to have made poetry more limited in scope, less conscious of the reader.

It is not only Larkin, among the Movement poets, who has expressed hostility towards the 'academic' audience. Four years before the appearance of 'The Pleasure Principle', D. J. Enright had warned that poetry was becoming 'a special interest--as specialized, as "academic", as certain branches of philosophy'. His essay 'The Poet, the Professor and the Public' (1953) described contemporary poetry as 'a game whose rules are known only to an ever-decreasing circle', and wondered 'whether the rightness that can only be enjoyed by a minority (and such a small one, at that) is worth having at all'.[28] Similar ideas appeared again in *The Apothecary's Shop* (1957), where Enright dismissed the idea that universities could play any part in 'nurturing' poetry: 'we need not deceive ourselves into believing that real poetry can ever be grown in academic hot-houses with the aid of "probes and scalpels" or watering-cans or artificial fertilisers'.[29]

Reservations about poetry aimed at an academic audience are related to a more general anti-academic impulse running through not only Movement essays and reviews, but Movement poems and novels. Enright's 'The Interpreters', for example, is a Movement tract 'against interpretation', condemning the minute exegesis which Anglo-American New Criticism has encouraged in the university teaching of literature. Like Yeats in 'The Scholars', Enright depicts critics as men who, far from being 'humanized' by their liberal education, have become insensitive to human suffering and passion. Critical exegesis is seen as a means of ignoring the 'real' human content of texts:

> The poet mentions suffering and even starvation;
> dead cats in the street and women slowly dying on the streets;
> the lot of a sizable part of a sizable nation —
> but dear me no! — that will not do for the critic, that
>   connoisseur of words
> who cannot abide the crude vulgarity of meaning . . .
>
> for it is not what a poem merely says that matters,
> elsewhere than here it finds its true signification:
>   whore, you may be sure,
> refers to some mysterious metaphysical temptation;
> hunger was his image for a broken dream; bread
> an old religious symbol; his typhoons the wind of God.
>
> Good lord, if a poet really meant what he said,
> we should all be out of a job . . .

It is not surprising that Conquest should have included this poem in *New Lines*, for Enright's last point is one that Conquest himself has also made. In a 1966 interview, he suggested that a conspiracy exists between poets and universities to esteem such qualities as ambiguity and difficulty in verse, since these keep university teachers employed: 'The feeling that if you say something in an oblique fashion, it is better than saying it straight, is definitely a highly-established fad, partly tying up with the old academics, because if you say it straight, there is nothing for them to sit and interpret for you—so their jobs are involved.'[30] This demeaning of the university profession appears, in more comic form, in Larkin's poems 'Naturally the Foundation Will Bear Your Expenses' and 'Posterity'. The speaker of the first travels widely and lives well on the basis of a lecture which he repeats at different institutions (Berkeley and Bombay), which he broadcasts on radio, and which he hopes eventually to have published. Jake Balokowsky in 'Posterity' is also an academic careerist: he works in a monastic 'air-conditioned cell at Kennedy', content to write the biography of a writer whom he regards as an 'old fart' because this is the only way to 'get tenure'. The academics in Movement novels are scarcely more attractive. In *Lucky Jim* the principal fraud figure is L. S. Caton, who steals an article which Dixon sends to him, though Professor Welch, who makes Dixon do unrewarded research work for him, is almost as culpable. Several Movement heroes are employed as academics—Dixon, Roger Micheldene in *One Fat Englishman*, Packet and Bacon in Enright's *Academic Year*, Roger Furnivall in Wain's *A Winter in the Hills*—but it is an essential part of their attractiveness that they lack interest in, or fail to be proficient at, their work. Most of them are buffoons or lechers, and the 'bungled lecture' is a common motif: Dixon and Bacon deliver drunken lectures to sober audiences, and in *Figures of Speech* Enright self-consciously reverses this—'current fiction was full of drunken lecturers'—by having a sober George Lester address a drunken audience.

It is true that this satirical treatment of the university is no less oriented towards Academe than are the Movement's poems about poetry: those employed in universities could be expected to take a special interest in it. But the Movement's campus novels and campus poems do show a spirit of impatience with academic life, even at times a philistinism, which is significantly different from the solemn view of the university as a 'centre of consciousness' passed down to the group by Leavis. Certain Movement poems, as we have seen, advertise the specialized knowledge of their author; but there is also an opposite tendency in Movement writing to resist specialization and disclaim intellectual achievement. This tendency is particularly noticeable in *Lucky Jim*, where Dixon feels bound to explain that he is a medieval history specialist purely because 'the medieval papers were a soft option in the Leicester course'. Each learned reference in *Lucky Jim* is accompanied by a disclaimer which assures the reader that Dixon is not to be regarded as an intellectual. He is reminded 'of a sentence in a book of Alfred Beesley's he'd once glanced at'; he 'remembered seeing in a book once' a statement about love by 'somebody like Plato or Rilke'; 'he'd read somewhere, or been told, that somebody like Aristotle or I. A. Richards had said that the sight of beauty makes us want to move towards it'; 'he remembered somebody once showing him a poem which ended something like "Accepting dearth, the shadow of death"'; 'he remembered a character in a modern novel Beesley had lent him who was always feeling pity moving in him like sickness, or some such jargon'. Dixon is surprisingly well-read, but, in order to avoid the taint of academicism, Amis keeps Dixon's memory vague and makes his encounters with literature appear in large measure painful and involuntary.

Dixon's precursor in this matter of the literary disclaimer is Orwell's George Bowling, who is in some respects well-read— he can identify 'that feeling you read about in the Bible when it says your bowels yearn'—but whose acquaintance with books is presented as casual and debunking: 'I was reading a novel I'd got out of Boots. *Wasted Passion* it was called. The chap in the story finds out that his girl has gone off with another chap. He's one of these chaps you read about in novels, that have pale sensitive faces and dark hair and a private income'. This extract points towards the kind of influence on the Movement which Orwell had: he encouraged a down-to-earth and plain-speaking intimacy with the Common Reader which was diametrically opposed to Leavis's (perhaps unintentional) encouragement of an erudite and 'knowing' intimacy with the fellow Eng.Lit. specialist. The Movement would not necessarily have thought of Leavis and Orwell as being in opposition—they could be admired equally for their 'English' pragmatism and sharpness—but they were nevertheless the key figures in the production of an academic/anti-academic tension in Movement discourse. Where Leavis exalted literary criticism, Orwell, though a skilful practitioner of it, could not overcome his suspicion that it was essentially 'fraudulent', and that 'every literary judgment consists in trumping up a set of rules to justify an instinctive preference'.[31] And where Leavis supported the idea of a minority culture in which poetry would be read by the responsive few, Orwell sought to remedy a situation in which he saw 'the common man becoming more and more anti-poetry, the poet more and more arrogant and unintelligible, until the divorce between poetry and popular culture is accepted as a sort of law of nature'.[32] Orwell helped to kindle the Movement's sense of responsibility towards the 'large' rather than the 'small' audience.

A good example of the Movement's concern to get on close terms with imagined members of the large audience is their use of the word 'chap'—a word which Orwell also liked to employ. The word functions to induce feelings of solidarity between writer and (male) reader: they are 'chaps together', good hearty English types who will tolerate no nonsense. But 'good chaps', like the writer and reader, must be distinguished from 'bad chaps': the latter, Amis's article 'That Certain Revulsion' suggests, are snobs, egotists, poseurs, or (a combination of all these) theatre-buffs: 'If chaps who go to the theatre are bad, chaps who study it, follow it, discuss it, act in it, go to schools of it, are worse. . . . In such people the flame of egotism burns brightly, so that if you find a theatre chap and a non-theatre chap talking together, the chances are immense that they are talking about the theatre, or rather one of them is.'[33] The intimacy invited in such passages is not that of the intellectual 'we' of some Movement poetry, which flatters the reader's sense of superior knowledge ('we are familiar with this allusion, are we not?'), but that of the homespun 'you and I', which appeals to the reader's sense of social decency ('You and I would not behave like that, would we?'). Indeed Movement writers sometimes use the phrase 'you and I' to make the reader side with them against academics and intellectuals. When Conquest, criticized by William Cookson for an attack on Ezra Pound, complains in his retort that criticism is becoming 'something only for the Expert, and no longer for you and me',[34] the suggestion is that 'you and I' are inevitably non-specialists. In a very similar fashion, Amis, reviewing Colin Wilson's *The Outsider* in 1956, invites his *Spectator* readers not to feel ashamed should they fail to be familiar with the intellectuals whom Wilson discusses:

Here they come — tramp, tramp, tramp — all those characters you thought were discredited, or had never read, or (if you are like me) had never heard of: Barbusse, Sartre, Camus, Kierkegaard, Nietzsche, Hermann Hesse, Hemingway, Van Gogh, Nijinsky, Tolstoy, Dostoievsky, George Fox, Blake, Sri Ramakrishna, George Gurdjieff, T. E. Hulme and a large number of bit players. The Legion of the Lost, they call us, the Legion of the Lost are we, as the old song has it. Marching on to hell with the drum playing — pick up the step there![35]

Amis's strategy in the passage clearly involves a good deal of pretence. It is unlikely that, as a university teacher, he had 'never read' or 'never heard of' these famous figures. It is equally improbable that his educated *Spectator* readers had never heard of them. The 'philistine' conspiracy, which is conducted by an intellectual and addressed as much to fellow intellectuals as to Common Readers, must not, therefore, be taken at face value: as the comic metaphor indicates—writers and artists as a marching legion—Amis intends to be playful. Nevertheless, the strategy does have a serious function. When Amis describes famous intellectuals as 'characters', or when, in a review of D. H. Lawrence, he wonders whether it is 'a good thing that these chaps continue to roll up',[36] he intends not to demean intellectual achievement, but to deglamorise it: great writers are reduced to the level of awkward human beings, and their resemblances to 'everyone else' are emphasized. Larkin's use of homely analogies and images in his discussion of poetry has a similar function, serving to demystify and democratize poetry: it is 'like knitting', it is 'pickled' experience, it is 'like a slot machine into which the reader inserts the penny of his attention', it can hope at best to 'keep the child from its television set and the old man from his pub':[37] such descriptions grant poetry a humble but secure place in the real world—'between the GARDENING and the COOKERY '. Kitchen and sporting analogies are particularly common in the Movement's critical statements: Wain, looking back on his composition of the novel *Hurry on Down*, compares it to the cooking of a meal; and he suggests that the situation of the writer in the 1950s is like that of 'a batsman going out to the wicket as fifth or sixth man, to follow a succession of giants who have all made centuries'.[38] The commonplace metaphors are part of an artistic programme in which 'ordinariness' was to be dignified.

The Movement writers' chatty familiarity with readers was also intended as an implicit rebuke to the Modernist writers against whom they were reacting. They detected in certain statements by Ezra Pound, for example, an arrogant disregard of the public: 'As for the "eyes of a too ruthless public": damn their eyes. No art ever yet grew by looking into the eyes of the public.' 'I quarrel with that infamous remark of Whitman's about poets needing an Audience'. For Pound, the popularity of the Georgian poetry anthologies, and failure to appreciate *Ulysses* and *The Waste Land*, testified to the corruption of public taste: he believed, quite understandably, that it was not beneficial for a poet to direct his work at such a public. But some of the Movement poets had an attitude to Modernism which made them side with the public rather than with Pound, and even Donald Davie, the Movement writer most sympathetic to Pound, accused him of 'scrapping the contracts traditionally observed between poet and reader' by failing to provide 'metrical landmarks to assist us'.[39]

The Movement believed indifference or hostility to the

reader to be responsible for what they saw as the obscurity of Modernist poetry. Awareness of the reader, they believed, helped the poet to 'restrain his oddities', and was a prerequisite for a relationship of equality and trust: as Enright puts it 'the poet should do the work, his fair share of it, and not leave it to the researching reader to seek clues on other ground.'[40] The Modernists destroyed this relationship by failing to concern themselves with the reader's likely reception of the poem, and his possible difficulties with its meaning. Now it was time to invert MacLeish, and to make poetry once again 'mean' rather than 'be'. T. S. Eliot had pleaded with readers to be patient if they found a poet's work obscure ('remember that what he may have been trying to do was put something into words which could not be said in another way'), but the Movement defended the rights of the reader to be bored by difficult poetry, declaring that patience with Modernist experimentation had worn thin. Larkin, for example, argued that the 'definitive characteristic' of Modernism was 'an obscurity unlike previous types in being deliberate and unnecessary', and looked back to the days when 'sales of "Georgian Poetry" went regularly into five figures.'[41]

The last sentence is particularly interesting, for it points towards the Movement's nostalgia not for the Augustan small audience but for the Georgian large one. 'Sometimes one reads with great envy about the average writer back in about 1910,' Wain said in an interview, and claimed—rejecting his previous stance—that 'there is no substitute for a large, interested reading public'.[42] Several of the Movement admire John Betjeman because he is one of the few poets since the Georgians to reach a large audience. Larkin's reviews of Betjeman's work nearly always contain awed reference to his sales figures, and attribute much of his popularity to his 'rejection of modernism': 'For him there has been no symbolism, no objective correlative, no T. S. Eliot or Ezra Pound.'[43]

The critic of the Movement is faced, then, with a series of divisions. On the one hand, the Movement enjoys and exploits the sense of belonging to an academic élite; on the other hand, it disapproves of writing aimed at such an élite. On the one hand, it asserts the importance of university teachers and critics; on the other, it questions and satirizes their function. On the one hand, it declares that to write for a large audience is damaging; on the other, it declares that it is valuable and necessary. On the one hand, its work is dense, allusive, intimate with fellow intellectuals; on the other, its work is simple, 'accessible', intimate with an imagined Common Reader. Previous critics of the Movement have tended to emphasize one side or the other, accusing it of 'academicism' or of 'philistinism'; the truth is that the work of the Movement is characterized by a tension between the two.

Why is it that the Movement should have worked in two opposite directions? A possible explanation would be to point to a conflict of personalities within the group, Davie, for example, representing an academic tendency, and Enright and Larkin an anti-academic one. This explanation has some plausibility, but would not account for the internal divisions in writers like Amis and Wain, who took up positions in both camps. Another explanation would be the chronological one: initially the Movement were academic, but gradually they saw the limitations of their position, and began to write for a larger audience. But, again, the explanation is only of partial use: one can detect increasing anti-academicism in Amis and Conquest, for example, but certainly none in Davie and Gunn. A third line of argument would be to suggest that the problem is an unreal one: it is perfectly natural that poets who enjoy only limited readership should occasionally hanker for a large audience, the desire for success and acclaim being something which all writers experience. But this general rule would not explain why 'the audience one writes for' was an issue of special importance to the Movement.

A better way to make sense of the Movement's divided attitude to audience is to look again at the group's socio-political identity. The Movement were an élite: they moved in the company of other intellectuals, and they wrote the kind of poetry that would be enjoyed in intellectual circles. But they were also identified as the 'new men' of a Welfare State post-war Britain in which élitism and privilege were coming to be regarded as ugly notions. In a period of democratic ideals, there were pressures, from both within and without the group, to be socially useful, to write not for privileged minorities, but for the general public. The newly instituted Arts Council, itself an example of the desire to 'bring the arts to the people', sometimes drew attention in its annual reports to the onus on writers to reach a growing audience for literature: there were mentions of 'the new audience emerging in industrial areas', and in 1950 a decision was taken to 'pursue an active policy of encouraging poetry'. Politicians sometimes made direct appeals to writers: in an inaugural address to the 1956 P.E.N. conference, R. A. Butler suggested that 'it is up to us here to go on widening the circle of those who admire the best'.[44]

The idea that a new public was waiting to be developed by contemporary writers also filtered into the universities. It appears, for example, in Vivian de Sola Pinto's *Crisis in English Poetry* (1951), which ends with the plea that poetry 'look outward, and regain contact with a wider audience ... It could reach a very much wider section of the "ordinary cultivated" public than it does at present. Through them it could play an important part in humanizing the classless (and at present cul-tureless) Welfare State.'[45] Even the critical writings of Leavis and F. W. Bateson, however 'élitist' their assumptions, could be felt to have a relevance to the current climate of political thought, because of their stress upon the responsibilities of intellectual minorities towards the public. Bateson encouraged the Movement to think of themselves as cultural ambassadors, 'missionaries of poetry in a world of prose'. Leavis depicted universities as 'collaborative communities', 'centres of con-sciousness' which beget and protect literary sensitivity: even-tually, through their efforts, an 'adequate' reading-public could be created. The notion of the responsible minority promised a reconciliation of the small audience and the large: as a member of the former, one was in an ideal position to instruct the latter.

The Movement's emphasis upon the writer's responsibility towards his public may partly be seen, therefore, as a reflection of contemporary ideology. When Larkin talks of leading the reader by the hand, when Davie admonishes Pound for breaking contracts and denying the reader assistance, and when Enright asks the poet to do his fair share of work, a socio-political code is transformed into a code for writer-reader relations: the poet or critic, privileged because of a superior knowledge of the text, must make special efforts to help the 'underprivileged' reader. That the terms in which these ambitions are expressed—'we' (the intelligentsia) are responsible for educating and humanizing 'them' (the public)—seem guaranteed to perpetuate existing divisions was a problem temporarily overlooked: it was a dominant part of Welfare State ideology that the gap between privileged and underprivileged could, as the result of the efforts of both creative writers and critics, eventually be closed. 'The critic', as Karl Miller puts it, when describing William Empson's increased 'public usefulness' during this period, 'could contribute his own sort of national assistance by undertaking to teach, and by respecting the opinions of the less sophisticated'.[46] The poet could put a new emphasis on clarity and rational meaning in poetry, 'helping' readers by remaining readily comprehensible.

The most concerted attempt to induce the intellectual élite to act responsibly towards the large audience is to be found in John Wain's *Interpretations* (1955). Only Davie and Wain of the Movement appear in this anthology of critical essays, but several of the contributors—A. Alvarez, G. S. Fraser, Iain Fletcher, Graham Martin and W. W. Robson—were not unsympathetic to the group, and Wain has said that, because of its concern with meaning and aversion to rhetoric, 'criticism of the kind represented by *Interpretations* is . . . linked closely with that coincidental style in poetry which became known, in retrospect, as "the Movement"'.[47] Wain's introduction sets the tone for the volume when it attacks academics who are 'only writing for each other; none of that intelligence is flowing into the common stock'. Literary criticism, he argues, should not consist of critics 'doing each other's laundry' and need not be remote and specialized; it is 'an activity that any sensible person can hope to train himself for, with not much more equipment than his native honesty and vitality'. Wain's almost Wordsworthian idealizing of the 'native honesty and vitality' of the Common Man is offset by his emphasis on the need for training—a training which the contributors to *Interpretations* undertake to provide.

Interpretations is a serious intellectual enterprise, much influenced by the close reading encouraged by Leavis, Empson and I. A. Richards, and its analyses of poems are long and detailed. But it eschews specialist language, preferring to make explanations through analogies of an everyday kind. Wain describes the first four stanzas of Yeats's 'Among School Children' as having 'a good head of steam to drive us along', and he depicts poetry in general in terms of a human face— 'the way the words are put together', 'the personal run of the rhythm' are 'what we learn to go by, just as we learn to size up human beings on first acquaintance'. Bernard Bergonzi, who has written excellently about the collection, notes the prevalence in *Interpretations* of mechanical imagery[48] —as well as Wain's 'head of steam', there are bridges, bulldozers, piers, concrete, tools and engines: the overall effect of such imagery is to suggest that the critic is not an ethereal 'highbrow', but a useful worker whose job is not unlike that of the civil engineer. At the end of his introduction Wain asks that literary criticism 'come down from the summit and allow itself to be seen as an affair of simple responsiveness and common sense,' since it is important 'to get people to be less frightened of literary criticism'. The critics in *Interpretations* accord with this aim by offering good-natured assistance; ingenious emendations and erudite allusions are less valued than a friendly tone and readily comprehensible prose style.

Many of the distinctive features of *Interpretations*—the matter-of-fact tone, the willingness to use cliché in order to 'communicate', the determination to get on terms with an imagined Common Reader—are visible again in Wain's own critical collection *Preliminary Essays* (1957). At one point, mixing his metaphors freely, Wain says that 'we want a little less gas about [Dylan] Thomas and some criticism that really talks turkey'. In another essay, 'The Literary Critic and the University' (1955), he describes criticism as 'one of the useful arts, not one of the fine arts', and defines it as 'the discussion between equals of works of literature, with a view to establishing common ground on which judgments of value can be based'. This definition clearly owes a good deal to Leavis's idea of the 'common pursuit' and 'collaborative community', but it is possible to detect in it an element of what Richard Hoggart has called 'false democratic bonhomie'.[49] Movement criticism is clearly instruction from above, and Wain in particular often seems to be talking *down to* rather than *with* the reader: his common mannerism, as was remarked on at the time, can make him seem very patronizing.

That the Movement's academicism sometimes militated against the attempt to reach a larger public is also clear from the work of Donald Davie. Davie, at least, was aware of the problem: he wrote in 1955 that it was 'dishonest nowadays simply to parrot Dr Johnson and "rejoice to concur with the common reader". Johnson knew what he meant by that, as we don't . . . And if the writer is uncertain about this, inevitably the uncertainty is transmitted to his tone, which will sometimes wobble and sometimes strain.'[50] Davie's acquaintance with this problem did not, however, prevent a certain amount of 'wobble and strain' from occurring in his own work. Where Wain had underestimated the Common Reader, Davie often overestimates him. Choosing 'Corrib. An Emblem' as his contribution to an anthology of poetry in 1962, he explains that although the poem was based on a painting by Tiepolo, he had not made this explicit in the poem, since to have done so would have been the mark of 'an intellectual snob, culture-vulture, and aesthete'.[51] It does not occur to Davie that to base a poem on a painting might in itself be considered an example of aestheticism; nor does it occur to him that to leave the Tiepolo allusion implicit is not necessarily any less 'intellectual' than to make it explicit. And how are we to reconcile Davie's appeal to the Common Reader with a poem that introduces, within its fifteen lines, the words and phrases 'Corrib', 'Connemara', 'tutelary', 'subcutaneous', 'pre-divinity', 'art Palladian', 'Hispanic through the Galway Lynches', 'Medici', 'virtù in freight' and 'Syrinx'. The choice of this poem, out of all his others, for an anthology certainly implies a severe mistaking of the degree of literacy which it presupposes. Davie is instinctively a learned and allusive poet, and there are poems of his ('Corrib. An Emblem' is not among them) which draw strength from this. But he also feels the need, as Pound and Eliot did not, to apologize for being learned and allusive: the gesture towards the 'Common Reader', the gruff no-nonsense attacks which the Movement make on aestheticism, 'obscurity' and minority art, exist sometimes as if to atone for being part of a charmed academic circle. As Lindsay Anderson said of Amis, the Movement poet 'will rather pose as a Philistine than run the risk of being despised as an intellectual'.[52]

There are cases, then, of the Movement falling between two stools: in trying to balance the interests of the large audience and the small, it sometimes failed to reach either. It would, though, be misleading to conclude that this was always so. In some respects, the Movement stood for the amalgamation of the two audiences, and in those poems where the intimacy learnt as a result of addressing a small, known group is brought into play when addressing a large, unknown one, amalgamation could be said to be achieved: public utterance in these poems seems the more forceful for being delivered simply and conversationally.

The Movement poem most successfully to reconcile the demands of the two audiences is Larkin's 'Dockery and Son'. Since it opens with the visit of the speaker to the university at which he was an undergraduate some twenty years earlier, the poem might be felt to have a special interest for the small audience. The black gowns, the 'canal and clouds and colleges', the Dean, the language of the Dean ('Dockery was junior to you/Wasn't he?') and of the speaker (he talks of people being 'up' at college): these identify the setting as an Oxford or Cambridge one. But to compare 'Dockery and Son' with, for example, Davie's 'On Bertrand Russell's "Portraits from Memory"', is to recognize how careful Larkin has been to avoid clannish or localized allusions. Oxford provides the initial setting, but the speaker's meditation on the divergence between his life and that of a near-contemporary gives the poem a much wider circumference. Indeed it is important to the development of the speaker, and to the broadening out of the poem, that he is on a train journey *away* from Oxford. Deterring at first, both in his 'death-suited' stiffness with the Dean and in his cosy memories of undergraduate naughtiness—

> Black-gowned, unbreakfasted, and still half-tight
> We used to stand before that desk, to give
> 'Our version' of 'these incidents last night'.

—he gains sympathy only once he has left Oxford, 'ignored', and travels towards the workaday world of Sheffield. It is then that he begins to ponder, vaguely and without much success, who Dockery might have been:

> Was he that withdrawn
>
> High-collared public-schoolboy, sharing rooms
> With Cartwright who was killed? Well, it just shows
> How much . . . How little . . . Yawning, I suppose
> I fell asleep, waking at the fumes
> And furnace-glares of Sheffield, where I changed,
> And ate an awful pie, and walked along
> The platform to its end to see the ranged
> Joining and parting lines reflect a strong·
>
> Unhindered moon.

A detail such as the 'awful pie' could have no place in a poetry that demands spareness, visual sharpness, and an eschewal of the prosaic. But that 'awful pie' is crucial here in establishing the poet as a man who notices such things—a man whose sure grasp of the commonplace encourages us to trust his insights into deeper and more serious questions about fate, free will, heredity, time, the purpose of life (according to the Movement's aesthetic, the less special or gifted a person, the more he is to be relied on). The speaker's 'ordinariness' becomes more apparent in the next lines, when he puzzles why he and Dockery should have come to lead such different lives. Freedom is what the speaker wanted (a freedom neatly expressed in the poem by the phrase 'unhindered moon', and its separation from the metrical confines of the previous stanza), and he believed he could find it by remaining unmarried and childless. But Dockery seems to have acted on quite different assumptions:

> Dockery, now:
> Only nineteen, he must have taken stock
> Of what he wanted, and been capable
> Of . . . No, that's not the difference: rather, how
>
> Convinced he was he should be added to:
> Why did he think adding meant increase?
> To me it was dilution. Where do these
> Innate assumptions come from? Not from what
> We think truest, or most want to do:
> Those warp tight-shut like doors. They're more a style
> Our lives bring with them: habit for a while,
> Suddenly they harden into all we've got . . .

The speaker's puzzling process is dramatized by the inclusion of hesitations and qualifications such as 'now', 'No, that's not . . . ', 'rather', and 'they're more a . . . ', which give the impression of a man earnestly struggling to make sense of a difficult problem. The problem, it is implied, is one faced by everbody: the introduction of the word 'we' in the lines above concludes the contrast between the speaker and Dockery, and begins the definition of what they, and everyone, have in common—an inability to prevent habit taking over our lives. In the last four lines of the poem, the pronoun 'we' recurs to reinforce the increasing fatalism—'we' are all at the mercy of irresistible forces—and creates a memorable universalizing of the poet's feelings:

> Life is first boredom, then fear.
> Whether or not we use it, it goes,
> And leaves what something hidden from us chose,
> And age, and then the only end of age.

Such is the power of these and other concluding lines in Larkin's work, that it is easy to forget how closed they make the poem: beyond the response 'Yes' or 'How true' there is, as a Larkin poem of that title puts it, 'nothing to be said'. This is because Larkin's poetry minimizes the interpretative process by including it within the text: what is inferred by the reader is limited by what has already been inferred by the speaker, whose own struggle to 'discover meaning' is what the poem dramatizes. The reader is 'helped' (he cannot be confused as to what the poem means), but he is also restricted (the only meaning he takes away from the poem is the one found for him by the speaker). In its treatment of the reader, Movement poetry offers a sharp contrast with Modernism. Pound and Eliot may sometimes give the reader few bearings, but they do at least allow him space to explore. Movement poetry, seeing Modernism not as 'open' but as 'obscure', is more conscious of the reader. But in providing him with an interpreter and guide, it also inhibits his movements—there is no opportunity to wander off the beaten track.

Once the strategies of Movement discourse are looked at closely, it becomes apparent that even Donald Davie's excellent account of them in 'Remembering the Movement' misses the point. Davie, it will be recalled, detected in the Movement a lamentable self-apology and social adaptiveness, and he believed that the group could therefore do no more than confirm the values of its readers. But phrases such as 'of course', 'surely', 'clearly' and so on, far from being pusillanimous in the way Davie suggests, are highly coercive. They imply by their very reasonableness and sociability that attitudes other than those held by the speaker are unreasonable and anti-social. They force our attention on the poet or critic (who seems moderate, genial and willing to stand corrected), and distract us from the implications of what is being said. They promise open-endedness, but like the famous formulation of communal critical endeavour from which they partly derive—Leavis's 'This is so, isn't it'—they are ultimately an instrument of persuasion. It would be going too far to call this tendency 'authoritarian'; Jonathan Raban's phrase for it—'the nicest and kindest form of paternal dictatorship'—seems preferable.[53] But one should be aware at least that beneath the sociable tone of Movement writing is a strong determination to inform, instruct, even manipulate.

4

Against Romanticism

After so many (in so many places) words,
It came to this one, No.
Epochs of parakeets, of peacocks, of paradisiac birds —
Then one bald owl croaked, No.

And now (in this one place, one time) to celebrate,
One sound will serve.
After the love-laced talk of art, philosophy and fate —
Just, No.

Enright, 'Saying No'

In 1952 there appeared in England a book of poetry which, in one respect at least, the Movement might have been expected to admire. The *Collected Poems* of a living British poet not only received considerable acclaim from academics and intellectuals, but sold extremely well. The traditional gap between the 'two audiences' had, it seemed, been closed: a poet of undoubted complexity had nevertheless succeeded in capturing the public imagination. The Movement, it might be thought, must have been satisfied; the Movement, however, was not. For the poet in question was Dylan Thomas, and over the next few years the Movement was to become known as a generation of writers with a shared aversion to Thomas's work.

The Movement's reservations about Thomas had been growing throughout the 1940s, and it would therefore be going too far to suggest, as one critic has done, that the Movement actually arose as a 'denunciation' of Thomas in 1952.[1] But it is certainly true that the success of Thomas's *Collected Poems,* followed closely by the publicity surrounding his death in America in 1953, provided an important impetus for the group: Thomas was identified as the major poetic reputation against whom any new generation of poets would have to react. This suggests, rightly, that some element of strategy was involved in the reaction: in the years 1952-4, the Movement poets were young and not yet properly established, and it was clearly in their interests to claim to be offering a departure from the leading figure of the day. But if the Movement tended to exaggerate their antipathy towards Thomas, the case against him was nevertheless crucial to the development of their own artistic programme: through resistance to his work, the Movement became more sure of their own aims in writing.

One must be careful to distinguish hostility to Thomas's work from hostility to the 'Thomas legend': it was the legend— Thomas as drunk, fornicator, rebel, etc—which most annoyed them. Davie in March 1954 said that the 'saddest thing' about Thomas's death was 'the fulsome ballyhoo which it evoked on both sides of the Atlantic', and later in the same year Wain also dissociated himself from the 'outburst of exhibitionist feeling' which followed Thomas's death: 'It's just necessary to make quite plain that one isn't in sympathy with any of it, all the way from the sentimental maundering in Soho pubs to the writers of sweat-making letters to the monthly press about "what Thomas meant to my generation".'[2] When the Movement discussed the legend, they could be surprisingly sympathetic to Thomas himself, presenting him as a provincial innocent ruined by the city—'a Bubbles who fell among literary touts', as Enright puts it[3] —and saving their venom for his hangers-on. Amis's memoir 'An Evening with Dylan Thomas', reprinted in *What Became of Jane Austen?*, is hostile not to Thomas but to a friend of his whom Amis calls 'Griffiths', and in his postscript to *Purity of Diction in English Verse* Davie speaks of 'the tawdy amoralism of a London Bohemia which had destroyed Dylan Thomas, the greatest talent of the generation before ours'. In such passages, the Movement maintains respect for Thomas's poetry, but shows a Leavis-like contempt for those in the literary world who contributed to, and cashed in on, his early death.

In addition to these attacks on the legend, there are, though, a number of Movement texts which express serious reservations about the quality of Thomas's poetry. One of the first of these, Wain's review of the *Collected Poems* for *Mandrake* in 1953,[4] paid tribute to Thomas's 'bold' and 'original' talent, but questioned its final worth, suggesting that Thomas was a careless poet who left the problem of 'making sense' to others: 'It is perfectly possible to furnish even his wildest pieces with a "meaning" (i.e. a paraphrasable content, or set of paraphrasable contents), but the gnawing doubt remains as to whether the writer really *cared* whether it meant anything precise or not'. Wain's implication that the good poet must be not only precise but fully conscious of all that he is putting into a poem is a characteristically Movement one, and it appears again in Amis's 1955 review of Thomas's posthumously-published *A Prospect of the Sea*.[5] Like Wain, Amis expresses some admiration for Thomas, praising that side of his work—'not ranting, canting Thomas the Rhymer, but comparatively disciplined, responsible Thomas'—which accords most closely to the Movement's own poetic ideals. But Amis is more severe than Wain on Thomas's 'wildness', arguing that he 'wasted his talent and integrity' in the pursuit of 'nightmarish reveries' which 'are not among those which many people in full possession of their faculties will find interesting or important'. Thomas's work, is

a sort of verbal free-for-all in which anything whatever may or may not be mentioned or seem to be mentiond. For long stretches very little can be extricated beyond a general air of bustling wildness allied to a vague sexiness or religiosity of subject-matter – if, again, 'subject-matter' is the proper term. The style is that blend of answerless riddle, outworn poeticism and careful linguistic folly which those immune to the spell of the Rhymer will salute with a groan of recognition.

Amis concludes that Thomas will satisfy only those who want from poetry 'something sublimer than thinking'. The use of this phrase suggests that Amis had been reading F. W. Bateson, who drew attention to its previous occurrence in 1805 (John Foster had applied it to Romantic poetry).[6] But the intended insult surely rebounds: poetry *should* be something sublimer than thinking, and the Movement's failure to recognize this was to be one of the limitations of its programme.

Amis's poetry and fiction also contain disparaging allusions to Thomas. There is an oblique description of him as 'our labour chief, our thick-lipped roarer' in 'To Eros', and a more blatant attack upon him in 'A Poet's Epitaph', where the central metaphor implies a rather boorish reference to the drinking problem which led to Thomas's death:

> They call you 'drunk with words'; but when we drink
> And fetch it up, we sluice it down the sink.
> You should have stuck to spewing beer, not ink.

The best known of Amis's criticisms of Thomas comes through his creation of the Welsh poet-dramatist, Probert, in *That Uncertain Feeling*. The intended similarity between Probert's play *The Martyr* and Thomas's *Under Milk Wood* can be inferred not only from the name of the town, Llados, which it features (the name reads backwards just as Thomas's town, Llareggub, reads backwards), but from the parody of Thomas's dramatic prose, which Amis once described as 'a tissue of irresponsible whimsy':[7] 'But, Bowen *bach*, they buried you at batlight in a dead winter. Deep, deep they buried you under the woman's hair of grass, you and your wound, the night Menna Pugh's fancy man from Tenby gave her four rum-and-peps and a packet of twenty and showed her the seaman's way . . .'. At other points in Probert's play, Amis parodies Thomas's poetry as well:

> When in time's double morning, meaning death,
> Denial's four-eyed bird, that Petrine cock,
> Crew junction down the sleepers of the breath,
> Iron bled that dry tree at the place of rock, . . .

As Amis's parody suggests, the Movement believed Thomas's poetry to be wilfully obscure, overladen with symbolism, and too reliant upon assonance and alliteration. Amis uses his protagonist, John Lewis, who is unimpressed by Probert's play—'Dear, dear, the thing was symbolical all right'—to raise Movement-like objections to Thomas's work. When, for example, Lewis complains that 'words like "death" and "life" and "man" cropped up every few lines, but were never attached to anything concrete or specific' he echoes the objection of Amis's poem 'Wrong Words' to the over-use in Romantic poetry of

> the word love, the word death, the word life,
> Rhyme-words of poets in a silver age.

Two other Movement poets to lay into Thomas were Enright and Davie. Enright's introduction to *Poets of the 1950's* criticized Thomas's poetry on the familiar Movement grounds that it lacked thought: 'Perhaps the kind of admiration which Thomas received encouraged him to leave "thinking" to the *New Verse* poets; but poetry is like the human body in needing bones as well as flesh and blood.' A similar premise can be found in Davie's *Articulate Energy,* also published in 1955, which looks back to a period in English poetry, the eighteenth century, where 'strong sense' was as common a term as 'strong feelings'. Davie sees Romantic and Modernist practice as having destroyed meaning and argument in poetry by over-emphasizing the importance of images. He is prepared to admit that in some poetry, notably that of Ezra Pound, such practice has had beneficial effects; but one poet whose pursuit of images he will not tolerate is Dylan Thomas: '. . . a sonnet by Dylan Thomas is unacceptable even on Hulme's terms. When concrete images are crowded upon each other, they lose their concreteness. The milk is soured by the magic, the bread has lost its tang, and the cloud its volume. The things will not stand still, but fluctuate and swim like weeds in a stream. A poem, it seems, can give way under the weight of the "things" that are crowded into it.'[8] Davie's criticisms are the most substantial, since they go beyond churlish complaints about Thomas's obscurity, and question whether he properly adhered to Modernist principles. But, in essence, Davie's case is the same: he asserts the need for control and intelligibility in poetry, and deplores the absence of these characteristics from Thomas's work.

The Movement's attack on Dylan Thomas was not, therefore, merely an attention-seeking revolt by young poets: there was a genuine belief that Thomas's work lacked certain qualities which it would be good for poetry to repossess. This conviction also lies behind a number of Movement poems which undertake not so much to parody Thomas as to 'revise' him, treating some of his favourite subjects in a new, and (it is implied) more salutary, manner. One such poem is Enright's 'On the Death of a Child', which revises Thomas's 'A Refusal to Mourn, the Death by Fire, of a Child in London'. Thomas's poem is distinguished by its daring metaphors ('the synagogue of the ear of corn', 'the least valley of sackcloth'), by its long, rolling sentences (suggestive of a 'flood of emotion'), and by its richly suggestive final ambiguity: 'After the first death, there is no other'. Enright's poem tries to counteract Thomas's. It eschews all but one simple image (that of a funeral); it consists of short sentences and stanzas (Thomas's opening sentence stretches for twelve lines, Enright's for just one); and it has a simple and unmistakable meaning:

> The greatest griefs shall find themselves inside the smallest cage.
> It's only then that we can hope to tame their rage,
>
> The monsters we must live with. For it will not do
> To hiss humanity because one human threw
> Us out of heart and home. Or part
>
> At odds with life because one baby failed to live.
> Indeed, as little as its subject, is the wreath we give —
>
> The big words fail to fit. Like giant boxes
> Round small bodies. Taking up improper room,
> Where so much withering is, and so much bloom.

Enright's poem offers repression of feeling as an alternative to Thomas's excess of feeling. It knowingly deviates from prevalent beliefs about the desirability of releasing emotion. It is, literally, a model of restraint: the tightness of its form enacts the speaker's advocation of controlled mourning. In place of Welsh *hwyl* comes English stiff upper lip.

But, as might be expected of a text so conscious of its predecessor, Enright's poem is not without its points of similarity to Thomas's. Not only does it end with the same kind of paradox—'After the first death there is no other': death contains 'bloom' (immortality or re-birth) as well as 'withering'—but it seeks to achieve the same contradiction of intent: that is, what claims to be a refusal to mourn (and what could therefore be taken to imply lack of feeling on the part of the refuser) must actually turn out to be a poem of heart-felt grief. Both Thomas and Enright refuse to mourn only in order to mourn more effectively than they could have done by agreeing to mourn; they both reject current conventions of mourning, and offer a new kind of mourning instead. Thus while the ways in which they choose to mourn are different from each other (and it had better be said that Enright's is the less successful way: the emotion is so much under control that we begin to suspect it cannot be deeply felt), Thomas and Enright work by similar principles: there is the same 'trick'—a contradiction of declared intention—within the structure of each poem. The similarity is a reminder that even the most militant rejection of literary precedent cannot prevent the incurring of debts. The reaction against Dylan Thomas was essential in enabling Movement poets to, in Harold Bloom's phrase, 'clear imaginative space for themselves';[9] but we should remember Bloom's point that the poet seeking to liberate himself from a 'Father' or 'Precursor' can never entirely succeed in doing so.

As 'On the Death of a Child' revises 'A Refusal to Mourn', so Larkin's 'I Remember, I Remember' revises 'Fern Hill'. This may seem an unduly narrow view of the impetus for a poem which takes its title from Thomas Hood, and which in certain lines seems to be alluding to Lawrence's *Sons and Lovers*. Larkin's poem seeks to dissociate itself from *any* treatment of childhood which is sentimental or idyllic. Nevertheless,

'Fern Hill' was arguably the text uppermost in Larkin's mind when he wrote 'I Remember, I Remember': as the most striking recent treatment of childhood, and as the best-known of all Thomas's poems, it was the one in most urgent need of revision. Another Movement poet, Donald Davie, certainly felt this to be the case: his 'A Baptist Childhood', a poem also written in the mid-1950s, begins by revising a phrase from the second line of 'Fern Hill' in order to emphasize the difference between Thomas's joyful and 'heedless ways' and his (Davie's) rather 'chill' Dissenter's upbringing: 'When some were happy as the grass was green,/I was as happy as a glass was dark'. Davie's disenchanted and even gloomy memories are echoed in other Movement texts, which consistently take an unsentimental approach both to children (pests rather than innocents) and to childhood ('a forgotten boredom'). The Movement's outlook seems once again to have been shaped by Orwell, whose George Bowling is careful to dissociate his nostalgia for Lower Binfield from what he calls 'that poetry of childhood stuff. I know that's all baloney . . . The truth is that kids aren't in any way poetic, they're merely savage little animals'.[10]

This is not a view of childhood and children encouraged by the great Romantic poets, nor by Dylan Thomas. Larkin's 'I Remember, I Remember' tries to substitute for the expansiveness of 'Fern Hill'—

> All the sun long it was running, it was lovely, the hay
> Fields high as the house, the tunes from the chimneys, it was air
>   And playing, lovely and watery

—a 'less deceived' sensibility, one that recognizes childhood, or certain childhoods, to be uneventful and even boring:

> Our garden, first: where I did not invent
> Blinding theologies of flowers and fruits,
> And wasn't spoken to by an old hat.
> And here we have that splendid family
>
> I never ran to when I got depressed,
> The boys all biceps and the girls all chest,

Their comic Ford, their farm where I could be
'Really myself'. I'll show you, come to that,
The bracken where I never trembling sat,

Determined to go through with it; where she
Lay back, and 'all became a burning mist'.

'I Remember, I Remember' is a poem written to be enjoyed by the Movement confederacy. Much as do phrases like 'of course' and 'surely' in other Movement poems, its inverted commas—'"have your roots"', '"mine"', '"really myself"', '"all became a burning mist"'—serve to create a consensus, inviting readers to recognize as cliché-d and derisory certain common notions about childhood and adolescence. Much of the energy of the poem is taken up in the demolition of these notions—so much, in fact, that while 'I Remember, I Remember' makes clear what the speaker's childhood *was not*, it fails to provide any description of what it *was*. Is, then, Larkin's poem merely negative and destructive? Surely not. For it makes a positive and constructive plea for the accommodation in poetry of a 'real' area of experience and of a 'real' tone of voice. Against Thomas's childhood 'honoured among foxes and pheasants' is set, simply, 'Coventry', a place which, obviously (Larkin's omission of any description of his Coventry childhood merely reinforces the impression that it must be obvious), would be unlikely to furnish childhood experience of the 'Fern Hill' kind. And against Thomas's rhetoric is set a level-toned scepticism—a scepticism which finally prevents the speaker from succumbing to the self-pitying error of seeing the 'nothing' of his childhood as entirely 'the place's fault': it is, he implies, his fault too.

The implied positives of 'I Remember, I Remember' need to be recognized, for the accusation of 'negativity' is one that has often been brought against Larkin and his Movement colleagues. The Movement, it is claimed, failed to offer anything to replace what it removed; its reaction against Dylan Thomas was purely destructive; it concerned itself only with, as the Enright poem which heads this chapter puts it, 'saying No'.

At least one of the Movement poets, Donald Davie, has acknowledged that the charge is a serious one:

> That so much more reaction
> Than action should have swayed
> My life and rhymes
> Must be the heaviest charge
> That can be brought against
> Me, or my times.   ('Revulsion')

But when the Movement writers accuse Thomas of rhetoric, or excess of feeling or over-reliance on metaphor, and when they incorporate into their own poems what are felt to be the opposite qualities of restraint, thought, plain statement, then a positive commitment to certain values is certainly present. The problem for the Movement, as a poem like 'I Remember, I Remember' suggests, was that the poetic tradition to which Thomas belonged had first to be destroyed if certain kinds of common experience and attitude were to be articulated. In order to say yes, it was necessary first of all to say no.

As far as the Movement was concerned Thomas's vices, and indeed the vices of all writers judged to have something in common with him, could best be summed up by the word 'Romantic'. 'Romantic', Davie has said, 'was for me and my friends the ugliest imputation that could be thrown at anyone or anything, a sentence of death from which there was no appeal.'[11] Not surprisingly, the term 'Romantic' was used very liberally by the Movement. At times it was applied, dismissively, to certain postures and attitudes—among them, idealism, rebelliousness, nature-worship, mysticism—which the group detected in 'life' as well as in literature. At other times, the term was used in a literary-historical sense, having reference to 'the Romantic period' of the late-eighteenth century and after. Much energy could be expended in demonstrating that the Movement's understanding of the term was drastically simplified, a misreading. But a more useful task for the critic or historian is to examine the ends to which the Movement's misreadings were put.

The first question to ask, though, is why the Movement should have felt the rejection of Romanticism to be a matter of such urgency. For it could reasonably be argued that English poets had been in reaction against Romanticism ever since the death of Keats, and that with the coming of the Modernist period, the rejection was decisively accomplished. Before the First World War, T. E. Hulme had hoped for the arrival of a new era of Classicism, and T. S. Eliot's work was often seen as a fulfilment of Hulme's predictions. This was not, however, a view which the Movement accepted. They believed—and other critics have since come to share this view—that Modernism was a development out of, rather than a departure from, Romanticism, and that Romantic assumptions about poetry had not only survived Hulme and Eliot, but had during the 1930s and 1940s actually been strengthened. This John Holloway termed

the great post-Eliot paradox of English poetical development: that the *avant-garde*, even while acclaiming him, were in the 1930s producing a public, political Romanticism (for such it was: Auden's 'Hearing of harvests rotting in the valleys', Spender thinking 'continually of those who were truly great', Day Lewis writing 'Do not desire again a Phoenix hour'); and in the 1940s, a private, Dylan Thomas-inspired, Id-Romanticism: Mr Barker, Mr Gascoyne and others. [12]

The Movement believed that Romanticism had reached a new peak, and poetry a nadir, during the 1940s, when 'neo-Romanticism' was the vogue and Dylan Thomas widely admired. Both Movement anthologies were highly critical of this decade: Enright's *Poets of the 1950's* called it a 'grim' period, and in *New Lines* Conquest claimed that during the 1940s 'the mistake was made of giving the Id, a sound player on the percussion side under a strict conductor, too much of a say in the doings of the orchestra as a whole . . . This led to a rapid collapse of public taste, from which we have not yet recovered'. As this suggests, the Movement regarded the influence of Freud on English poetry to have been largely pernicious: the use of his ideas by the Surrealists had, Conquest went on to say, encouraged poets in the 1940s 'to regard their task simply as one of making an arrangement of images of sex and violence tapped straight from the unconscious (a sort of upper-middle-brow equivalent of the horror-comic), or to evoke without comment the *naïvetés* and nostalgias of childhood'.

Comments such as these were aimed not only at Dylan Thomas, but at other poets believed to be working in the neo-Romantic tradition— W. R. Rodgers, Edith Sitwell, and the group of writers who were known as the 'New Apocalypse'. In his introduction to the 1941 'New Apocalypse' anthology *The White Horseman,* G. S. Fraser had claimed that 'Freud's main discovery is that it is impossible really to talk nonsense'.[13] The Movement writers believed that this vulgarization of Freud had legitimized a damaging randomness in poetry, and they emphasized in contrast that it was difficult really to talk sense: as Amis put it in a 1954 review, 'thinking is a notoriously difficult exercise, and there are always inducements to giving it up as soon as convenient'.[14] They believed that the subconscious had recently received an excessive amount of attention, and that it was time to restore the virtues of 'conscious' writing—reason, order, argument.

The commitment to these qualities also lay behind the Movement's attacks on W. R. Rodgers, an Irish poet who enjoyed some popularity in the late 1940s and early 1950s. The Movement thought that Rodgers shared Dylan Thomas's fault of emphasizing 'sound' in poetry at the expense of 'meaning'. In a 1952 *Observer* review, Wain saw Rodgers's popularity as indicative of a 'disastrous situation in contemporary verse', and asked for 'poems written in a quieter style that does not continually advertise itself like a man wearing a loud check suit'.[15] Wain's parody of experimental writing in *Hurry on Down* may have had particular reference to Rodgers, whose 'Christ Walking the Water', for example, is similarly alliterative and assonant:

> 'A king ringed with slings,' began Froulish without more ado,
> 'a thing without wings but brings strings and sings. No, the

slow foe! Show me the crow toe I know, a beech root on the
beach, fruit of a rich bitch, loot in a ditch, shoot a witch,
which foot? . . . Clout bell, shout well, pell-mell about a tout,
get the hell out. About nowt.'

(Wain)

Slowly, O so slowly, longing rose up
In the forenoon of his face, till only
A ringlet of fog lingered round his loins;
And fast he went down beaches all weeping
With weed, and waded out. Twelve tall waves
Sequent and equated, hollowed and followed.

(Rodgers)

Kingsley Amis, in a 1953 essay, titled 'Ulster Bull: The Case
of W. R. Rodgers' (the suggestion of 'bullshit' is intended),
argued that in Rodgers's work 'attention to the meaning is
disastrous, and, much more important with verse like this,
attention to the sound is, ultimately, just as disastrous'.[16]
Similar conclusions were reached in a Donald Davie essay of
the same year, which suggested that Rodgers's work, and the
emphasis placed on sound in neo-Romantic poetry generally,
was a debasement of Pater's famous suggestion that 'all art
constantly aspires to the condition of music'. Davie found
in the criticism of Suzanne Langer a definition of the poetry-
music relationship which would place importance not upon
'sound' (euphony, alliteration, assonance, onomatopoeia),
but upon the Movement-like qualities of 'meaning', structure,
strict syntax:

When poets say that poetry is or ought to be like music, they often
turn out to have only a naive idea of what music is. They take such
musical freaks as the imitations of cuckoo-calls, or clocks, or peals of
bells, as if they were central to music's nature; and so build up a theory
of poetry around the equally freakish poetical device of onomatopoeia...
    What distinguishes Mrs Langer's from all these other accounts of the
poetry-music relationship is her insistence on music as pre-eminently
articulation. In her view a poem is like a piece of music in that it articulates itself . . . In other words, the central act of poetry as of music,
is the creation of syntax, of meaningful arrangement. And hence (this
seems to me the most salutary implication) the unit of poetry is not the
'passage', not (thank God) the 'image', but *the poem.*[17]

Davie's is a scholarly article, but one in which he admits his relief ('thank God') at finding intellectual support for the kind of poetry he wishes to reinstate.

Further intellectual support of this kind came, if somewhat less directly, from the Logical Positivist school of philosophy, a school which was enjoying such prestige in the early 1950s that it was spoken of as 'the official English philosophy of the time'. The most influential work of English Logical Positivism was A. J. Ayer's *Language, Truth and Logic,* first published in 1936, and re-issued in a revised edition in 1946. Appealing to 'empiricism', 'verification' and 'analysis', Ayer's book was a jauntily confident attack on metaphysics. It maintained that 'no statement which refers to a reality transcending the limits of all possible sense-experience can possibly have any literal significance'; that 'the philosopher has no right to despise the beliefs of common sense', and that 'the mystic, so far from producing propositions which are empirically verified, is unable to produce any intelligible propositions at all'.[18] In 'Mr Sharp in Florence', Davie talks of being 'grounded and ground in logic-chopping schools', and most of the Movement were acquainted with Ayer's work. Even if not fully conversant with the specialized philosophical problems in *Language, Truth and Logic,* they could admire its general temper.

Ayer's only reference to poetry in *Language, Truth and Logic* is significant: he denies the suggestion that poetry has a close connection with metaphysics, and argues that 'in the vast majority of cases the sentences which are produced by poets do have literal meaning'.[19] This argument lent support to the Movement's belief that poetry should have a clear meaning and be susceptible to critical analysis. It gave them the kind of confidence which one finds in Donald Davie's 1955 essay 'Poetry, or Poems?', which attacks R. P. Blackmur for having dared to suggest (in a betrayal of New Critical Principles) that poetry is 'magical', 'mysterious', 'metaphysical', and not therefore always able to be analysed:

Yes, we would all agree of course that something escapes analysis, is mysterious. But where, how soon in our reflections, how near the surface of the poem, does the magic start, the mystery supervene? And nearly always one finds,when people take up this position, that they mean the magic starts from the word go. The magic and the mystery are the smoke-screen for the enemies of criticism and of poetry . . . For it nearly always turns out that the smoke-screen is really covering the getaway of some poet or poets whose work, as their apologists know very well, won't stand up to the critic's scrutiny.[20]

Logical Positivism encouraged the Movement to be sceptical, alert, suspicious of being taken in. It also encouraged them to offer instead of neo-Romantic 'evocation', poems that would proceed, or would give the impression of proceeding, by logical argument. Movement poetry contains an unusually large number of arguing connectives—words like 'for', 'still', 'yet', 'because' and 'so'. Wain's 'Eighth Type of Ambiguity' for example, is a poem which, though not finally reducible to strict logical paraphrase, seems to have constructed a logical argument. The opening words of each of the ten stanzas in this poem function to suggest that it is constructing a logical case almost as meticulously as a philosopher might:

1 'Love is . . . '	(quoted assertion)
2 'Yet even . . . '	(counter-argument)
3 'For love . . . '	(explanation)
4 'So understanding love . . . '	(preliminary conclusion)
5 'For love . . . '	(further explanation)
6 'But still . . . '	(qualification)
7 'When love . . . '	(illustration)
8 'Then all . . . '	(further illustration)
9 'And so . . . '	(conclusion)
10 'It seems . . . '	(case proven)

Wain's poem is anti-Romantic not because of its choice of subject, but because of its handling of that subject: he takes the 'ultimate' emotional experience, love, and tries to subject it to a dispassionate and witty treatment. He is not successful: sentimentality and cliché intrude. But his poem betrays the influence of Empson and Logical Positivism, and dissociates itself from the 'vagueness' and 'illogicality' of poets like Dylan Thomas and W. R. Rodgers.

This immediate background to the Movement's anti-Romanticism—the poetic and intellectual climate of the 1940s and 1950s—needs to be kept in mind. It puts into perspective what might otherwise seem to be a presumptuous claim to discredit the whole Romantic tradition. There exist, however, a number of Movement texts which *are* presumptuous—texts which represent the Movement as a revolt not against the last ten years but against the last 150. One such text (even its title sounds, by Movement standards, reckless in the extreme) is Amis's 'Against Romanticism'. An indication of the authority which this poem purports to carry is the fact that John Press felt it necessary to reprimand it for failing to discriminate 'between the valid principles of Romanticism and the quagmire into which it may lead the less talented of its adherents'.[21] The obvious retort to Press is that Amis is not, as a poet, under any obligation to make such discriminations; they are a matter for the critic. But Press has some justification in seeing 'Against Romanticism' not as a poem but as a literary-critical essay in verse-form. It has, for example, not only a poetic source but a critical one. The poetic source is Robert Graves's 'An English Wood', which like Amis's poem features a determinedly temperate landscape, one devoid of danger, unrest and legendary beasts:

> This valley wood is pledged
> To the set shape of things,
> And reasonably hedged:
> Here are no harpies fledged,
> No rocs may clap their wings,
> No gryphons wave their stings . . .
> Here nothing is that harms —
> No bulls with lungs of brass . . .
> No mount of glass;
> No bardic tongues unfold
> Satires or charms.

A more direct source for Amis's poem, though, seems to have been F. W. Bateson's *English Poetry,* a critical study which makes a strong case against Romanticism, and which is prefaced by a poem with a title very similar to Amis's, 'The Anti-Romantics':

> So we are the music-unmakers, it seems —
> Of Pastoral Park disinfecting your dreams,
> At La Belle Sauvage the sardonic irregulars,
> Of skylarks the scarers, the nobblers of Pegasus.[22]

Bateson describes himself and his like-minded contemporaries (the Movement 'we' appears again) as 'nobblers of Pegasus'; Amis, in an equally disrespectful reference to mythical beasts, looks forward to a poetic world 'not trampled by the havering unicorn'. Both poems are debunking manifestos aimed at an intellectual audience. Amis's poem, moreover, is tightly argued and developed in the manner of a literary essay, presenting first an analysis of the development of Romanticism, secondly a critical case against it, and thirdly a tentative programme for future poetry.

'Against Romanticism' begins by impugning the origins of Romanticism, suggesting that it comes into being when poets find the 'temperate zone' and 'decent surface' of the everyday world to be lacking in excitement, and therefore 'discard real time and place' for a sensuous fantasy world:

> To please an ingrown taste for anarchy
> 　Torrid images circle in the wood, . . .
> 　Bodies rich with heat wriggle to the touch,
> And verbal scents made real spellbind the nose:
> 　Incense, frankincense: legendary the taste
> Of drinks or fruits or tongues laid on the tongue.
> 　Over all, a grand meaning fills the scene,
> And sets the brain raging with prophecy,
> 　Raging to discard real time and place . . .

The poem is set in the present tense, and as such might be seen as an attack on contemporary neo-Romanticism, with its excess of 'torrid images'. But Amis is principally concerned with the development of English poetry between about 1780 and 1820. That development is seen as the replacement of the Augustan virtues of order, reason and moderation with the Romantic vices of disorder, irrationalism and rage. No names are mentioned, but there are strong suggestions that Amis has specific personalities in mind: 'verbal scents' is almost certainly a reference to Keats, whose 'Eve of St Agnes' Amis once dismissed as a 'sugary erotic extravaganza';[23] the 'brain raging with prophecy' may be Blake's, whose elaborate myths or 'grand meaning' the Movement writers have shown little regard for; 'an ingrown taste for anarchy' may be aimed at Shelley, 'bookish cries' at Coleridge, 'tickled up with ghosts' at exponents of the Gothic novel. In Amis's view, the Romantic poets were disrupters, replacing the stability and solidity of the eighteenth century with a 'frantic' fantasy world. It is the lost environment of eighteenth-century poetry which, though it cannot return, Amis would like to see being in some measure recaptured in poetry. He imagines a 'temperate zone' which, with its clean buildings, cut grass, and pleasant roads recalls the world of Pope's 'Windsor Forest', where ordered lawns and gentle glades are preferred to the untamed alternative, a 'dreary desert, and a gloomy waste/To savage beasts and savage laws a prey'. With its ideals of civility and order, the age of Pope offered a pleasing alternative to Romantic celebration of the wild. One of Larkin's *XX Poems*, 'The Dedicated', draws attention to those who 'employ the scythe/ Upon the grasses/That the walks be smooth'. Holloway's 'The Petty Testament of Peter the Clerk' makes explicit the Movement's nostalgia for the eighteenth century:

> I desire to leave
> A formal garden, clipped and clean
> — Something out of the Age of Sense —
> Not just more racket, dirt and jumble
> Where footsore men can blind and stumble.

These images of an environment under control are images also of a poetry under control: the Augustan qualities of discipline and urbanity must be rediscovered. Davie in 'Homage to William Cowper' describes himself as 'a pasticheur of late-Augustan styles': while 'most poets let the morbid fancy roam', Davie writes in a controlled, though not complacent, manner about domestic subjects, 'the sofa and the hare'. Modesty, simplicity and familiarity are highly prized. Davie suggests that the poet should begin 'at home'; Amis agrees with him:

> Better, of course, if images were plain,
>> Warnings clearly said, shapes put down quite still
> Within the fingers' reach, or else nowhere.

For most of its forty-four lines, then, 'Against Romanticism' follows a Movement tendency to uphold the Augustan as against the Romantic, and the Classical as against the Gothic. But there are also lines which suggest that Amis means to contrast Romanticism with a different kind of discourse: Realism. The Romantic poet is seen as someone 'raging to discard real time and place', mistakenly occupying himself with 'visions' and 'prophecy'. Amis, in contrast, is pragmatic and utilitarian: 'Let us at least have visions that we need'. Such insistence on the poet's duty to 'real time and place' is a common feature of Movement work. In the introduction to *New Lines,* Conquest suggests that the Movement poets have learnt from 'the principle of real, rather than ideological, honesty' which distinguishes the work of Orwell, and exhibit, as a result, a 'reverence for the real person or event'. The word 'real'—as when Amis in 'Wrong Words' calls attention to the 'real ladies' and 'real defeats' that lie behind the 'conceits' of love poetry, or when Enright in 'The Noodle-Vendor's Flute' celebrates 'real cities, real houses, real time'—occupies an unusually large place in the Movement's poetic vocabulary, and reveals a characteristically 1950-ish confidence that there exists, as Malcolm Bradbury puts it, 'a common and shareable reality' which people can possess.[24] It is this confidence which enables Amis, in a 1956 review of William Golding's *Pincher Martin,* to attack Golding for failing to 'turn his gifts of originality, of intransigence, and above all of passion, to the world where we have to live'.[25]

Their use of the word 'real' often carries the implication

that the Movement have uncovered some situation which has tended to be overlooked or distorted by writers in the Romantic tradition. 'Idealizing' Romantic attitudes are to be replaced with an art of the real. The aesthetic to which the Movement aspired is very like the condition of 'photography' described in Larkin's 'Lines on a Young Lady's Photograph Album':

> But o, photography! as no art is,
> Faithful and disappointing! that records
> Dull days as dull, and hold-it smiles as frauds,
> And will not censor blemishes
> Like washing-lines, and Hall's-Distemper boards,
>
> But shows the cat as disinclined, and shades
> A chin as doubled when it is . . .

The Movement fiction of Amis and Wain belongs to a tradition of comic Realism in the English novel. The Movement poetry of Larkin and Davie can also be thought of as Realist in tendency because of its marked preference for metonymy over metaphor: it sets itself against what Conquest in *New Lines* calls 'the debilitating theory that poetry must be metaphorical'. It observes 'a real girl in a real place,/In every sense empirically true'. It makes small commonplace detail—the bed, upright chair, sixty-watt bulb, in Mr Bleaney's bedsitting room—carry great emotional weight, believing that, in Wain's words, 'the right kind of reader can extract a rich experience from the heaviest and most matter-of-fact compilation, *so long as it is honest*'.[26] Larkin insists on the 'realities' of quotidian existence to the extent of incorporating brand names in his poems,[27] or of reeling off the contents of shops:

> Cheap suits, red kitchen-ware, sharp shoes, iced lollies,
> Electric mixers, toasters, washers, driers— . . .
>
> ('Here')

> . . . cheap clothes
> Set out in simple sizes plainly
> (Knitwear, Summer Casuals, Hose,
> In browns and greys, maroon and navy) . . .
>
> ('The Large Cool Store')

The Movement's anti-Romanticism expresses itself, therefore, not only through nostalgia for ordered Classical landscapes, but by virtue of a 'realistic' attention to the disfigured townscapes of the present—housing estates, shops, advertising boards, clothes lines, allotments. Where they feature at all, rural landscapes are less likely to be wandered through than seen from a train window, and the overall approach to environment is habitually a 'less deceived' one determined to reflect the fact that many people in advanced Western societies live or work in industrial towns or cities. Movement texts are 'realistic' in another sense, too: in contrast to many late-nineteenth and early-twentieth-century texts, they make little protest against the ruination or pollution of the English landscape by industry: rather, there prevails what Davie calls a 'level-toned acceptance of that England as the only one we have, violated and subtopianised and poisoned as it is'.[28]

Implicit in all this is the suggestion that the Movement's approach to landscape is necessarily more mature and relevant than that of the 'naïve' Romantics: 'How,' Holloway asks, 'can we look at scenery with the same eyes as Wordsworth, who had never heard the noise of a petrol engine, claxon or transistor . . .?'[29] Seeing themselves as the first representatives of the machine age (it hardly needs emphasizing what a distortion this was), the Movement poets are quick to condemn any appearance of 'nature-worship'. The 'Reason for Not Writing Orthodox Nature Poetry' given in John Wain's poem of that title, is that, although the poet would like to speak of the 'beauty' of the landscape facing him, to do so would necessitate speaking 'by rote', so conventionalized has the language for describing nature become. The early Romantics may have been quite 'genuine', but according to Wain the nature poetry of the Victorians and Moderns has its eye on the market:

> And like a spectacled curator showing
> The wares of his museum to the crowd,
> They yearly waxed more eloquent and knowing

> More slick, more photographic, and more proud:
> From Tennyson with notebook in his hand
> (His truth to Nature fits him like a shroud)
>
> To moderns who devoutly hymn the land . . .

Amis's 'Here is Where' is similarly cynical about nature poetry.
It begins with a parody of how a conventional nature poem
might begin—

> *Here, where the ragged water*
> *Is twilled and spun over*
> *Pebbles backed like beetles . . .*

—but then rudely interrupts the description ('Going well so
far, eh?') to suggest that such descriptions seem nowadays to
exist merely to pander to the sentimentalities of town-dwellers:

> The country, to townies,
> Is hardly more than nice,
> A window-box, pretty
> When the afternoon's empty.[30]

Amis here is following Orwell, who wrote in his essay 'Inside
the Whale' that 'over-civilized people enjoy reading about
rustics (key phrase, "close to the soil") because they imagine
them to be more primitive and passionate than themselves',
and whose heroes Bowling and Comstock are determined not
to be 'soppy about "the country"'. An Orwellian scepticism
can also be detected in Enright's 'A Polished Performance',
which suggests that Rousseau's notion of the 'noble savage'
has become a marketable myth, pleasing to town-dwellers,
but having little basis in fact. The poem examines the exploi-
tation of 'a simple unspoilt girl/Living alone, deep in the
bush' by a successful film director. His film works by appealing to urban taste for the 'innocent simplicity' of rural life,
but it conceals the realities of the girl's condition:

> Deep in the bush we found her,
>   Large and innocent of eye,
> Among gentle gibbons and mountain ferns.

Perfect for the part, perfect,
    Except for the dropsy
Which comes from polished rice.

In the capital our film is much admired,
    Its gentle gibbons and mountain ferns,
Unspoilt, unpolished, large and innocent of eye.

So concerned are the Movement writers to avoid erroneous attitudes towards nature that, when they come to treat it themselves, they are often acutely self-conscious. Wain's 'Reason for Not Writing Orthodox Nature Poetry', Amis's 'Here is Where', Davie's 'Oak Openings' and 'Woodpigeons at Raheny', Enright's 'Nature Poetry' and 'Changing the Subject', Conquest's 'Antheor': all these are awkwardly aware of the difficulties involved in writing what they call (usually in embarrassed inverted commas) 'nature poetry'. Conquest's poem, for example, asks: 'What can a poem do with a land-scape?' The answer seems to be that if it is a Movement poem, not very much, for the Movement poet is too conscious of poetic convention, and too afraid of resorting to cliché, to write freely. Often, as Conquest does in 'Antheor', he will protest that he is unable to 'do justice' to nature:

The emblems are too crude. The poetry sees
A giant static set-piece where the trees'
Variety shows a single streak of green.

Conquest's phrase 'set-piece' is echoed in Wain's *Hurry on Down*, where the hero, Lumley, sees the Sussex countryside as 'a stage set, a fake'. In part, this is because Lumley has 'grown up accustomed to the countryside of the middle of England, which earns its own living': thus the landscapes of the South, with their 'groomed cottages in Hollywood black and white', are 'not what Charles secretly considered the "real" country-side'. Such contrasting of 'real' Northern or Midland landscapes with 'soft' or 'artificial' Southern ones is a common feature of mid-1950s writing, and reflects the importance of the Movement's lower-middle-class, provincial identity.[31] But in part, also, Wain's use of the phrase 'stage set' seems typical

of the Movement writer's habit of projecting his own embarrassment back onto the landscape itself: if the landscape has
made him feel self-conscious, then (the suggestion is) it must
be deliberately arranging and contriving its effects. The Movement in these instances substitutes one kind of mystification
about the natural world for another: nature is seen not as an
autonomous organism which sometimes inspires 'sublime'
feelings but as a mechanism calculated to induce, and existing
solely for, human pleasure. In Wain's 'Reason for Not Writing
. . .', nature is described in terms of food and drink, 'a recipe'
and 'brew'; in his *Hurry on Down*, the beauty spot to which
Lumley takes his girlfriend, Veronica, is described in terms of
a theatrical performance specially put on for tourists and
young lovers:

The sunlight on the water knew exactly how to behave; after so many
centuries it could produce the precisely needed effect as it flickered in
reflection on the dark underneath of the leaves which the trees held out
at just the correct height above it. The birds were rehearsed, the flowers
and grass knew precisely what to do; the cool grey shapes of revered
buildings formed, in the background, a perfectly contrived contrast and
balance for the calm, heavy cattle lying down in the fields. So slick, so
confident in its much-photographed guide-book-and-calendar charm,
the ensemble ought to have been a flop. But in fact, it worked, and
Charles had to admit that its method was the only one; like all beautiful old fakes, it had ended by believing in itself, and that conviction
could not, ultimately, be resisted.

The knowingness of both Wain and his hero Lumley bears
out Donald Davie's suggestion, in his essay 'Remembering the
Movement', that the typical Movement writer 'is never so
surrendered to his experience, never so far gone out of himself in his response, as not to be aware of the attitude he is
taking up'. Davie in 1959 was critical of this self-consciousness,
but he and his confederates originally saw it as a necessary
reaction against the Romantic tendency to submit weakly to
the 'awesome', the 'sublime', the 'unknown'. This tendency
was thought to be especially pronounced in Shelley, whom
Leavis had criticized in *Revaluation* for 'surrendering to a kind

of hypnotic rote of favourite images, associations and words'.[32] Leavis's criticism set the tone for a number of Movement attacks on Shelley. Lumley in Wain's *Hurry on Down* refers to his 'namby-pamby dribblings', while Gunn in 'Lerici' contrasts Byron's brave and 'masterful' drowning ('such/ Dignify death by thriftless violence') with Shelley's puny and surrendering one:

> Shelley was drowned near here. Arms at his side
> He fell submissive through the waves, and he
> Was but a minor conquest of the sea:
> The darkness that he met was nurse not bride.

Davie's 'Hypochondriac Logic' sees 'the Shelleyan failing' less as weakness than as vagueness: Shelley is judged to be one of those poets

> who have thought
> A truth more true as more remote,
> Or in poetic worlds confide
> The more the air is rarefied . . .
> Whose poems infect his readers too,
> Who, since they're vague, suppose them true.

The most sustained Movement attempt to criticize and revise Shelley is Amis's 'Ode to the East-North-East-by-East Wind'. The pedantic geography of the title is intended as a reproach to what Amis regards as the extravagant pantheism of Shelley's 'Ode to the West Wind', which depicts the wind as an 'unseen presence' and 'wild spirit', 'tameless, and swift, and proud'. Leavis had attacked Shelley's 'weak grasp upon the actual' in this poem.[33] Amis in his revision tries to incorporate the actual by depicting the wind in more familiar human terms as 'a cheery chap I can't avoid', a 'sweating, empty-handed labourer', a 'mailless courier'. A final personification has the added dimension of an attack upon what Amis sees as Shelley's boyish anarchism. He addresses the wind not (as Shelley does) in hushed reverence, but as a parent admonishing a destructive child:

> Well now, since blowing things apart's your scheme,
>   The crying child your metaphor,

> Poetic egotists make you their theme,
>   Finding in you their hatred for
> A world that will not mirror their desire.
> Silly yourself, you flatter and inspire
>   Some of the silliest of us.
>   And is that worth the fuss?

Amis's use of the word 'silly', and earlier endearment to
the 'darling' wind, suggest the influence of Auden whose
later poetry makes similar attempts to get on familiar terms
with, and thereby to domesticate, the natural world. It is
a ploy which Amis also uses in *That Uncertain Feeling,* where
Lewis greets the wind as 'an old enemy of mine . . . bringing
its crony, the rain, up in support', and it suggests a certain
nervousness about granting the natural world autonomy. This
is a characteristic of the Movement poets generally: they tend
to dislike or fear the lack of a human presence in nature.
Holloway's 'Warning to a Guest', for example, contrasts a
warm, domestic interior with a threatening exterior of darkness, fog and storms. Though Holloway shows some fascination
with 'the fabulous/Things of the moon's dark side', he warns
his companion not to wander out, but to remain secure in the
house:

>   . . . stay with us.
>   Do not demand a walk tonight
>   Down to the sea. It makes no place for those
>   Like you and me who, to sustain our pose,
>   Need wine and conversation, colour and light.

As an alternative to a wild and depopulated outdoors, the
Movement offer cheerful and populated interiors—the living-
room, the teashop, the pub. Nature is, as far as possible,
accommodated to the human: Larkin poems like 'Wires',
'Myxomatosis', 'First Sight' and 'At Grass' do not attempt to
explore, as the poetry of Lawrence and Ted Hughes would do,
the 'inner being' of the creatures under consideration. Rather,
Larkin's interest is in drawing a human parallel, and in pointing
a moral (it is noticeable, too, that he concentrates on farm
animals or pets). This indifference, even insensitivity, to the

non-human world—nature *qua* nature is of little interest to them—might be seen as a serious limitation in the Movement writers, but they themselves saw it as a necessary part of their programme. They detected in the poetry of the Romantics (with the exception, perhaps, of Wordsworth) a dangerous anti-humanist tendency, and they sought to correct it. As Davie says in defence of Larkin, the Movement poet 'makes himself numb to nonhuman creation in order to stay compassionate towards the human'.[34]

The Movement conceived of compassion towards the human as involving, also, a reaction against Romantic cults of the hero and of the artist. Romantic heroes and artists, like Romantic landscapes, are intended to inspire feelings of sublimity and awe: the reader is invited to admire their exceptional gifts. In this way Romantic poets, so the Movement believed, minimized the responsibility of individuals towards their fellow-citizens, making deviance from social norms into a virtue. The 'new heroes' of Movement fiction are rarely outstanding individuals: they are likely to be awkward, vulnerable, conformist, even cowardly—all they have to offer is a fundamental Orwellian 'decency'. When traditional heroes appear in Movement verse, they are re-interpreted in this light: Enright presents Coriolanus (in his poem of that title) as ' a candidate for civil service, but he failed some simple test'. And John Holloway's Ulysses is 'an old man . . . just an elderly pierrot', whose travelling looks not courageous but mildly eccentric:

> Sixty was hardly the age for such youthful excesses! —
> Colleagues would primly suggest: all those trips and weekends,
> Lighthearted postcards that came from outlandish addresses . . .
>
> ('Ulysses')

The intention of this demythologizing treatment is not to diminish the stature of heroes, but to stress their similarities to 'everyone else': heroes are interesting to the Movement at those points where they resemble the rest of humanity.

The anti-hero is such a dominant figure in Modernist fiction and poetry that it could be argued that there is nothing unusual, and indeed that there is much that seems conventional and dated, in the Movement's rejection of the Romantic hero. But the protagonists of Movement literature differ from Modernist protagonists in being what might be termed 'non-heroes' rather than anti-heroes. The anti-hero of Modernist literature is, typically, someone who lacks the physical endowment of the traditional hero, but who remains a rebel or outsider because of his artistic gifts. A good example would be Joyce's Stephen Dedalus, a physically undistinguished person, but heroic in his defiant pursuit of art. Movement protagonists have no more in common with Dedalus than with traditional heroes, seeing him as a new example of, rather than departure from, the heroic type. Enright's *Packet* considers that 'of all the unpleasant characters in literature, Stephen Dedalus was the worst';[35] and Kingsley Amis, in a typically pragmatic onslaught, notes that 'a lot of people get a bit fed up from time to time . . . But they do not on this account go round considering themselves as, or behaving like, Stephen Dedalus; at least they try not to, and rightly'.[36] The Movement writers have little regard for Dedalus's creed of *non serviam*: they want their artists not to rebel, but to go along with the aims of their community.

The Movement regarded its rejection of the Romantic cult of hero and artist as itself an example of serving the community. In a Britain more intent on pursuing communal and egalitarian ideals than it had been before the Second World War, celebration of the hero or artist was judged to be misplaced, and, as Rubin Rabinovitz notes, 'movements which stress[ed] the value of the individual over social values were on a decline'.[37] What was needed from writers was the suggestion that in a Welfare State democracy everyone was of equal importance, that everyone had an equally vital part to play: 'Exit the hero'. Romantic archetypes like the Promethean challenger or the Odyssean quester seemed inappropriate, and even dangerous. Enright's poem 'After the Gods, After the

Heroes' suggests that the post-war era is one in which humbler mortals may become the subject for poetic treatment:

> It hurts to say so, but in our time
> Perhaps you will have to rely on others, on
> Paterfamilias and materfamilias, clerks bored by their
> Desks, graduates with pass degrees and no special field,
> Grandads out for a last fling, girls with odd fancies,
> Boys who would write verse, if they could . . .
> These non-heroes that the poorest country's rich in.

The reaction against the Romantic celebration of individuality was strengthened by interpretations of recent history. Rather than linking Romanticism with Rousseau, the French Revolution and the slogan 'Liberty! Equality! Fraternity!', many intellectuals now saw a connection between Romantic individualist ideology and the rise of Nazism and Fascism. This connection was persuasively argued for by Peter Viereck, an American whose poetry and ideas have been linked to the Movement's. In his study *Metapolitics: From the Romantics to Hitler* (1941), Viereck traced the development of an ideology seen to originate in early Germanic Romantic theory, to continue through the work of Nietzsche and Wagner, and to be realized with the coming to power of Hitler. He concluded that 'Wagnerian Romanticism is the most important single fountainhead of Nazi ideas and ideals'.[38] Such arguments were influential: it was widely felt that Hitler's rise to power had been intimately bound up with the 'overreaching' or 'too much daring' which Romantic poetry enshrines. There was a growing distrust of rhetoric and charismatic individualism. Churchill's failure to be re-elected as Prime Minister in 1945 may have been due, as Paul Addison argues throughout his study *The Road to 1945,* to unrealistic policies and a poor electoral campaign; but it also symbolized an increased immunity to the attractiveness of 'great men'.

This immunity was reflected in the culture of the post-war period. Poets reacted against the work of Dylan Thomas because it seemed to work, much as wartime speeches had, through rhetoric and feeling. The present, Wain claimed, was a time for 'keeping one's head';[39] the heart, said Davie was 'not to be solicited'. In novels, as James Gindin has argued, 'the unheroic figure [became] the standard fictional representation of the age',[40] while in drama and in painting there was talk of a 'kitchen sink' manner. Ordinariness became something to pursue rather than evade. Dispensing with a Yeats-like prayer for fortune and success, Larkin in 'Born Yesterday', a poem to Amis's baby daughter, wished for the child a dullness and ordinariness that could make her happy:

> May you be ordinary;
> Have, like other women
> An average of talents:
> Not ugly, not good-looking,
> Nothing uncustomary
> To pull you off your balance,
> That, unworkable itself,
> Stops all the rest from working.
> In fact, may you be dull —
> If that is what a skilled,
> Vigilant, flexible,
> Unemphasized, enthralled
> Catching of happiness is called.

The belief that, as Enright puts it in 'After the Dinner', 'ordinariness has much to be said for it,/Is reasonably precious even', also influenced the Movement's characterization of 'the poet'. The typical Movement persona, as it appears in the work of Larkin, Amis or Enright, is that of a man not marked off from his contemporaries, but indistinguishable from them. The Movement poet is, as A. Alvarez put it, 'just like the man next door—in fact, he probably *is* the man next door'.[41] His work is aimed at the Common Reader because he is himself a Common Man—an ordinary person whose feelings and experiences are those of 'everyone else'. One of Archie Rice's songs from John Osborne's *The Entertainer* brilliantly caricatures the kind of protagonist which the Movement tried to create:

Now I'm just an ordinary bloke
The same as you out there. . . .
I'm what you call a moderate,
I weigh all the pros. and the cons.
I don't push and shove. . . .
Thank God I'm normal, normal, normal.
Thank God I'm normal,
I'm just like the rest of you chaps.
Thank God I'm normal,
I'm just like the rest of you chaps,
Decent and full of good sense,
I'm not one of these extremist saps,
For I'm sure you'll agree,
That a fellow like me
Is the salt of our dear old country,
        of our dear old country.

A sensible, decent, normal, moderate, ordinary 'chap' or 'bloke', 'the same as you out there': for the Movement poets to achieve this image it was necessary first of all to reject traditional Romantic or Bohemian interpretations of the poet as a man apart. They tended to understate rather than advertise their poetic activities, as if anxious not to look like poets. There was special hostility to the notion that in order to be a poet one has first to behave or dress like one. In a letter to the *London Magazine* in March 1954, Davie sneered at those admirers of Dylan Thomas who prefer their 'poets in blatant technicolour . . . I know I take my poets more seriously'. Davie had perhaps been reading Amis's recently published *Lucky Jim*: the idea of the technicolour artist receives literal and satirical treatment in that novel when Amis describes 'the entry of a tall man wearing a lemon-yellow sportscoat, all three buttons of which were fastened, and displaying a large beard which came down further on one side than on the other, half-hiding a vine patterned tie. Dixon guessed with surging exultation that this must be the pacifist painting Bertrand'. Implicit in Amis's description is a confident expectation that contemporary readers would place and find ridiculous Bertrand's Bohemian garb, and would therefore share Dixon's desire to demand of Bertrand 'an apology, humbly offered, for his personal appearance'. Artists or writers who 'look the part' reappear in Amis's next four novels in the shape of Probert, Buckmaster, Anna le Page, and Irving Macher. In Wain's *Hurry on Down* the role is filled by Edwin Froulish, whose studied eccentricities and 'gift for self-advertisement' annoy the hero Lumley. The suggestion is that artists like Bertrand and Froulish 'put on an act' in order to attract attention they would not otherwise receive. As Wain puts it, 'the last thirty years have been the hey-day of the poetic charlatan . . . It's so easy: announce, as loudly and as often as possible, 'I AM A POET!' and begin immediately to make personal claims which imply you can't be expected to live under the same restraint as ordinary non-poetic humanity. For some time, this alone will suffice . . .'.[42]

The Movement's emphasis that the poet must live under the same restraint as other people began as a reaction against Romantic notions of the poet as a special being or genius. Such beliefs had been prevalent in the late-eighteenth and early-nineteenth century, and were reasserted in the 1940s, when the neo-Apocalyptic Henry Treece distinguished between 'poets' and 'people', suggesting that 'to be a poet is to have your blood running a different way from other men's blood'.[43] To the Movement such ideas were wholly offensive. Conquest deplored the tendency in the 1940s 'for poets to pose as Poets—beings apart from and superior to life'.[44] The suggestion that poets or artists are in some way special also comes under attack in *Lucky Jim* when Christine makes the Treece-like comment that 'a relationship with an artist's a very different kettle of fish to having a relationship with an ordinary man . . . I think he's sort of got special needs, you know, and it's up to others to supply them'; Dixon's response to this is to make his 'lemon-sucking face', and to reflect how repugnant he finds 'any notion of anyone having any special needs for anything at any time, except for such needs as could be readily gratified with a tattoo of kicks on the bottom'. Virtually the same scene occurs in *That Uncertain Feeling* when Mr Gruffyd-Williams and Lewis argue over the behaviour of the local poet Probert. '"He's rude," I said. "And don't you think that being a poet entitles him to be a bit different from other people in that way?" "On the contrary"'. Ideally, to adapt Orwell, all people are the same, but poets are more the same than other people. The Movement insists that there is, in Davie's words, 'no necessary connection between the poetic vocation, on the one hand, and, on the other, exhibitionism, egotism and licence'.[45]

Another belief about the 'special needs' of the poet which the Movement rejected was the one which lays down that a poet, if he is to retain his skill and integrity, must avoid the fetters of conventional employment. Wain, putting it with his usual bluster, remarked that in a modern Welfare State 'starving authors aren't romantic figures any more: they just stand in line with all the other floperoos'.[46] Since nearly all the Movement poets held full-time academic posts themselves, it was understandable that they should stress the desirability of combining writing with other work: 'why,' Amis asked in 1954, 'do people talk as if having a job is bad (even though economically necessary) for a novelist? It's lack of a job that can be bad.'[47] Several of the Movement came, moreover, from backgrounds in which hard work and paying one's way were highly prized, and in which 'dropping out' was unthinkable: Larkin, for instance, talks of his as 'a solid background in which everybody worked. No question of it. It was immoral not to work'.[48] Rather than reject and despise the work-ethic, then, the Movement tried to incorporate it into their artistic programme: poetry was to be a matter of graft and craft, not of luck and inspiration. 'Regarding poetry as hard work,' Amis said, '. . . strikes me as less dangerous than feeling it ought to possess or obsess one.'[49] Poetry was to be earned; if it was a matter of inspiration, if it came as naturally as leaves to a tree, it could not be poetry at all. Poetry must, moreover, be seen to be earned, and could do this by observing the accepted laws of form and metre; organic form and free verse were largely to be avoided. The provincial, lower-middle-class identity of some of the Movement poets thus had an important bearing on the artistic assumptions of the group. 'In the ridings,' Davie later wrote in 'Six Epistles to Eva Hesse' (1970), 'we admire/The man with expertise for hire', and he went on to draw a picture of

> Yorkshire bards who take perverse
> Pride in writing metred verse,
> All their hopes invested in
> One patent, brilliant discipline.

One of the central tenets of the Movement programme, then, was the revival of the tradition of the poet as 'clericus' or clerk. The poet was to be not seer but civil servant, a responsible citizen responsibly employed. Though it contradicted much Romantic theory, the Movement believed that this tradition of the poet had a respectable heritage. Amis suggested 'all previous writers except a few 19th-century freaks' had to work for a living.[50] Even Elizabeth Jennings, the Movement poet most sympathetic to Romantic images of the poet as a mystic or visionary removed from society, argued that

the best poets have usually been the most busy and practical people . . . Chaucer was involved with affairs of state, Shakespeare lived the hectic life of both playwright and worker in the theatre, Donne was a hard-working priest, and, in our own time, T. S. Eliot worked for many years in a bank and, even today is a director of a publishing house . . . At other times in history, poets have been considered slightly mad and their poetry has been put down to their madness. It would be a mistake to be deceived by this sort of idea.[51]

Some Movement texts extend the notion of the worldly and routinely-employed poet to the point of making their persona or protagonist a businessman. Following Orwell, whose George Bowling is a salesman, Amis, Larkin, and Wain in particular involve their speakers in commercial realities from which most writers would shrink (the post-Romantic tradition being that poetry is, in Auden's words, a place 'where executives/Would never want to tamper'). Even the title of Amis's 1956 collection of poems, *A Case of Samples,* seems intended to challenge that tradition: it implies that the poet is a sales representative who offers his goods to the public. The business-man type appears in 'A Song of Experience' (the poem from which *A Case of Samples* takes its title) and in Amis's later 'Evans Country' sequence. He also appears in Larkin's two 'Toads' poems, and in Wain's *The Contenders.*

The Movement also found the businessman type to be a handy synonym for *l'homme moyen sensuel,* and thus a useful weapon in their reaction against what they understood to be Romanticism's unduly solemn treatment of sexual relationships. In this instance, the Movement saw themselves in opposition not to the nineteenth-century Romantic poets but to D. H. Lawrence and Dylan Thomas: these two, it was believed, had treated sex in a mystifying and portentous manner. The Movement approach, in contrast, was that sex was 'fun'—a simple pleasure rather than a sacred mystery, and therefore to be treated in light and entertaining fashion. 'The virtue . . . of the anti-romantic view of life,' Amis claimed in 1954, is that 'it expresses itself in ways which appeal to humour as well as reason.'[52] Hence Amis's dislike of what he sees as Lawrence's humourlessness—a dislike to be found not only in his 1956 review 'Phoenix Too Frequent' (reprinted in *What Became of Jane Austen*), but in Jenny Bunn's response to Lawrence's novels in *Take a Girl Like You*: 'she had not got much out of them, except that you had no chance at all with any of it unless you were sensitive and warm and proud and naturally aristocratic and heavy and dark (especially that), and not much of a chance even then. They were very long books and very hard to find your place in'. Hence, too, the approach of Evans, the hero of Amis's sequence 'The Evans Country', who is careful to distinguish his fun-loving treatment of sex from that of his Lawrentian friend Haydn. In Amis's fiction sex has its complications, but they are handled in a comical and debunking manner. A motif which recurs

through the first four novels is the farcical interruption of a
seduction scene—Dixon's expulsion from Margaret's bedroom,
Lewis's hurried escape in Welsh costume from the Gruffyd-
Williams's house, the wasp sting which terminates Garnet
Bowen's outdoor encounter with a *senhorita,* and Patrick
Standish's drink-induced impotence on his 'dirty weekend'
in London.

In sexual matters, Movement texts often see things from
the point of view of a male seducer impatient with conventional pieties: 'Why pretend/Love must accompany erection?'
asks the speaker of Gunn's 'Modes of Pleasure'. Amis's men
are usually keen to take women to bed, but will not tolerate
much discussion of sex: talking about sex is associated with
sexual inactivity. One of the tributes to the travelling salesman
in Amis's 'A Song of Experience' is that 'What Blake presaged,
what Lawrence took a stand on,/What Yeats looked up in
fable, he performed'. Excess of thought, word or sensitivity
incapacitates: 'bang's the way to get things done', Amis suggests in 'Mightier than the Pen', and his Evans is seen going
'in like a whippet' for 'a fearsome thrash with Mrs No-holds-
barred'. Similar attitudes are discernible in Gunn's 'Carnal
Knowledge', where the male speaker is cynically inattentive
to his mistress's feelings ('If you have tears, prepare to cry
elsewhere') and insults her intelligence (he notes the 'space
between the thighs and head,/So great, we might as well not
be in bed'), but makes use of her for sexual pleasure. In this
poem and 'A Village Edmund'—the latter with its hero 'swag-
gering up the high street, thumb in belt'—Gunn offers an
aggressive masculinity which dissociates itself both from the
'tender' heterosexuality of Lawrence's gamekeeper, Mellors,
and from the covert homosexuality of Auden and Spender.

It is doubtful, however, whether the Movement attempt
to take a funny-but-tough approach to sexual relationships
can be adjudged a success. In the first place, the priggishness
against which Amis and Gunn were imagined to be reacting
is still present in other Movement texts. Lumley in Wain's

Hurry on Down, for example, seems intimidated by, and disapproving of, first Betty, the woman who lives with Froulish—'he had little experience of the particular type of slut she represented, and was afraid that if given any encouragement she might offer him a share in her favours'—and then June Veeber, whose offer to stay the night with him makes Lumley feel 'defiled'. Similarly prim and maidenly feelings about sex are discernible in Davie's 'Three Moral Discoveries': 'I dared occasion, and came off intact,/Unharmed, not therefore unashamed'. Larkin is not priggish about sex (in their awkward, self-deprecating and rather romantic approach, his speakers might more properly be called Prufrockian), but nor does he present sex as a pleasure, dwelling instead on post-coital disillusion—'fulfilment's desolate attic', as he puts it in 'Deceptions', or the 'sad scapes' of 'Dry-Point':

> The wet spark comes, the bright-blown walls collapse,
>
> But what sad scapes we cannot turn from then:
> What ashen hills! what salted, shrunken lakes!

Even in the work of Gunn and Amis, the two Movement writers most associated with the 'new' tough-mindedness of the post-war era, uneasiness of certain kinds is evident. In Gunn it shows up in the very insistence with which he presents males like 'A Village Edmund' as 'randy and rowdy and rough'. The concern with symbols of *machismo*— motorbikes, knives, leather belts, tattoos—seems obsessive, even fetishistic. Ritualistic and sado-masochistic elements in sex—the 'whip, cords, and strap, and toiling toward despair' described in 'The Beaters'—exert an increasing fascination for him, and by the time of *My Sad Captains* (1961) he sees a darker side to *l'homme moyen sensuel,* observing in 'Modes of Pleasure'

> The Fallen Rake, being fallen from
> The heights of twenty to middle age,
> And helpless to control his rage,
> So mean, so few the chances come.

Even in the very early 'Lofty in the Palais de Danse', Gunn's

treatment of sexual relationships is darker and more complex
than we might expect. On the face of it, this poem's approach
to sex is as tough and as pragmatic as the Movement determined it should be. The speaker has picked up a girl at a local
dance-hall, and afterwards takes her into the street for sexual
intercourse:

> You praise my strength. The muscle on my arm.
> Yes, Now the other. Yes, about the same.
> I've got another muscle you can feel.
> Dare say you knew. Only expected harm
> Falls from a khaki man. That's why you came
> With me and when I go you follow still.
>
> Now that we sway here in the shadowed street
> Why can't I keep my mind clenched on the job?
> Your body is a good one, not without
> Earlier performance, but in this repeat
> The pictures are unwilled that I see bob
> Out of the dark, and you can't turn them out.

In the 1950s, the poem could be taken as a daringly frank
treatment of casual sex, and as a reflection of changes in the
sexual mores of the young. The speaker is crude, as a soldier
might be expected to be, and Gunn reinforces the crudity
with some raw and shocking effects: the joke about 'another
muscle', the tone of male bravado, the contrived cinematic
imagery at the end. But even leaving aside the question of the
speaker's attitude to women—an exploitative attitude to be
found elsewhere in the Movement (especially in Amis), and
one which, from the perspective of the present, looks sexist
and even misogynistic—one would be hard pressed to describe
this as a poem in which sex is presented as a 'simple' or 'normal'
pleasure. Restless, 'gone to bad' in a 'deadly world', Gunn's
speaker has been driven to promiscuity in order to find a
replacement for a dead girlfriend—'one I knew before that
died'. Sex for him is thus intimately bound up with loss and
death; it is not 'fun'. The final image of 'unwilled' forces
which 'bob/Out of the dark' leaves a disturbing impression.

Gunn, it could be argued, never attempted to conceal disturbing aspects of sexual experience: on the basis of the 'demon lovers' of 'A Village Edmund', or of the 'werewolf lust' of 'The Beach Head', critics could and should have detected the dark, Gothic elements in his treatment. Amis, on the other hand, has made concerted efforts to present sex as a simple pleasure: post-coital conversation in his novels always purports to confirm that what has just taken place is 'good' and 'splendid'. At the same time, it seeks to persuade us that the Amis hero is a proficient sexual performer:

> 'That was good, wasn't it, darling?'
> 'Yes, it was good all right.'
> 'You're quite a man, aren't you?'
> 'Oh, I don't know. It's just that you love it.'
> 'Well, don't you love it?'
> 'Yes, as a rule. I did then, anyway.'   (*That Uncertain Feeling*)

> 'Maurice,' she said now, 'that was ab-so-lute-ly terr-i-fic. I don't know *how* . . . you do it. Was it nice for you? You certainly deserved it to be.'
> 'It was splendid.'   (*The Green Man*)

The anxiety that such passages might be thought to conceal (later confirmed in *Jake's Thing*) first became noticeable in Amis's *Take a Girl Like You* (1960). In this novel, the pleasure-seeking Movement male is Patrick Standish, who seeks to persuade Jenny Bunn that sex is 'fun', and that her valuation of virginity is 'a fuss about nothing'. But not only does Patrick's argument meet resistance from Jenny, whose point of view is sympathetically presented by Amis, but it fails convincingly to receive the assent of Patrick himself. For Patrick, sex is a means of warding off thoughts of death, 'meditations on the old last end', and he comes to disapprove of people who seek a 'demonstration of how clean and straightforward and entertaining and part-of-a-spending-spree and good-fun-for-all-concerned sex *really* is, not all those peculiar old other things they're liable to suspect it may possibly be when they read the *News of the World,* or pass a girls' school at playtime, or cut across the common last thing at night'. Like Gunn's Lofty, Patrick fails to disentangle sex from thoughts of death. Immediately before his anticipated seduction of Jenny (and it is part of the book's dark undercurrent that he will eventually have to take her virginity by what amounts to rape), he finds sexual excitement turning into a terrifying contemplation of his own death:

At that moment a sharp uneasiness started up somewhere inside him. His breathing quickened and deepened as at the onset of sexual excitement, but this was not his condition. He felt his heart speeding up again and becoming irregular, like a bird making shorter and longer hops. There was a faint, hollow rolling and grinding in his ears, while a rapid prickling spread over his skin from a point midway between his shoulderblades. Nothing in his thoughts or his situation accounted for these symptoms which, the accompaniments of terror, stirred in him more than one kind of teror, as they had recently been doing every other night or so while he lay awake in bed. This was the first time they had come on in the day . . . At this point his own vision of death, refined and extended nightly for years, was directly before him . . .: thick water, then thin mud, then thick mud, just mud and the struggle to breathe, a gradual loss of consciousness followed by dreams of water and mud and the struggle to breathe, dreams superseded by identical dreams, a death prolonged for ever.

To point to these elements of darkness and anxiety in the Movement's treatment of sex is to begin to raise questions about the extent of the Movement's anti-Romantic reaction. One of the axioms of the Movement had been that, as Dixon put it in *Lucky Jim,* 'nice things are nicer than nasty ones', sex being 'nice', death 'nasty'. Where Dylan Thomas's poetry had often merged images of sex and death, as if to suggest the inseparability of the two, Movement poets were to show that a clear line could be drawn between them. Their failure to draw this line is part of a more general failure to dissociate themselves from that preoccupation with the dark, the anarchic, the irrational, the chaotic, which they took to be characteristic of the Romantic sensibility. It would be a partial reading of the Movement which ignored the points at which the reaction against Romanticism faltered, at which the attempt to affirm 'ordinariness', 'normality' and 'common sense' collapsed. In the work of Gunn, Amis, and Larkin especially, there is a continuing participation in the Romantic tradition.

That Thom Gunn felt at least some prejudice *against* Romanticism is clear from his poem 'To Yvor Winters, 1955', which in its disparagement of 'the neurotic vision' and assertion of the need to maintain an 'empire over thought and speech' is very reminiscent of Amis's 'Against Romanticism'. Gunn dedicated the poem to Winters (he is its 'you') because Winters's critical work, like the Movement's, had emphasized the importance of intelligence and order in poetry. The poem is itself a 'defence of reason':

> You keep both Rule and Energy in view,
> Much power in each, most in the balanced two:
> Ferocity existing in the fence
> Built by an exercised intelligence.

Gunn's emphasis on 'Rule'—his argument that, as he put it in a 1957 review, 'it is only by the control of energy that energy can ever be defined or conveyed'[53]—is typical of the Movement's anti-Romanticism. But his use of words like 'energy' and 'ferocity' also puts him at a slight distance from the rest of the group, and makes it understandable that he should also have been associated with Ted Hughes. Gunn's admiration for 'energy' had from the beginning made him more sympathetic to Romanticism than were his Movement confederates. In November 1952, he praised the 'energy' of Dylan Thomas, suggesting that 'the very fact he has such vitality as to be incoherent is refreshing'.[54] He also, in that same month, distinguished between a 'true' and valuable Romanticism, and the false and effete version of it which he found being propounded by Paul Dehn in *Romantic Landscape*: 'In his title he [Dehn] claims, healthily, to be a Romantic; but then so did many earlier Georgians . . . But your true Romantic looks forward as well as backward. Mr Dehn lacks muscle, he lacks recklessness, he lacks arrogance, he lacks that indiscriminate energy which is the mark of any Romantic who is not called so sneeringly.'[55] 'Muscle', 'recklessness', 'arrogance', 'indiscriminate energy', respect for Dylan Thomas: these are not characteristics we associate with the Movement programme.

Another feature of Gunn's work which divides it from the Movement is its interest in Existentialism, a philosophy which is often thought to be related to Romantic individualism. Gunn had spent some time in Paris before going to Cambridge, and, being slightly younger than most of the other Movement poets, was part of the 'National Service generation' for whom Sartre's work became fashionable in the 1950s. Sartrean notions of 'risk', 'choice', 'will' and 'action' appear frequently in his first two collections, *Fighting Terms* (1954) and *The Sense of Movement* (1957), and there is praise for those who 'regret nothing' and who can declare 'I am being what I please'. Such praise leads, in turn, to a worship of Romantic overreaching. Gunn praises both traditional heroes—'Alexander or Mark Antony/Or Coriolanus, whom I most admire'—and modern figures, like Elvis Presley, who adopt a 'posture for combat'. It is impossible to imagine any of the other Movement poets, with their intuitive equation of hero-worship and Fascism, paying such tributes.

The co-existence of Romantic and anti-Romantic tendencies in Gunn is best illustrated in the most famous of his early poems, 'On the Move'. The strictness of metre and rhyme-scheme; the speaker's admiration for the motorcyclists' exertion of control; the tentative, self-qualifying, explanatory tone-of-voice; the fact that the poem is written from the point-of-view of a stationary observer, not of an active participant: all these features of the poem give it a Movement quality. Less typical of the Movement, and more indicative of a Romantic sensibility, are the 'robust' assonances of the language—'gust', 'spurts', 'dull thunder', 'hum', 'bulges', 'hurler', 'hurled'; the existential implications of words like 'purpose', 'will', 'dare', 'choosing' and 'self-defined'; and, above all, the sympathy shown towards the 'uncertain violence' of a social group which others in the Movement might have regarded as dangerously rebellious. Gunn's poem 'justifies' the gang, giving it an intellectual respectability, and it ends with a celebration of movement which is most un-Movement-like:

> A minute holds them, who have come to go:
> The self-defined, astride the created will
> They burst away . . .
> At worst, one is in motion: and at best,
> Reaching no absolute, in which to rest,
> One is always nearer by not keeping still.

Kingsley Amis's 'On Staying Still', which was written about the same time as 'On the Move', is a characteristically Movement corrective to the outlook expressed in Gunn's poem. Gunn praises movement-for-the-sake-of-movement, not minding whether it is directed or not; but Amis unfavourably contrasts the 'changeless tidal fury' of the sea with the immobility of an old 'broken boat' or 'hulk' on the shoreline:

> . . . staying still is more,
> When all else is moving
> To no end, whether
> Or not choice is free.
> Good that decay recalls
> (By being slow and steady)
> Blossom, fruitful change
> Of tree to coal, not any
> Changeless tidal fury.

The poem is a corrective not only because of its defence of inaction and stoicism (these being the recommended Movement responses to the decay of the 'old hulk' that is England), but because it questions 'whether/Or not choice is free'. For Gunn choice is all important, but Amis and Larkin often see choice as futile, individual destinies being determined by some unseen force. In Larkin's work, the first tentative expression of fatalism came as early as 1946, when John Kemp, finding

it impossible to decide whether his love for Jill has been fulfilled or unfulfilled, wonders whether he has not been

'freed, for the rest of his life, from choice?'
   For what could it matter? Let him take this course, or this course,
but still behind the mind, on some other level, the way he had rejected
was being simultaneously worked out and the same conclusion was
being reached. What did it matter which road he took if they both led
to the same place? . . . What control could he hope to have over the
maddened surface of things?

This passage, as David Timms notes,[56] anticipates the conclusion of 'Dockery and Son', where our lives are said to be
determined by 'what something hidden from us chose'. Fatalism also pervades 'As Bad as a Mile' where, in an image suggestive of the Fall (and implying that we are condemned to
fail because of man's Original Sin), failure is seen 'spreading
back up the arm/Earlier and earlier' to 'the apple unbitten in
the palm'. In a more recent and blatant expression of fatalism,
Larkin depicts life as

> an immobile, locked,
> Three-handed struggle between
> Your wants, the world's for you, and (worse)
> The unbeatable slow machine
> That brings you what you'll get.[57]

Amis's protagonists are also convinced that self-determination
is an illusion. In *That Uncertain Feeling* John Lewis decides
that 'it wasn't doing what you wanted to that was important...
as wanting to do what you did'. In *Take a Girl Like You* the
determinism is stronger and bleaker. Patrick Standish, who
'had often thought that the fatalist boys were on to something', invents the phrase 'Bastards' H.Q.' to express his
feeling that there may exist a malevolent Creator who governs
human lives.
   Though the work of Amis and Larkin thus offers a fatalistic
contrast to Gunn's celebration of choice and free will, it is
doubtful whether their corrective is any less 'Romantic' than
what it seeks to correct. Yvor Winters has suggested that

'determinism is Romanticism in a disillusioned mood',[58] and really the Gunn position (choice is all-important) and the Larkin-Amis position (choice is of no importance) are two sides of the same Romantic coin: a true Movement position would be somewhere between the two extremes. It is clear, at any rate, that the fatalism pervading the work of Larkin and Amis, however lightly worn, betrays an element of superstition which is not consonant with the Movement's declared reaction against Romantic irrationalism, and which indicates an inability wholly to submit to a 'rational' and 'realistic' philosophy.

This failure is also evident in Larkin's continuing urge to transcend the limits he imposes upon himself. Movement reason and realism ordain an acceptance of limits: 'living as the art of the possible', as Patrick Standish puts it. But Larkin's poetry remains too attracted to the unbounded alternatives ever to accept such ordinances with conviction. A characteristic tension in his verse is the conflict between a disappointed resignation in the face of what life is, and a continuing awareness of what it 'should' or 'might' or 'could' or 'ought to' have been. As its title hints, it would not be fanciful to see a poem like 'Essential Beauty', with its 'sharply-pictured groves/Of how life should be', as the work of a Platonist. Larkin's are

> live imperfect eyes
> That stare beyond this world, where nothing's made
> As new or washed quite clean . . .

The tension between 'is' and 'could have been' is particularly noticeable in poems like 'Toads' and 'Poetry of Departures', where Larkin takes on the role of the Movement-like responsibly-employed citizen, but pines for a life beyond nine-to-five routine. 'Toads' begins with a cry against the fetters of conventional employment—'Why should I let the toad *work*/Squat on my life?'—and its speaker gazes enviously at those who

> live up lanes
> With fires in a bucket,
> Eat windfalls and tinned sardines —
> They seem to like it.

As a Romantic poet, Larkin yearns to rebel; as a Movement poet, he must persuade himself that he is unsuited to rebellion. The conflict is visible again in 'Poetry of Departures', where the speaker is left 'flushed and stirred' by examples of social deviance, but hears of such behaviour only at 'fifth-hand': the phrase tells us, not only how remote the speaker is from scenes of such a kind (his is a life of correctness and fidelity, 'the good books, the good bed'), but that he is sceptical as to whether they actually take place—may they not be subject to ornamentation? This scepticism, and some specious reasoning, enable the speaker to convince himself that to break out would be for him, and is perhaps for others, as 'artificial' as remaining 'sober and industrious'. He might as well stay as he is:

> But I'd go today,
>
> Yes, swagger the nut-strewn roads,
> Crouch in the fo'c'sle
> Stubbly with goodness, if
> It weren't so artificial,
> Such a deliberate step backwards
> To create an object:
> Books; china; a life
> Reprehensibly perfect.

The archaic and 'artificial' imagery—'swagger', 'nut-strewn', 'fo'c'sle', 'stubbly with goodness'—helps the speaker to make the point that, as Orwell's George Bowling puts it when he considers walking out on his family, 'that kind of thing only happens in books': the Movement persona could never take to the road in the manner of a Rimbaud or a Kerouac. But the vigour of the imagery also indicates that the speaker continues to find the Romantic alternative painfully attractive, and is not wholly resigned (however much he may claim to be) to the limited life which he leads.

In itself, this quiet resentment of limits, this 'blunder up against the wires', would not be sufficient to allow us to speak of Larkin as a Romantic poet. In his essay 'Romanticism and

Classicism', T. E. Hulme argues that the 'classical in verse' does not preclude 'imaginative flights': the crucial point is that although the classical poet 'may jump', he 'always returns back'.[59] But the imaginative flights we have observed are a pointer to other Larkin poems in which, by contrast, there is no less deceived consciousness to effect a return to earth. Such poems would be 'Here', with its movement through and out from the city towards a solitary and 'unfenced existence'; 'Wants', with its 'wish to be alone' and 'desire of oblivion'; and 'Age', 'Absences' and 'Water', where the poet's gaze is lifted upwards, and his transcendental longing expressed through images of light and space. In these and other texts, Larkin writes, quite unmistakably, as a Romantic poet.

The Movement's declared reaction against Romanticism was, then, valuable in assisting the group to define its artistic aims. But it was also to some extent an act of will working against the instincts of the group's major figures. In the early 1950s it was important for the group to offer an alternative to prevailing Romantic modes. In doing so, the Movement contributed valuably to a 'democratizing' of poetry, presenting the poet as ordinary citizen rather than privileged seer. Once this aim had been achieved, however, the Movement were liberated from their role as anti-Romantics. They could acknowledge that not all elements of Romanticism were pernicious, and that some were indeed quite compatible with the Movement programme. Certain aspects of Romantic theory have still been met with resistance, but since 1960 the Movement's participation in a continuing Romantic tradition has become more apparent.

5

Tradition and Belief

> As a guiding principle I believe that every poem must be its own sole freshly-created universe, and therefore have no belief in 'tradition' or a common myth-kitty or casual allusions in poems to other poems or poets, which last I find unpleasantly like the talk of literary understrappers letting you see they know the right people. A poet's only guide is his own judgment...
>
> Larkin, in *Poets of the 1950's*

Larkin's declaration of disbelief in tradition, allusion and myth is the best-known of all his statements about poetry. Ironically, it may also have been the least carefully pondered: he claims that he made it in response to a request from D. J. Enright, but never imagined that it would be quoted: 'the phrase has pursued me ever since. It just shows how careful you should be.'[1] It is not surprising, though, that the statement should have become famous, for in making it Larkin sets himself against a considerable body of literature and literary theory. In particular, he calls into question the importance placed upon tradition, allusion and myth by Modernist writers: implicitly under attack are works like Eliot's *The Waste Land* and 'Tradition and the Individual Talent', Joyce's *Ulysses*, Pound's *Cantos* and 'How to Read', Yeats's *The Tower* and *A Vision*. The position, whether it was intended to be made public or not, is a presumptuous one.

Larkin's sentiments would not, however, have been found strange or uncongenial by his Movement colleagues. In his introduction to that same anthology, Enright made a similar attack on 'the shadow of "Tradition", which apparently takes the form of tasteful quotations from the Greek with an odd nymph or two thrown in'. And Amis, whose 'Against Romanticism' calls for a poetry 'free from all the grime of history' and 'not trampled by the havering unicorn', had anticipated Larkin's views on myth in 'Sonnet from Orpheus', a poem from his 1953 collection *A Frame of Mind*. Orpheus, the subject of so many writers' attentions down the ages, is heard speaking out angrily against all those who have made use of him:

> And now I'm tired of being the trade-name
> on boxes of assorted junk; tired of
> conscription as the mouthpiece of your brash
> theories, of jigging to your symbol-crash.
> Speak for yourselves, or not at all; this game
> is up — your mannikin has had enough.

Larkin's and Amis's attack on myth is, in its broadest sense, anti-Modernist, but it may also reflect a particular animus against the over-use of Christian and Classical myth by British poets of the 1940s. Several of the most famous Second World War poems—Edith Sitwell's 'Still Falls the Rain', Dylan Thomas's 'Among Those Killed in the Dawn Raid', F. T. Prince's 'Soldiers Bathing', David Gascoyne's 'Ecce Homo'— had used the image of the crucifixion to express the plight of man in wartime. The Movement regarded such use of myth as uninstructive: to explain World War Two in terms of man's crucifixion of Christ did not make for insight and illumination. To talk about 'real time and place' it would be necessary to eschew myth, as Larkin, Amis, and Enright largely did.

Larkin's statement, then, represents an important current of feeling within the Movement. But once again, there is no simple consensus on the matter. In the first place, the practice of several other Movement poets goes against Larkin: Davie, for example, writes a densely allusive poetry, and Gunn makes extensive use of myth ('Lazarus Not Raised', 'Helen's Rape', 'Merlin in the Cave', and 'Jesus and His Mother' are titles from his first two collections). More importantly, the views of

Larkin, Amis and Enright are more complex than might at first appear. Larkin seems not to be opposed to allusions so long as they are fairly covert: he himself alludes to Tennyson's 'The Princess', with its 'sweet girl-graduates', in 'Lines on a Young Lady's Photograph Album'. What he and other Movement poets object to are poems which, if they are to be intelligible, *require* the reader to recognize an allusion: Movement poems do not make detection of an allusion essential to their understanding, but offer a 'bonus' to those readers who do manage to spot a reference. (The technique seems typical of the Movement's attempt to meet the need of the 'two audiences': provision for the intellectual audience does not alienate the non-intellectual one.) It is also noticeable that both Larkin and Enright place the word 'tradition' in inverted commas: this is a hint that it may be a particular interpretation of tradition which they mean to disparage. Again, it is not actually myth but rather 'a common myth-kitty' which Larkin fails to believe in: does this mean that it is only certain myths which he believes have been over-exploited? and would he accept the possibility of poets contributing to, or creating, new myths of their own?

It is important to ask these questions because it is arguable that, in one of his poems, Larkin does all that he seemingly undertook not to do when he made his statement for *Poets of the 1950's*: that is, draw on tradition, allude to other poets, and create a myth. This poem is Larkin's 'MCMXIV', which looks back to what is imagined to have been the 'innocence' of English society immediately before the onset of the First World War:

> . . . the countryside not caring:
> The place-names all hazed over
> With flowering grasses, and fields
> Shadowing Domesday lines
> Under wheat's restless silence;
> The differently-dressed servants
> With tiny rooms in huge houses . . .
>
> Never such innocence again.

The most obvious way to treat 'MCMXIV' is not as a mythical poem but as a historical one. The poem concerns itself with a specific moment of history, and even includes period detail—

> The tin advertisements
> For cocoa and twist, and the pubs
> Wide open all day.

But to read the poem in this way almost inevitably requires one to feel strong reservations about it. A common objection to the poem is that put by Graham Martin when he argues that in 'MCMXIV' Larkin reveals a 'deeply conventional "historical sense"', and concludes that Larkin is 'at his weakest when he moves away from the personal and immediate to the historical'.[2] In criticizing Larkin, Martin invokes not only Eliot (the phrase 'historical sense' comes from 'Tradition and the Individual Talent'), but also Pound, whose method in the *Cantos* is adjudged to provide 'sounder' history than Larkin's method in 'MCMXIV'. But as Martin's word 'conventional' unwittingly indicates, Larkin's method in 'MCMXIV' is clearly *not* that of a historian: his is a poem written out of, and enshrining, a convention of belief about 1914, not a poem undertaking to provide new historical insights. 'MCMXIV' expects to receive, not intellectual, but emotional assent; it offers itself not as historical fact but as myth.

What exactly is the myth articulated in 'MCMXIV'? Possibly, it is a new version of the myth of the Fall. The Great War is the equivalent of the serpent, enticing man from his paradisal home amongst the 'flowering grasses' of England, and depriving him of his 'innocence' (a key word in the poem): Larkin's pity is for a race of innocents about to be exposed to experience. Less grandiosely (the Movement would certainly have regarded direct use of the myth of the Fall as grandiose), 'MCMXIV' is a termination myth, a myth about the end of something: it identifies at a particular point of history (as Eliot's theory of the 'dissociation of sensibility' did, as Leavis's theory of the 'organic community' did) a decisive break in English consciousness and experience. Both the choice of the images in

'MCMXIV'—'place names', children 'called after kings and queens', 'crowns' of hats, 'lines' of volunteers—and the adjectives and adverbs used—'long', 'established', 'patiently'—embody the idea of a tradition or continuity extending (the word 'stretched' is used at one point) far into the past, but about for the first time and finally to be broken. The 'moustached archaic faces' are archaic not just because they seem to us outdated in appearance; they are archaic, also, in the sense that they do have connections with an earlier England—an England which stretches back to 'Domesday'. This deeper level of suggestion in the poem seems almost to contradict the surface historical level: for while the period detail and the claim that there has 'never before' been such innocence give the impression that it is specifically the Georgian culture whose loss Larkin mourns, the use of images such as 'Domesday', 'kings and queens' and 'place names' imply that Larkin is mourning the loss of something much greater: a long-standing English tradition of which the Georgians are the last representatives. Thus when David Timms argues in his account of the poem that 'it is the simultaneous apprehension of reality and their [the volunteers'] false ideal which moves us',[3] he is mistaking the origins of the poem's emotional force. Larkin is not interested in the question of whether the men are about to die for a false ideal; he is interested in them as privileged participants in an English tradition from which we, because of the intervention of the Great War, are forever excluded.

This myth of 1914 as the end of something reappears in other texts produced by writers in the Movement generation. When in *Take a Girl Like You,* for instance, Patrick Standish ridicules Jennie Bunn's outdated attitudes to pre-marital sex, it is natural that he should refer to 1914 as the date at which (so he must persuade her if she is to go to bed with him) the moral values to which she appeals became obsolete. The kind of man whom she wants, he suggests, is one who would respect her virginity, who 'wouldn't have given you any trouble trying to get you into bed before the day. The snag about him is he's dead. He died in 1914 or thereabouts. He isn't ever going to turn up, Jenny, that bloke with the manners and the respect and the honour and the bunches of flowers *and* the attraction'. Jimmy Porter in John Osborne's *Look Back in Anger* (1956) is more sceptical than Standish about the notion of a clean 1914 break, describing the idea of pre-war innocence as a 'phoney' memory promulgated by the 'old Edwardian brigade'. But, as Movement protagonists often do, Porter remains susceptible to the idea:

Always the same picture: high summer, the long days in the sun, slim volumes of verse, crisp linen, the smell of starch. What a romantic picture. Phoney too, of course. It must have rained sometimes. Still, even I regret it somehow, phoney or not. If you've no world of your own, it's rather pleasant to regret the passing of someone else's.

It is to the community of belief represented in such quotations that Larkin's 'MCMXIV' appeals. The poem addresses itself to a generation of writers who, having been born in the decade or so following 1914, and therefore having come so close to pre-war England without actually experiencing it, felt with peculiar force the idea that England before the Great War had possessed an irrecoverable 'innocence'. While those writers who were children during the Great War—the 1930s generation of Auden, Spender and Isherwood—focused attention on the war itself (expressing both pacifist tendencies inspired by Wilfred Owen, and ideas of heroism caused by frustration at having missed out on the Great War), the Movement generation looked back on the world which was imagined to have existed just before the war. As a near contemporary of the Movement's, Kenneth Allsop, puts it in a comment that reads almost as a gloss on 'MCMXIV': 'I personally have, and I believe a great many men and women in my age group have, an intense longing for the security and the innocence that seems to have been present in Britain before the 1914 war.'[4]

'MCMXIV' is therefore myth rather than social history, and tells us more about the Movement than it does about the Georgian society which it describes. Larkin, it is true, would resist such a reading of the poem. He has spoken of it as a 'monument' to the dead of the Great War,[5] and has tried to keep its form and content impersonal, so that our attention will be on the subject rather than on the speaker; he intends there to be nothing obtrusive to remind us that it is the work of a mid-twentieth-century writer. But is clear that part of the sadness of 'MCMXIV' is the sadness of a latecomer: Larkin not only commemorates the Great War volunteers, he pities himself and his contemporaries for never having had the opportunity to experience the social order of 1914. More indicative still of the post-1945 origins of the poem is the guise in which that social order appears: Larkin's vision of strictly observed hierarchy—'servants' and 'limousines', 'farthings and sovereigns', 'tiny rooms in huge houses'—may have some basis in historical fact, but it also reveals a great deal about Larkin's, and the Movement's, nostalgia for the stability provided by a clearly defined class hierarchy. In his essay 'Who Talks of My Nation' (1955), Wain claims that 'something in every English breast hankers for the medieval chain of relationships, with everyone paying feudal homage to the person next above and receiving it from the person next below'.[6] The claim is dubious, but it does point to the kind of sensibility which underlies Larkin's poem. 'MCMXIV' appeals to that tendency in the Movement (increasingly in evidence in the late 1950s and early 1960s) to regret rather than welcome changes in the class-structure. It provides an image of hierarchic 'innocence' which will dignify Movement conservatism. It locates the decisive break in English continuity as 1914, but it would not be fanciful to suppose that certain unsettling aspects of post-1945 history—the H-bomb, the end of Empire, the promise of a classless democracy—were the real cause of the feelings of discontinuity to which the poem attests.

The myth of 1914 had, then, special meaning for the Movement generation. But as Paul Fussell has shown in his book *The Great War and Modern Memory* (1975), the idea of 1914 as the last moment of innocence before the harsh arrival of a new world was not one on which the Movement had a monopoly. There was, in fact, a substantial English tradition of writing about the Edenic innocence of 1914 on which Larkin could draw for his poem; and in presenting the myth, Larkin alludes to that tradition. Even while the Great War was still being fought, the myth began to be created. J. C. Squire's 'To a Bull-Dog', a poem included in the 1916–17 *Georgian Poetry* anthology, looks back to a time of companionship 'before the old life stopped'. Edward Thomas's 'As the Team's Head Brass' records a conversation about a young man going out to fight which suggests that if he had not gone

> 'Everything
> Would have been different. For it would have been
> Another world.' 'Ay, and a better . . .'

Wilfred Owen's 'From My Diary, July 1914', a wartime transformation of pre-war jottings, presents an idyllic picture of the summer of 1914, with 'Flashes/Of swimmers carving through the sparkling cold'. Robert Graves's 'The Last Day of Leave' (1916), though set during rather than before the Great War, presents a similar idyll—'no clouds; larks and heath-butterflies,/And herons undisturbed fishing the streams'—which is shattered by the intrusion of the fact of war in the final lines:

> 'Do you remember the lily lake?
> We were all there, all five of us in love,
> Not one yet killed, widowed, or broken hearted.'

Larkin could draw on prose as well as on poetry. There were the memoirs of Siegfried Sassoon, which recalled the pastoral splendours of the summer of 1914—'the apple-scented orchards, and all those fertilities which the harrassed farmer was gathering in while stupendous events were developing across the Channel. Never before had I known how much I had to lose'.[7] Later, in the 1930s, Orwell made nostalgia for pre-1914 England the basis of *Coming Up for Air*. George Bowling remembers the period as 'summer all the year round' and poignantly recalls its rural charm—'the dust in the lane, and the warm greeny light coming through the hazel boughs'. Bowling is so captivated by these memories that he is driven to re-visit his childhood village, Lower Binfield, and reflects on the meaning of his nostalgia: '1913! My God! 1913: The stillness, the green water, the rushing of the weir! It'll never come again . . ., the feeling inside you, the feeling of not being in a hurry and not being frightened, the feeling you've either had and don't need to be told about, or haven't had and won't ever have the chance to learn'.

These accounts of pre-war England provided Larkin with images not just of pastoral innocence, but of discontinuity. The phrase 'never again', for example, so crucial to Larkin's expression of the irrecoverability of 1914, can be found not only in the Orwell passage above, but in a number of English poems written around the time of 1914. Edward Thomas's 'In Memoriam (Easter 1915)' describes spring flowers which

> call into mind the men
> Now far from home, who, with their sweethearts, should
> Have gathered them and will do never again.

Similarly his 'It Rains' recalls the poet walking in the rain with his lover,

> Drenched, yet forgetting the kisses of the rain:
> Sad, too, to think that never, never again
>
> Unless alone, so happy shall I walk
> In the rain.

There are the wheelchair victims in Wilfred Owen's 'Disabled', who 'will never feel again how slim/Girls' waists are'. The phrase also appears frequently in Hardy's poems written on the death of his wife just before the Great War, where the regret for loss of an 'old life' is of a more personal kind. The dead Emma 'nor knows nor cares for Beeny, and will laugh there nevermore'; the scene of her 'last drive' is one 'that never again would beam on' her; Hardy himself will 'traverse old love's domain/Never again.' Larkin has said that 'the dominant emotion in Hardy is sadness',[8] and the sadness which pervades another of Hardy's poems for Emma, 'This Summer and Last', is very similar to the sadness which pervades 'MCMXIV':

> Unhappy summer you,
>   Who do not see
> What your yester-summer saw!
> Never, never will you be
>   Its match to me,
>   Never, never draw
> Smiles your forerunner drew,
>   Know what it knew!

Variations on the refrain 'never again' had also been used, some twenty years earlier, by A. E. Housman in *A Shropshire Lad*. The persona of 'Loveliest of trees . . .' regrets that of his 'threescore years and ten,/Twenty will not come again', and 'Into my heart an air that kills' describes 'the happy highways where I went/And cannot come again'. Housman's phrasing here seems to have made an early impact on Larkin: an unpublished poem in his notebook for the years 1944–50 describes the death of someone whose 'final summer' has been symbolically preserved in the form of bottled jam:

> Behind the glass, under the cellophane,
> Remains your final summer—sweet
> And meaningless, and not to come again.

It is true that the phrases 'nevermore' and 'never again' are a common feature of poems from the Romantic period (the 'nevermore' of Poe's raven is a famous example), and it might therefore be unwise to suggest that in using the construction 'never . . . again' in 'MCMXIV' Larkin was deliberately alluding to the poems I have mentioned. But it is clear that, in composing the poem, he was in a general way drawing on an English tradition of writing about the immediate pre-1914 period—a tradition which would include such figures as Thomas Hardy, Edward Thomas, Robert Graves and Wilfred Owen. This gives 'MCMXIV' an added dimension: it is not only a monument to the English 'flower of youth' that died in the Great War; it is also a monument to an English poetic tradition. The 'moustached archaic faces' are those not just of anonymous volunteers, but of Hardy, Owen and others.

To read 'MCMXIV' as a poem about a poetic as well as a social tradition might seem implausible, but there is an extremely good reason for doing so. This is the tendency, common in the Movement generation, to think of 1914 as the date at which an indigenous tradition in poetry ended, and at which the Modernist tradition began. From a strict historical point of view, this association is questionable. In English poetry, Modernism had begun to make itself felt by 1909, the date of Eliot's 'Portrait of a Lady', and of Pound's first influential activities in London. In other arts and countries, Modernism can be seen developing in the late-nineteenth century. But Wyndham Lewis spoke of himself, Pound, Eliot and Joyce as the 'men of 1914', and the presumption of a connection between the Great War and Modernism is still usual among critics. The connection was very influential on Movement thinking, encouraging them to see 1914 as a turning-point in the literary, as well as social, history of the nation. It helped to produce the theory that because of the Great War a central tradition in English poetry had been discontinued. The yearning for stability in 'MCMXIV'—'established names', 'tidy gardens'—is more than nostalgia for a secure social order: it is nostalgia for the 'tidy' and 'established' forms of pre-Modernist English poetry. And the 'long uneven lines' are not just those of enlisting soldiers; they are (one might rather whimsically suggest) the 'long uneven lines' of Eliot's and Pound's poetry, waiting to replace the 'Domesday lines' of Hardy, Housman, Edward Thomas and their forefathers.

Had the Movement accepted that the coming of Modernism was a valuable liberating force for English poetry, then their nostalgia for 1914 might have been more temperate. But the Movement believed that Modernist poets had perpetuated the Romantic vice of presenting the poet as a special being or genius removed from 'ordinary' society, and that they had initiated an unproductive era of experimentalism. 'The modern movement,' Enright claimed in his introduction to *Poets of the 1950's,* 'began with a brilliant blaze. Unfortunately the flames got out of control, and ever since we have been warming ourselves at the embers'. Most damaging of all, the Movement believed, had been Modernism's near-destruction of an English poetic tradition. Fortunately, just as there were survivors of the Great War, so there were certain English poets—Hardy and Graves, for example—who had 'survived' the coming of Modernism, and whose work, it was thought, might provide a line back to pre-Modernist literature. To look to such poets would be to restore the interrupted, temporarily discontinued, but not completely devastated tradition of 1914. The Georgian social order was irrecoverable, would 'never again' be experienced, but the values associated with it might be passed on through its poets.

This theory that there might exist an interrupted English tradition underlay much of the Movement's work in the 1950s and 1960s. It was in two books published in 1973, however, that the theory was first propounded at length. In that year Larkin's anthology *The Oxford Book of Twentieth Century English Verse* and Davie's critical study *Thomas Hardy and British Poetry* put forward the idea that an English poetic tradition stemming from Thomas Hardy, and taking in a number of other poets outside the Modern movement, is of considerably more importance than has generally been allowed. During an interview in which he explained his choices for the Oxford anthology, Larkin said that the discovery or definition of an 'interrupted' tradition had been of primary importance to him:

I had in my mind a notion that there might have been what I'll call, for want of a better phrase, an English tradition coming from the nineteenth century with people like Hardy, which was interrupted partly by the Great War, when many English poets were killed off, and partly by the really tremendous impact of Yeats, whom I think of as Celtic, and Eliot, whom I think of as American.[9]

Larkin's conflation, in a single sentence, of the Great War and Modernism is a typical Movement procedure: Eliot and Yeats (or, as Larkin prefers it in an interview with Ian Hamilton, Eliot and Pound)[10] are seen as the literary equivalent of the Somme, killing off through the fragmentation and foreignness of their work a secure and settled native continuity. The native continuity is emphatically English, not British or Anglo-American: Celts and Americans are felt to be disrupters. Larkin includes Yeats and Eliot (though not Pound) in his anthology, but his main purpose is to bring attention to poets whom he sees as being outside the Modern movement. Hardy, Housman, Kipling, de la Mare, Edward Thomas, Graves, Betjeman and Roy Fuller are among those generously represented. In this way tradition is re-ordered so that the Modernists have less of a role than that usually allotted to them.

Donald Davie was one of the fiercest critics of Larkin's Oxford anthology, arguing in the *Listener* on 29 March 1973 that its attention to a large number of minor poets had condoned the amateurish and second-rate. Through the 1960s, when he was largely in reaction against the Movement, Davie frequently expressed the view that the rejection of Modernism by contemporary poets was an act of insularity and retrogression: 'The British imagination, it may be, has never to this day recovered from the shock of Passchendaele; and the damage to it there puts the British writer out of step with the American, not just Graves out of step with Eliot, but at the present day Larkin and Hughes out of step with Charles Olson and William Stafford.'[11] Nevertheless, as the reasoning above makes clear, much the same assumptions as influenced Larkin's Oxford choices—the interruption of native literature by the Great War, the opposition between English and American traditions which has followed ever since— control Davie's critical thinking. When in 1973 he came to reconsider the difference between English and American verse in *Thomas Hardy and British Poetry* ('British' sounds more acceptable to Davie because less insular, but the writers whom he chooses to study are all English),

Davie was prepared to make larger claims for the non-Modernist tradition coming from Hardy. Though ambivalence runs through it, his essential enterprise is to legitimize the procedures of contemporary English poets by establishing their pedigree:

> Some of the features of later British poetry which have baffled and offended readers, especially in America — I have in mind an apparent meanness of spirit, a painful modesty of intention, extremely limited objectives — fall into place if they are seen as part of an inheritance from Hardy, an attempt to work out problems, especially social and political problems, which Hardy's poetry has posed for the twentieth century. And I hope to do more than merely excuse these characteristics of writing in the Hardyesque tradition; I want to present them as challenging, and to ask in effect, 'Are not Hardy and his successors right in severely curtailing for themselves the liberties that other poets continue to take? Does not the example of the Hardyesque poets make some of those other poets look childishly irresponsible?'[12]

Davie, it will be noticed is not primarily concerned with the reputation of Hardy. Rather, he is concerned to demonstrate the existence of a 'Hardyesque tradition' into which contemporary writers fit, and thereby to show that seemingly regrettable features of contemporary writing are, after all, acceptable. This seems a very odd way to justify contemporary writing—the Movement is to be presented as 'challenging' not because it has broken with the past, but because it has remained faithful to it; vices are to become virtues if precedents for them can be established—and the assumptions behind the procedure point, once again, to a conservatism within the Movement group: in poetry and in politics, and increasingly so after 1956, the Movement tendency is to be reverential towards long-established English traditions. A political equivalent to Davie's concern with tradition can be found, for instance, in John Wain's essay 'How It Strikes a Contemporary' (1957), where despite not being an attender of public schools himself (few Movement poets were), and despite feeling the public school-system to be unjust, Wain defends public schools on the grounds that they provide a much-needed 'continuity' and 'tradition' in English life. The 'Establishment'—'the property-owning aristocracy and *bourgeoisie*'—must also be preserved, since, 'wasteful and clumsy as it is, it does at least provide a channel through which, in this perilous passage of our history, a native, 'English' set of attitudes can flow, relatively intact, from the past towards the future.'[13] Wain and Davie believe that they can justify the reprehensible by placing it within a tradition.

The Movement's literary conservatism was partly a consequence of their exposure, as undergraduates at Oxford and Cambridge, and later as lecturers in English, to the criticism of F. R. Leavis and T. S. Eliot, both of whom laid great emphasis upon tradition. 'From the moment I got to Cambridge,' Davie has said, 'nothing did I hear from my teachers but "tradition". It was represented as something problematical, hard to get hold of, easily confounded with impostures. In particular it was supposed that I began with a prejudice against it.'[14] Leavis was one of Davie's teachers at Cambridge, and it may have been his stress on the social responsibilities involved in it which gave the undergraduate Davie the impression that tradition was a matter of great importance. In his 'Towards Standards of Criticism' (1933), for example, Leavis had brought tradition within his theory of cultural disintegration, arguing that the preservation of literary tradition has a more than literary significance: 'The fact that the other traditional continuities have . . . so completely disintegrated makes the literary tradition correspondingly more important, since the continuity of consciousness, the conservation of collective experience, is the more dependent on it: if the literary tradition is allowed to lapse, the gap is complete.'[15] It is easy to see how Leavis's dialectic of continuity and gap, preservation and disintegration, might lie behind Movement texts like 'MCMXIV', *Thomas Hardy and British Poetry,* and Wain's 'How It Strikes a Contemporary'.

Leavis was himself indebted to T. S. Eliot, whose essay 'Tradition and the Individual Talent' (1919) had removed the pejorative connotations of the word 'tradition'—'blind and timid adherence' to outdated conventions—by introducing the idea of an active and fruitful relationship between present and past. For Eliot, the good contemporary writer is always very aware of the past; his 'significance' lies in his 'appreciation of his relation to the dead poets and artists', and this involves him in 'great difficulties and responsibilities':

The existing monuments form an ideal order among themselves, which is modified by the introduction of the new (the really new) work of art among them. The existing order is complete before the new work arrives; for order to persist after the supervention of novelty, the *whole* existing order must be, if ever so slightly, altered . . . The past should be altered by the present as much as the present is directed by the past. And the poet who is aware of this will be aware of great difficulties and responsibilities.

The gravity of the tone and phrasing here is Eliot's way of making his at the time controversial theory of tradition acceptable to the academies. The gravity certainly communicated itself to Leavis, and thence to the Movement: tradition, they learnt, was a serious matter. Similarly influential were Eliot's decrees that a poet 'cohere' and 'conform' with predecessors, and his reassurances that 'really new' works did not destroy or dislodge tradition, but rather 'ever so slightly altered' it. These ideas the Movement seem at times to have vulgarized, interpreting them so as to suggest that 'really new' works are the same as old ones, that writers become 'really new' by modelling themselves on their forebears. Eliot's essay might in this way be seen as contributing towards the Movement tendency to look backwards rather than forwards: the group slogan, 'consolidation', was one which the more cautious elements in Eliot's essay made possible. When Wain, for example, as early as 1953, claims that 'for years' in his literary work he has been 'focusing on those elements in the past which can, or could, vitalize the present',[16] he is bearing witness to the impact of Eliot's essay.

There was one aspect of Eliot's essay which caused disagreement in the group, however, and which may help to explain why Larkin should have made what seems by now to be the implausible claim that he had 'no belief in "tradition"'. The disagreement originated in Eliot's suggestion that a sense of tradition must be acquired consciously and laboriously: tradition 'cannot be inherited, and if you want it you must obtain it by great labour', 'the poet must be very conscious of the main current'. This divided the Movement, for while Davie and Wain, at one extreme, argued that any redefinition of tradition must be conscious and deliberate, and that a poet must have a sound grasp of literary history before he can write anything of distinction, Larkin, Enright and Holloway, at the other extreme, saw this as a too mechanical notion of tradition, and argued that any reordering that occurred would be unconscious and intuitive, and would come out of and after the poet's struggles to create a distinctive manner.

The flashpoint for this disagreement was Wain's essay 'The Writer's Prospect' (1956), which argued, with a rigidity which provoked Enright and Holloway to instant replies, that a poet must be fully conversant with his place in literary history in order to begin writing: 'The fact is that a grip on contemporary literary history is a necessity for anyone wishing to know what can usefully be done *next*. The time has gone by when a writer could just soldier on. Given the initial creative spark, there has to be some idea of the chart we are sailing by.'[17] In a letter to the next-but-one issue of the *London Magazine* (and later expanded into an essay), Enright objected to this picture of 'the writer sitting in a control tower, planning his life's work with maps and pins', suggesting that a procedure so self-conscious 'wasn't what Eliot intended'.[18] But the idea of conscious selection also recurs in Davie's broadcast, 'The Poet in the Imaginary Museum' (1957), where the poet (less in the control tower than in the ivory tower) is seen 'picking and choosing from among the styles of the past'[19] and, earlier, in Wain's 'The Reputation of Ezra Pound' (1955), which sets out to explain the specific problems of redefining tradition faced by post-1945 poets:

After the war, there was a good deal of reconstruction to be done in the arts, and the poet who was just setting out on his life's work had a pretty hard job of selection to do. His first question was the hardest: where was help and technical guidance to come from? . . . It was rather like being confronted with a smashed-up tangle of railway lines and wondering which one to repair first. . . . The '30's were no use, at any rate as far as the main line was concerned, the Auden line: it was worn out even before it got smashed, and what smashed it decisively was not the war, but Auden's renunciation of English nationality . . . My own answer, which certainly got plenty of support once it was voiced, was that the Empson track was the best one to repair . . . The Empson boom that followed took me, and I think everyone, by surprise, but at least it showed that there had been some sense in the suggestion . . .[20]

Wain's imagery in these two articles—the poet as navigator, the poet as railway engineer—suggests a literally too mechanical application of what Leavis and Eliot had had to say about 'lines' of tradition. Though he did not name Wain, it was clearly to him that Holloway was referring when, in 1957, he parodied what he was later to call the 'rollingstock' theory of tradition: 'Tradition, or rather, more tendentiously, *the* tradition (chosen one among rejected many) is a writer's forebears, who have taken writing as if along a railway line to a point N. The new writer then identifies the line, and follows out the communal direction to N + I . . . There is no need to press this further. The kind of achievement one can hope, and the kind one cannot hope, to get from it is clear enough.'[21] Holloway's views were shared by Larkin, who in an interview in 1964 ridiculed the notion 'that every poem must include all previous poems, in the same way that a Ford Zephyr has somewhere in it a Ford T Model.'[22]

Though Wain and Davie were the immediate targets for Larkin here, it is Eliot's view of tradition which he means to reject. Eliot had talked in 'Tradition and the Individual Talent' of the need for a poet to be aware of 'the mind of Europe', arguing that no poet of worth 'can form himself wholly on private admirations'. Larkin, in deliberate contrast, has said that 'a style is much more likely to be formed from partial slipshod sampling than from the coherent acquisition of a literary education'.[23] He has also emphasized his own dependence upon private admirations. His description of how he changed allegiance from Yeats to Hardy, for instance, seems designed to provoke those who represent the reorientation of tradition as a matter of solemn and carefully pondered choice. Until 1946, Larkin explains in his introduction to *The North Ship,* he had been writing like Yeats, partly because he was 'isolated in Shropshire with a complete Yeats stolen from the local girls' school' but 'in early 1946 I had some new digs in which the bedroom faced east, so that the sun woke me inconveniently early. I used to read. One book I had at my bedside was the little blue *Chosen Poems of Thomas Hardy'.* This leading example of an important 'adjustment' of literary tradition--Larkin's rejection of Yeats for Hardy, and the change in mid-twentieth century English poetry which resulted from it—is represented as a matter of chance, not choice.

These disagreements with Eliot help to explain why Larkin should have declared a lack of belief in 'tradition'. They also point towards the divergences in attitude which were eventually to 'break up' the Movement; the varying sympathies shown towards Eliot and Modernism (with Davie and Larkin, for example, ranged on opposite sides) were to become increasingly important in the 1960s. But in the 1950s these differences seemed of less consequence than the consensus over 'what had to be done'. There might be disagreement about Eliot's criticism but there was agreement that the direction taken by Eliot's poetry was not one which contemporary poets should follow. The 'new' tradition to be followed was the 'old' tradition of 1914—an English tradition which Eliot, Pound, and the Great War had seemingly interrupted, and one in which Larkin would certainly have been willing to declare his belief.

II

> . . . some lump of English clay
> Grounds me, and makes me grudge the play
> Of mind, the freedom of it.
> > Davie, 'Six Epistles to Eva Hesse'

Larkin's image of Georgian England in 'MCMXIV' is an image not just of 'innocence', but of stability: the gardens are 'tidy', the marriages unbroken, the names 'established'. To the Movement, one of the most important features of the pre-Modernist English tradition was, likewise, its stability. It was this which had Amis and Wain looking back in their novels to the Realist tradition of Bennett, Wells and Orwell: here was felt to be an order and comprehensibility missing from Modernist novelists like Virginia Woolf. As fiction reviewer for the *Spectator* in the mid-1950s, Amis attacked what he called 'the idea about experiment being the life-blood of the English novel',[24] and in *I Like It Here* he sends his hero Garnet Bowen to visit Fielding's tomb and to pay respect to that novelist's moral decency—'he had been a good chap'. As Wain has said, the typical Movement novel 'did not try to continue the work of James, Proust, Joyce, et al . . . . Instead, older models neglected for a century, were reverted to'.[25]

In poetry there was a similar emphasis on restoring what was thought of as being the unity and order of pre-Modernism. After a period in which the possibilities of free verse had been opened up, 'tidy' forms (villanelle, sonnet, quatrain) and 'established' metrical laws (full rhyme, iambic pentameter) were once again the norm. In their statements for Enright's *Poets of the 1950's,* Amis talked about 'a desire to be lucid if nothing else, and a liking for strict and fairly simple verse forms'; Wain said that he aimed for 'poise, coherence, and a logical *raison d'être* for every word, image and metaphor used'; and Davie said that while he 'honour[ed] the poets, English, Irish and American, who revolutionized English poetry', he

had in his own poetry 'tried to reinstate some of the traditional disciplines (e.g. strict metric)'. When, in a 1956 special
issue of the Cambridge magazine *Delta*, it was mooted that,
because of its refusal of the 'open' forms made available by
Modernist poetry, the Movement might be thought of as
reactionary and archaic, Davie vigorously disputed the point:
'The metrical and other habits of English verse seem to me to
be in no sense "arbitrary", but rather to be rooted in the
nature of English as a spoken and written language; I can see
no other explanation of the fact that the rules which, say, Mr
Amis and Mr Graves observe are the rules which have governed
ninety percent of English poetry for more than 500 years.'[26]

This is not a particularly distinguished defence of the Movement: put crudely, it sounds as if Davie is saying that what
was good enough for his grandfathers and great-grandfathers
(though not for his fathers, the Modernists) is good enough
for him. But in his discussions of syntax in *Purity of Diction
in English Verse* and *Articulate Energy,* he had produced more
ingenious defences of the Movement's reversion to pre-Modernist tradition. To observe rules of traditional syntax, rather
than to abandon them as the Modernists had done, was, he
suggested, to act in the interests of social order and continuity:
'Systems of syntax are part of the heritable property of past
civilization, and to hold firm to them is to be traditional in
the best and most important sense'.[27] Developing Leavis,
who in *The Great Tradition* had described Joyce's *Ulysses*
as 'a pointer to disintegration', Davie connects Modernism
less with the 'fragmentation' of the Great War, than with the
development of Fascism. In a remarkable passage in *Purity of
Diction* he argues that Pound's Imagist disruption of syntax
was intimately bound up with his support for Mussolini:

By hunting his own sort of 'definiteness' (truth only in the particular)
he [Pound] is led to put his trust not in human institutions but in individuals. Similarly he pins his faith on individual words, grunts, broken
phrases, half-uttered exclamations (as we find them in the *Cantos*), on
speech atomized, all syllogistic and syntactical forms broken down.

Hence his own esteem of the definite lands him at last in yawning vagueness, the 'intuitive' welcome to Mussolini . . .

It would be too much to say that this is the logical end of abandoning prose syntax. But at least·the development from imagism in poetry to fascism in politics is clear and unbroken . . . It is impossible not to trace a connection between the laws of syntax and the laws of society, between bodies of usage in speech and in social life, between tearing a word from its context and choosing a leader out of the ruck. One could almost say, on this showing, that to dislocate syntax in poetry is to threaten the rule of law in the civilized community.[28]

'On this showing' (to use one of Davie's favourite phrases), the Movement's restoration of ordered syntax and rational modes becomes a democratic ·act. And whereas Modernism is associated with the outrages of recent history, the English tradition which preceded it (and which the Movement intends to make follow it) is endowed with political 'innocence' and goodness. A writer like Thomas Hardy might occasionally sound jingoistic, but his politics did not seem to the Movement to be 'dangerous' in the way that the politics of Yeats, Lawrence, Pound and Wyndham Lewis were dangerous. Hardy's tight forms and his level tone guaranteed his political reliability: as Davie puts it, 'Hardy is the one poetic imagination of the first magnitude in the present century who writes out of, and embodies in his poems, political and social attitudes which a social democrat recognizes as "liberal"'.[29]

Most of the writers to whom the Movement looked back were judged to be 'liberal' or 'liberal humanist' in their outlook—moderate, tolerant, democratic, as progressive as an instinctive wariness of progress allowed. Their tone is warm, sympathetic, even compassionate, but they are doubtful of the power of political reform to eradicate human suffering, and tend to avoid becoming too 'involved' in politics. Hardy was felt to be father of this tradition, and a poem like Davie's 'Among Artisans' Houses' might be seen as Hardyesque in principle. Published in 1950, it is the earliest example of Davie's concern with civic responsibility—or what he here calls 'civil sense'. The poem describes Plymouth, a town which survived heavy Second World War bombing, and where, Davie suggests, 'continuity is clear/From Drake to now'. In the town's architectural arrangements, Davie identifies the presence of 'mutual respect'; the closely-packed 'terraced houses' are a 'moral shape of politics', symbolizing communal and democratic values:

> There are not many notice this
> Resourcefulness of citizens,
> And few esteem it. But it is
> An outcome of the civil sense,
> Its small and mean utilities;
> A civilization, in its way,
> Its rudiments or its decay.

Davie's poem makes no reference to Hardy, and its one striking parallel is not to Hardy but to Roy Fuller: the line 'plots are furiously neat' echoes Fuller's poem 'The Emotion of Fiction', which admires plots—not of houses, but of novels—which have 'virtues of furious neatness'. But Davie's poem contains several of the characteristics which he has since come to call Hardyesque. It is concerned to find 'continuity', to show the persistence of 'the past'. It is level-toned, self-qualifying and sceptical, knowing that democratic 'mutual respect' is unexciting but upholding it nevertheless. And it is resigned to the limitations of the actual, rather than, as a Modernist poem might be, dazzled by an image of the 'Just City' which makes the existing order seem tawdry and contemptible. Davie might have worried that his 'cramped and cramping tone' in the poem represented, as he has since said Hardy's did, a selling short of the poetic vocation; but he would like to believe that the poem's political vision is 'decent' and 'liberal' in a Hardyesque, and perhaps Orwellian, way.

The liberalism of the English tradition which the Movement wished to restore is importantly related to the poet's general stance: he writes as an observer who pities those (usually less fortunate than himself) whom he sees around him. Here the key precursor was less Hardy than Wilfred Owen, a poet who has often been seen as a Modernist, but whom the Movement writers tended to think of as a descendant of Hardy.[30] They also linked him to the Georgians, feeling that this was not to diminish his reputation since the Georgians had been an under-rated literary movement (Owen himself had boasted 'I am held peer by the Georgians'). Owen and the Georgians, it was thought, shared the view that a poem could serve as a vehicle for compassion or 'pity'. Conquest praised them because 'they spoke as man to man, not as priest to acolyte', and Larkin has said that their movement 'represented a robust, zestful upsurge of realism'.[31] The Georgian poets, like the Movement, lived through a period of Welfare reform (Lloyd George as Chancellor of the Exchequer pushed through several taxation and national insurance measures), and their poems are often about some 'underdog' and victim. De la Mare's 'Miss Loo', W. H. Davies's 'The Heaps of Rags' and 'The Bird of Paradise', Wilfred Gibson's 'Geraniums' and 'The Gorse', the war poems of Siegfried Sassoon and Wilfred Owen: these formed a liberal and (in Larkin's sense) 'realist' tradition which the Movement admired.

Larkin's 'Mr Bleaney' is a poem indebted to this English tradition. In its pity for a passive victim, it resembles, for example, Owen's 'Disabled'. The literal disability of Owen's youth becomes the figurative disability of Larkin's Bleaney, a man with very limited control over his movements and desires. Both are imprisoned in a bleak interior and controlled by an unseen 'they':

> How cold and late it is! Why don't they come
> And put him into bed? Why don't they come?
>
> (Owen)

> 'This was Mr Bleaney's room. He stayed
> The whole time he was at the Bodies, till
> They moved him.'
>
> (Larkin)

Both poems communicate the 'disability' of their victim through the imagery of death, isolation and sterility. Owen's youth is pictured 'waiting for dark' in a 'ghastly suit of grey', and although he wants to be 'put into bed' he is now deprived of sexual experience: girls 'touch him like some queer disease'. Bleaney's room is described as a coffin-like 'hired box', his bed is 'fusty', and the only social contact he has is with his landlady, his sister, and 'the Frinton folk/Who put him up for summer holidays'. Coldness is another image crucial to both poems. Owen uses the word 'shivered' in the second line, and in the penultimate one the speaker reflects 'How cold and late it is!' The words 'shivered' and 'frigid' also occur in the last two stanzas of 'Mr Bleaney':

> But if he stood and watched the frigid wind
> Tousling the clouds, lay on the fusty bed
> Telling himself that this was home, and grinned,
> And shivered, without shaking off the dread
>
> That how we live measures our own nature,
> And at his age having no more to show
> Than one hired box should make him pretty sure
> He warranted no better, I don't know.

The syntactical incompleteness of these stanzas (though modified by the balance of 'I don't know' with the earlier 'I know'), is perhaps the equivalent of a shiver of 'dread' which passes through the speaker as he realizes that, though different from Bleaney, he may himself continue the cycle of passivity. In this introduction of a second person (the persona), Larkin's poem is richer than Owen's, more than merely 'pitying'. But the sympathy which it extends, and the realistic detail, are very similar to Owen's. The language, too, occasionally recalls that of Georgian verse: the phrase 'shaking off the dread' echoes the following lines from Sassoon's 'Haunted', which appears in the 1916–17 *Georgian Poetry* anthology:

> He thought: 'Somewhere there's thunder,' as he strove
> To shake off dread; he dared not look behind him.

Hilary Corke's view of 1950s poetry as being 'Georgian' in tendency[32] therefore has some appropriateness, but would not have seemed to the poets concerned to be a self-evident criticism: as Davie puts it, 'if only today we could write as well as these men did at their best!'[33] What the Movement most valuably derived from Owen and the Georgians was a capacity to enter imaginatively into the lives of others. Larkin's 'Deceptions', 'Love Songs in Age', 'Afternoons' and 'The Building'; Enright's 'Black Country Women' and 'Children Killed in War'; Gunn's 'From the Highest Camp', 'Black Jackets' and *Positives*; Jennings's 'My Grandmother' and 'Old Women': these are Movement texts whose sympathies and insights can be seen as part of a liberal humanist tradition to which, in the inaugural years of the Welfare State, it seemed appropriate to return.

The liberal humanist strain in the English tradition was often invoked when the Movement tried to meet the objection that they were promoting a minor and insular literature. In a 1964 review, Davie admitted that English poetry 'had suffered' through following Owen's 'humanitarian' example, but argued that 'failure on these terms is almost more honourable than success'.[34] Amis, too, believed that 'minor' English literature possessed qualities missing from Modernist literature: 'The one unifying characteristic of our giants—the Jameses, the Woolfs, the Lawrences—was the immense seriousness with which they took themselves . . . To be spared all that for the time being, even if it means forgoing some real talent, is not total disaster. There is some ground for equanimity in looking foward to an era of minor literature.'[35] To be small was to be both beautiful and humane. Irony, modesty, humour, sensitivity, attention to the 'ordinary' and domestic (rather than to the grand and heroic): these, it was thought, were more likely to be found in 'minor' than in 'major' literature. Long and ambitious works were often, Amis suggested, the mark of a poet lacking concern for the 'human': 'A correlation emerges between a proneness to the more spacious or inflatable poetic forms and an indifference to what has often been considered the prime literary subject, relations between human beings.'[36]

The Movement was also prepared to affirm that certain writers had managed to work outside the Modernist tradition, and yet to write poetry which was neither trivial nor backward-looking. The figure most often cited in such instances was Robert Graves, whose example several Movement poets applauded. The Movement's view of Graves as an anti-Modernist required a certain amount of distortion. In the 1920s Graves had collaborated with Laura Riding on *A Survey of Modernist Poetry* (1927), a work which was critical of the Georgians and 'Modern' in spirit. On the other hand, Graves had been a contributor to the Georgian anthologies and by the 1950s began to express hostility to Modernism. In his 1955 Clark lectures he attacked the 'idolatry' of Modernism and its 'five living idols—namely Yeats, Pound, Eliot, Auden, and Dylan Thomas', and was more willing to acknowledge his participation in the Georgian movement: 'it has meant a great deal to me that I once lived on terms of friendship with my elders Thomas Hardy and William Davies, and with men of my own age like Wilfred Owen and Norman Cameron.'[37] The Movement seized on the implications of Graves's disenchantment with Modernism. Enright, for example, in an essay called 'Robert Graves and the Decline of Modernism' (1960), claimed that 'as you can trace in the work of one poet, Yeats, the decline of late romanticism and the rise of modernism, . . . so in the history of Graves's reputation you can trace the rise of modernism and its present decline.'[38] Modernism, the Movement used Graves to suggest, was no longer modern. 'The innovations of that time,' Conquest claimed, 'are seen to be peripheral additions to the main tradition of English poetry'. Wain made a similar point: 'already some of the characteristically modern poetry, making the most whole-hearted use of those techniques and attitudes which first earned the name, is beginning to seem old-fashioned.'[39]

Though all the Movement looked to Graves as a poet who had shown the possibilities inherent in a non-Modernist tradition, different members of the group responded to different qualities in his work. Gunn was the Movement poet most responsive to Graves's use of riddle, emblem and magic. His 'A Secret Sharer', though partly based on a personal experience,[40] may owe something to 'The Foreboding', which appeared in Graves's *Poems, 1953*. Graves describes a disembodied speaker observing himself:

> Looking by chance in at the open window
> I saw my own self seated in his chair
> With gaze abstracted, furrowed forehead,
> Unkempt hair.

Gunn's poem, which takes its title from a Conrad short story, also uses the idea of the Gothic *doppelgänger*. The speaker gazes up at the window hoping that his 'other self' will appear:

> Over the ankles in snow and numb past pain
> I stared up at my window three stories high:
> From a white street unconcerned as a dead eye,
> I patiently called my name again and again.
>
> The curtains were lit, through glass were lit by doubt.
> And there was I, within the room alone.
> In the empty wind I stood and shouted on:
> But O, what if the strange head should peer out?

But in preferring the 'enchanted' to the 'disenchanted' Graves, Gunn is an exception. As Holloway points out, 'the imaginativeness and strangeness of Robert Graves' were largely 'ignored' by the Movement: 'what has been learnt from him is a less remarkable but less tricky quality, his dry, depreciatory, yet often tolerant tone.'[41] In particular, the Movement turned to him for instruction in the art of disabusement. His poems are often sceptically structured, an initial statement of false or facile sentiment (often presented in italics or within quotation marks) being quickly checked: 'At First Sight', for example, deflates romantic cliché: '"Love at first sight" some say, misnaming/Discovery of twinned helplessness'. 'Change' works rather similarly:

'This year she has changed greatly' — meaning you —
My sanguine friends agree,
Hoping thereby to reassure me.

No, child, you never change; neither do I.

Graves's unmaskings look forward to Movement poems like
Larkin's 'Next Please' and Jennings's 'Summer and Time', both
of which follow a conventional superficiality—'we say'—with
a disillusioned rejoinder—'But we are wrong'. A considerable
number of Movement poems are, indeed, simple Gravesian
unmaskings of deceit. That memory is unreliable, that fulfilment rarely matches expectation, that other people's characters are our own projections, that things, in short, are not
what they seem: these pieces of conventional wisdom occupy
a large, indeed an unduly large, place in Movement poetry.
Over half the poems in Amis's *A Case of Samples,* for example,
make it their duty to expose the gap between a purported
and an actual truth, and a good many of these are indebted
to Graves. 'Departure', 'The End', 'The Silent Room', and
'The Sources of the Past' all have their origins in Graves's
work, and make it understandable why, to his description of
Amis as an 'utterly original' poet, Larkin should have added
the important qualification' '(this is when he is being himself,
not when he's Robert Graves)'.[42]

The Movement believed that Graves's ability to see through
deception was a typical characteristic of the native temperament. Modernist poets, precisely because so few of them were
English, had ignored the value to poetry of scepticism and
empiricism; they had interested themselves in transcendental
religions, mystical philosophies, utopian politics. As a result,
Davie argues, Modernist writers 'claim, by implication or else
explicitly, to give us entry through their poems into a world
that is truer and more real than the world we know from
statistics or scientific induction or common sense'. But in
the English tradition dominated by Hardy, he suggests, notions
of transcendence are regarded with suspicion: 'Hardy appears
to have mistrusted, and certainly leads other poets to mistrust,

the claims of poetry to transcend the linear unrolling of recorded time'.[43] After the mysticism and dramatic urgency of Yeats, Larkin came to Hardy with what he calls a 'sense of relief that I didn't have to try and jack myself up to a concept of poetry that lay outside my own life.'[44] Hardy and Graves helped the Movement to have the courage of their temperamental and professional leaning towards scepticism, empiricism, verification. Holloway, for example, seems to exalt on several occasions in his poetry a 'modest, half-indifferent trust/ In down to earth things, common sense', defiantly asserting as poetic qualities normally held to be prosaic or 'academic':

> Look, we desire evidence. Evidence is found
> By thought; persistence; suspicion; enquiry. Drudging
> Through rubbish for the occasional jewel. Trudging
> Backwards and forwards over the same ground
> Till people ask you satirically what you've found.
>
> ('Two Friendly Sonnets')

> But I have other virtues that
> I've cultivated here and there:
> Industry, pride and tolerance,
> A love of detail, and a care
> For what is true rather than what
> Just seems to be so at first glance . . .
>
> ('The Petty Testament of Peter the Clerk')

A poem with the kind of scepticism to which the Movement was attracted is Hardy's 'In Church'. This is not one of his most famous poems, nor one of his best, but its unmasking of the 'guile' of a religious preacher was influential:

> 'And now to God the Father,' he ends,
> And his voice thrills up to the topmost tiles:
> Each listener chokes as he bows and bends,
> And emotion pervades the crowded aisles.
> The preacher glides to the vestry-door,
> And shuts it, and thinks he is seen no more.

> The door swings softly ajar meanwhile,
> And a pupil of his in the Bible class,

> Who adores him without gloss or guile,
> Sees her idol stand with a satisfied smile
> And re-enact at the vestry-glass
> Each pulpit gesture in the deft dumb-show
> That had moved the congregation so.

The exposure is lightly handled: Hardy is amused by, rather than outraged at, one of life's little ironies. But a concern to show 'what is true rather than what/Just seems so at first glance' is what determines his poem's form. The critic who recently detected in Larkin's poems a 'tripartite structure' ('situation—impulsive response—"less deceived" response')[45] could have added that such a structure reproduces that to be found in many of Hardy's poems. It is not, at any rate, hard to see how 'In Church' might lie behind two Movement poems about religious guile, Davie's 'The Evangelist' and Larkin's 'Faith Healing'. Davie's speaker may well be a believer (he is certainly someone sufficiently concerned with religion to be a church-attender), but he refuses to 'believe' in a Dissenting minister whose sermon he attends. Like Hardy, Davie exposes the dissembling which he perceives in the minister's performance:

> 'My brethren . . .' And a bland, elastic smile
> Basks on the mobile features of Dissent.
> No hypocrite, you understand. The style
> Befits a church that's based on sentiment.
>
> Solicitations of a swirling gown,
> The sudden vox humana, and the pause,
> The expert orchestration of a frown
> Deserve, no doubt, a murmur of applause . . .
>
> You round upon me, generously keen:
> The man, you say, is patently sincere.
> Because he is so eloquent, you mean?
> That test was never patented, my dear.

The 'you' here is the poet's wife, but might equally well be an imaginary reader: Davie challenges that 'you', daring to affirm mistrust as a virtue, and remaining unmoved by 'the tides of feeling' around him. He is, in his own words, 'fastidious', but does not feel this to be a matter for apology.

Larkin's 'Faith Healing' has in common with Davie's poem a sceptical Movement persona: that of someone who stands apart from, and remains unimpressed by, a religious ceremony. Like Davie's, Larkin's speaker mistrusts pulpit eloquence: to him it is synonymous with insincerity. (A similar view can also be found in 'Sunday', from Enright's *The Terrible Shears*: 'The churches were run by a picked crew/Of bad actors radiating insincerity'.) The streamlined efficiency of the American salvationist (for Larkin, 'American' is in itself sufficient to denote blandness) is contrasted with the hesitancy and awkwardness of the women who are brought to him. They are 'stiff, twitching', 'hoarse', 'dumb', and 'their thick tongues blort'; the healer scarcely pauses to listen to them before offering a prayer:

> Slowly the women file to where he stands
> Upright in rimless glasses, silver hair,
> Dark suit, white collar. Stewards tirelessly
> Persuade them onwards to his voice and hands,
> Within whose warm spring rain of loving care
> Each dwells some twenty seconds. *Now, dear child,*
> *What's wrong*, the deep American voice demands,
> And, scarcely pausing, goes into a prayer
> Directing God about this eye, that knee.

'Faith Healing' does not sustain the almost satirical note of this opening stanza, a note which was probably prompted by Billy Graham's visits to England in the 1950s. Larkin's conviction that what brings people to seek religion is an unquenchable need for love—'a sense of life lived according to love', a sense of 'all they might have done had they been loved', but a sense which 'nothing cures'—makes his climax more moving than Davie's. Larkin is also more concerned than Davie to focus sympathetic attention on those abused by the religious ceremony: he identifies with the clumsiness of the women by leaving the last sentence of his poem syntactically confused

and awkward. Larkin's poem is for this reason a richer contribution to the English tradition than Davie's. It draws not only
on Hardy's scepticism, but on his sadness and 'beautiful
clumsiness'.[46] It is not only 'sense', but what Graves called
(in his definition of poetry) 'sense; good sense; penetrating,
often heart-rending sense'.[47]

But 'sense', the central feature of that English tradition
rediscovered by the Movement, is not something which it is
very easy to admire in poetry. When the Movement poets
dramatize themselves as stubborn, pragmatic, dragged down-
wards by a 'lump of English clay', when critics accuse them
of failing to be generous or uplifting, when Davie, in his recent
book, ponders whether Hardy and Larkin may not have 'sold
poetry short'—in all these instances one can see the same basic
questions being asked: how can a poetry so concerned to
unmask and deny also be in some degree affirmative? how can
an empirical, obstinately 'sensible' poetic temperament nevertheless be capable of providing its audience with some kind
of faith (faith being a venture beyond what can be verified
and proved)? These questions are clearly of importance in
poems where the context is a religious one, where a refusal to
believe becomes a matter of more-than-ordinary significance.
Hardy's 'In Church', Davie's 'The Evangelist' and Larkin's
'Faith Healing' are poems in which this issue of tradition and
belief are touched on. There is one other poem, Larkin's
'Church Going', in which it is central.

III

He says he thinks there is no God
And yet he comes . . . it's rather odd.
                    John Betjeman, 'Diary of a Church Mouse'

Strange, that a sense of religion should
Somehow survive all this grim buffoonery!
                    Enright, 'Sunday'

'Church Going' was published in the *Spectator* on 18 November 1955, appeared also in Larkin's collection of that year, *The Less Deceived* and in 1956 was anthologized in *New Lines*. Although written at the time of the Movement's greatest coherence, made available through a Movement periodical and anthology, and widely regarded as one of the best poems by any writer associated with the Movement, 'Church Going' has not been seen as a characteristically Movement work. David Timms, speaking for those critics who prefer to see Larkin as an individual talent rather than as someone who drew on a group identity, questions whether it is really 'in the Movement manner', and a TLS reviewer in 1958, while conceding that the poem's uniqueness did not prevent it from being the product of a literary movement, insisted that the poem ran contrary to the Movement's critical theory: 'The best poems, in fact, of any "movement" tend to break the theoretical mould of that movement (neither "Tintern Abbey" nor "The Ancient Mariner", it has been pointed out, can really be justified on the critical principles of Wordsworth's Preface to *Lyrical Ballads*).'[48] But 'Church Going' *does* observe the best principles of the Movement programme. In it Larkin expresses something of the social identity of the group; he addresses himself to the inner confederacy while writing a public poem for the community; he remains true, especially in his dramatization of the poet as an 'ordinary', fallible citizen, to the Movement's anti-Romantic aesthetic; and he embodies many of the values of the 'interrupted' English tradition.

'Church Going' was written out of, and in the act of being written gave clearer expression to, an interesting division in the Movement's religious identity. That identity was, on the one hand, firmly agnostic. Only Elizabeth Jennings of the group was a practising Christian, and there are several Movement texts which repudiate traditional Christian belief. In Larkin's work, for instance, there is no sense of an after-life. His 'Next Please' suggests that in the 'wake' of death 'no waters breed or break'; 'The Old Fools' that when you die 'you can't pretend/There'll be anything else'; the recent 'Aubade', published in the TLS on 23 December 1977, that religion is a 'vast moth-eaten musical brocade/Created to pretend we never die', and that the after-life is really 'total emptiness for ever':

> . . . this is what we fear — no sight, no sound,
> No touch or taste or smell, nothing to think with,
> Nothing to love or link with,
> The anaesthetic from which none come round.

Larkin is usually fearful but stoical in the face of mortality— as Hardy and Owen were in much of their verse. But Hardy and Owen are also occasionally indignant towards an Unseen Creator or Immanent Will, and this pose of indignation can be found in the work of Amis. His 'New Approach Needed' asks Christ to 'get some service in' before returning to earth, and in 'The Huge Artifice' Amis depicts God as a novelist whose fiction has 'not often been surpassed/For ignorance or downright nastiness'. 'To believe at all deeply in the Christian God,' Ayscue announces in *The Anti-Death League* (1966), '. . . is a disgrace to human decency and intelligence'. Other Movement writers might put it less strongly, but their scepticism largely restrains them from subscribing to Christian belief. A conversation in Amis's *The Green Man* (1969) seems to sum it up: '"Maurice, I take it you don't allow any possibility of survival after death?" "Christ no. I've never believed in any of that crap"'.

Working against this disbelief, though, were a number of

factors which made the Movement more preoccupied with religion than might be expected of a group of mid-twentieth-century agnostics. In the first place, the Movement writers tended to come from homes in which religion was still treated as a matter of seriousness and importance. Several of them had had Nonconformist upbringings, and liked to think of Nonconformists not as petty bourgeois and conventionalized but as an embattled minority vigorously asserting independence. Davie, for example, has recently explored the cultural and religious heritage of Dissent, presenting it as rich and challenging.[49] In such families, memories were passed down of a period when religion was a major part of most lives. Wain, who in *Sprightly Running* described his parents as 'Christians of the extreme Low-Church variety'—adding, as if seeking the associations of the Movement's 'Nonconformist' label, 'why they were not actually Nonconformists I shall never understand'—draws on such family memories in a 1957 essay 'Along the Tightrope'. Once again, the year 1914 is seen as a crucial turning-point:

Before 1914, if a tradesman wanted the custom of solid citizens, he had to turn up at church, and see to it that his family turned up with him; a doctor or solicitor who wanted to establish his practice couldn't afford to be known as a Freethinker; his place was at morning service with the respectable world. So the churches were always full. Then came the war, and a general untying of this kind of social corsetry; the churches attracted one in ten of their previous congregations, mostly older people.[50]

The Movement writers knew that Church had once brought people together, and they tended to regret that (a play on words which Larkin exploits) instead of regular church-going, church was now going.

Wain also makes clear in *Sprightly Running* that the Oxford which he (and thus Larkin, Amis, Holloway and Jennings also) experienced as an undergraduate had 'a very considerable respect for Christianity'. Wain argues that partly because of the influence of C. S. Lewis, whose debating skills in defence of Christianity were much admired, partly because of the growing acceptance of T. S. Eliot's *Four Quartets* as a major work, and partly because of a 'sense of crisis and suffering' caused by the Second World War, Christianity exerted a powerful influence at Oxford in the 1940s: 'Everbody to whom an imaginative and bookish youth naturally looked up, every figure who radiated intellectual glamour of any kind, was in the Christian camp.' Wain adds that for him Christianity was intimately associated with the literature which he was reading at Oxford, so that the English Church seemed to be 'a mysterious and sacred building reared by our ancestors, including the men whose works I was studying with such loving concern'. Church for the Movement was yet another example of an English continuity now threatened with extinction.

It was this which modified the Movement impulse towards defiance and irreverence. Though agnostic, the Movement did not feel it appropriate to make actively anti-Christian gestures. 'I wouldn't have professed myself a practising and believing Christian,' Davie has said of those years, 'yet on the other hand I've never shared or understood the animus against Christianity as a hypocritical cheat.' Amis has made a similar comment about his army experiences in the 1940s: 'it was a point of honour with my generation never to opt for the slightest inconvenience on conscientious grounds of this kind. We let the army have its way and put "CE" on our identity discs, and were rather sophisticated with the occasional militant who insisted on "AGN(ostic)" or "N(o) R(eligion)". There seemed to be enough fuss about most things already'.[51]

The Movement identity is balanced, therefore, between an undemonstrative agnosticism on the one hand, and a susceptibility to the continuities of Christianity on the other: it is reverent as well as irreverent. One reason why 'Church Going' is a poem for the Movement confederacy is that it articulates this tension by featuring as its speaker someone who is at first bored and derisive—entering the church only when he is 'sure there's nothing going on', he briefly fools around inside it, before leaving with the thought 'the place was not worth stopping for'—but who, through his meditations on the function and history of the church, gradually gains a sense of its importance. Those who have found it difficult to reconcile the irreverent behaviour of the persona at the beginning of the poem with his solemnity at the end could do so more easily if they were aware of this characteristic Movement tension. 'Church Going' is a Movement poem because, while remaining, as Larkin says, 'entirely secular',[52] it nevertheless manages to justify if not the ways of God, then at least the place of church.

'Church Going' is not merely a poem for the Movement confederacy, however. Indeed, part of its success is the way in which it broadens an initially 'personal' experience into something much wider and more public in scope. The first two stanzas confine themselves to the details of a particular individual's church visit. But in the third stanza, through a barely perceptible replacement of 'I' with 'we', Larkin begins to universalize the experience. The problem of the place of church in a modern agnostic society is represented as one with which 'we' are all concerned:

> Yet stop I did: in fact I often do,
> And always end much at a loss like this,
> Wondering what to look for; wondering, too,
> When churches fall completely out of use
> What we shall turn them into, if we shall keep
> A few cathedrals chronically on show,
> Their parchment, plate and pyx in locked cases,
> And let the rest rent-free to rain and sheep.
> Shall we avoid them as unlucky places?

The attempt to reach out from the little audience to the large one is only one of several ways in which Larkin's poem might be seen as acting upon principles central to the Movement programme. It builds up in a series of clearly defined 'blocks' (seven stanzas with a regular ababcadcd rhyme-scheme and iambic pentameter), a structure which permits a lucid and rational argument to be developed. It is in places colloquial, but also revives outworn language in the manner prescribed by Davie in *Purity of Diction,* exploiting the unusual—'accoutred', 'frowsty', 'simples'—and reinforcing the solemn tone of the last stanza with a piece of poetic diction, 'blent', which appears in Yeats's 'Among Schoolchildren' ('it seemed that our two natures blent/Into a sphere from youthful sympathy') and in several poems by Hardy. Most important, 'Church Going' dramatizes the poetic persona not as a Romantic hero or outsider but as someone 'ordinary', fallible, clumsy:

> Hatless, I take off
> My cycle-clips in awkward reverence,
>
> Move forward, run my hand around the font.
> From where I stand, the roof looks almost new —
> Cleaned, or restored? Someone would know: I don't.

Larkin's debunking, uninformed and awkward persona prompted one reviewer to call 'Church Going' 'very much Lucky Jim's poem'.[53] This was disputed by John Wain, who wanted to show that the 'withdrawn, ironic, self-parodying persona' of 'Church Going' had a longer lineage than Dixon's buffoonery: 'in terms of ancestry, the central figure is descended from late nineteenth-century French poetry (Laforgue, Corbière), the intermediary being Mr Eliot's *Prufrock.*'[54] There are certainly connections between Eliot's Prufrock and the persona of 'Church Going', and since Larkin has been criticized for his 'refusal to take note of what had been done before 1890 in the ironic self-deprecating vein by Laforgue and Corbière, and to take his bearings accordingly',[55] it is useful of Wain to point to Larkin's possible participation in this tradition. Yet it is not at all clear that Larkin would have needed to look outside an exclusively English tradition to have learnt how to manage self-deprecation. For the awkwardness, self-derogation and discomfort in church of the 'Church Going' persona, Larkin might have looked not to Corbière's 'Le Poète Contumace', but to the stuttering choir boy who features in an early English poem called 'A Choir Training':

> Uncomly in cloistre I cowre ful of care;
> I looke as a lurdein and — listne til my lare —
> The song of ce-sol-fa does me silken sare
> And sitte stotiand on a song a moneth and mare.[56]

The point is not that Larkin had seen this particular poem when he wrote 'Church Going', but that there existed an indigenous tradition of which these 'Domesday lines' are an expression. Upon more recent texts from that tradition he certainly did draw. Hardy and Graves, for example, were able to provide him with precedents for his 'bored, uninformed' speaker. Hardy's 'Afternoon Service in Mellstock' describes a childhood experience in church which is both uninformed ('mindless') and bored (the boy's attention wanders to the scene outside); yet from the hindsight of later life, Hardy affirms the importance of the experience:

> We watched the elms, we watched the rooks,
>   The clouds upon the breeze,
> Between the whiles of glancing at our books,
>   And swaying like the trees.
>
> So mindless were those outpourings! —
>   Though I am not aware
> That I have gained by subtle thought on things
>   Since we stood psalming there.

Graves's 'The Boy in Church' also recounts a childhood experience of church, and follows the same development from boredom and detachment—

> 'Gabble-gabble . . . brethren . . . gabble-gabble!'
>   My window glimpses larch and heather.
> I hardly hear the tuneful babble,
>   Not knowing nor much caring whether
> The text is praise or exhortation
> Prayer or thanksgiving or damnation.

—to appreciation of the solidity which the church provides:

> . . . I like this church.
> The pews are staid, they never shiver,
>   They never bend or sway or lurch.

These two poems might be thought too slight, because mainly childhood reminiscences, to have had an appreciable effect on Larkin, but their affirmative direction was one to which he would have responded. A sceptical affirmativeness can also be found in two other possible sources for 'Church Going', John Betjeman's 'Sunday Afternoon Service in St Enodoc Church, Cornwall' and Norman Cameron's 'The Disused Temple'. Though the speaker in Betjeman's poem is a church enthusiast who goes 'Biking in high-banked lanes from tower to tower/On sunny antiquarian afternoons', he prefers, like Graves's speaker, to gaze at the seascape and 'deep cliffs' outside than watch the 'weary clergyman' preach. Gradually, however, the idea of the church's continuity and relationship with the seascape takes hold, and he pays homage to the building:

> Oh lichened slate in walls, they knew your worth
> Who raised you up to make this House of God
> What faith was his, that dim, that Cornish saint,
> Small rushlight of a long-forgotten church,
> Who lived with God on this unfriendly shore,
> Who knew He made the Atlantic and the stones
> And destined seamen here to end their lives
> Dashed on a rock, rolled over in the surf,
> And not one hair forgotten. Now they lie
> In centuries of sand beside the church.

'Church Going' owes to this poem the idea of a church visit (which appears elsewhere in Betjeman's work too), the final image of the dead who 'lie round', and the word 'destinies' (possibly inspired by Betjeman's equally sonorous 'destined'). But for the agnosticism of 'Church Going', and the image of a disused rather than thriving building, Larkin might have looked instead to Cameron's 'The Disused Temple': its inclusion in Larkin's Oxford anthology confirms that it at some time made an impression on him. As a close friend of Graves, an anti-Modernist, and an ironical self-examiner, Cameron has obvious affinities with the Movement. Like Larkin's his poem considers the problem of what to do with an 'unfrequented' place of religion in an age which has little use for it, and shows that such places continue to have a disturbing effect even on the non-religious:

> Since it was unfrequented and left out
> Of living, what was there to do except
> Make fast the door, destroy the key? (No doubt
> One of our number did it while we slept.)
>
> It stays as a disquieting encumbrance.
> We moved the market-place out of its shade;
> But still it overhangs our whole remembrance,
> Making us both inquisitive and afraid.

Cameron's poem embodies that tension between reverence and irreverence which the Movement found so meaningful: the evocation of the temple's disquieting presence is balanced by a joke about 'shrewd acousticians [who] hammer on the door'. Larkin's 'serious house' is also subject to invasion by odd characters—'dubious women', 'Christmas addict[s]' and 'ruin-bibber[s], randy for antique'. For development of these comic possibilities within a solemn context Larkin may have also found useful, as John Fuller has noted,[57] Auden's poem 'Not in Baedeker', published in *Nones* (1951). Larkin is on record as preferring the pre-1939 'English' Auden, but he would have responded to this 1949 poem because of its study of a 'certain' (particular, but also secure) English place (a lead mine area) undergoing decline—

> A certain place
> Has gone back to being (what most of the earth is
> Most of the time) in the country somewhere

—and because of the anecdote with which the poem concludes:

> One September Thursday two English cyclists
> Stopped here for a *fine* and afterwards strolled
> Along the no longer polluted stream
> As far as the Shot Tower (indirectly
> Responsible in its day for the deaths
> Of goodness knows how many grouse, wild duck
> And magnificent stags) where the younger

> (Whose promise one might have guessed even then
> Would come to nothing), using a rotting
> Rickety gallery for a lectern,
> To amuse his friend gave an imitation
> Of a clergyman with a cleft palate.

Larkin's speaker carries out a similarly parodying performance, though, as often happens in Larkin's poems, he must
do so in solitude. For an audience he has only his own 'echoes':

> Mounting the lectern I peruse a few
> Hectoring large-scale verses, and pronounce
> 'Here endeth' much more loudly than I'd meant.
> The echoes snigger briefly. Back at the door
> I sign the book, donate an Irish sixpence,
> Reflect the place was not worth stopping for.

The donation of an Irish sixpence has been the cause of
dispute among critics, those who feel unsettled by its apparent
disrespect holding to the theory that since Larkin was in
Ireland in the early 1950s, the donation may have been legitimate.[58] But there are clearly other irreverent elements in the
poem with which this reference is compatible. Besides, like
many others in the poem, this reference has a literary precedent. In George Orwell's *Coming Up For Air,* George Bowling
briefly enjoys a return to his old parish church ('The same
dusty, sweetish corpse-smell. And by God! the same hole in
the window'), but then is disturbed by the vicar: 'He said good
evening and promptly started on the usual line of talk — was
I interested in architecture, remarkable old building this,
foundations go back to Saxon times and so on and so forth . . .
As soon as I decently could I dropped sixpence in the Church
expenses box and bunked.'

Though Bowling provides a good model for the 'ordinary',
'middling' and initially irreverent speaker of 'Church Going',
Orwell's impulse in religious matters is not always to bunk or
debunk. His most sustained consideration of church, the novel
A Clergyman's Daughter (1935), shows Dorothy rebelling
against her clergyman-father, but eventually coming to accept

church on the recognisably Orwellian grounds of its 'decency': 'However absurd and cowardly its supposed purpose may be, there is something — it is hard to define, but something of decency, of spiritual comeliness — that is not easily found in the world outside. It seemed to her that even though you no longer believe, it is better to go to church than not; better to follow in the ancient ways than to drift in rootless freedom'. Her friend Mr Warburton later defines Dorothy's position as 'Anglican Atheist', a term that well suits the speaker of 'Church Going': '"I suppose if the truth were known, there are quite a lot of your kind wandering about the ruins of the C. of E. You're practically a set in yourselves", he added reflectively: "The Anglican Atheists"'.

Larkin's explanation of the importance of church is not, however, quite the same as Orwell's. He would probably accept Dorothy's view that church is 'decent' and that it is best 'to follow in the ancient ways', but this is not the reason for the importance of church which his poem gives. To Larkin's speaker, church matters because it alone of all institutions was once able to unite the various stages of life,

> because it held unspilt
> So long and equably what since is found
> Only in separation — marriage, and birth,
> And death, and thoughts of these.

Larkin's achievement in 'Church Going' is to provide a justification for church which is his own, and yet to work out of a common tradition. Even in the last stanza, where the verse might appear to be at its most personal and idiosyncratic, Larkin speaks with the weight of predecessors behind him. The tradition includes, as has been seen, Hardy, Graves, Betjeman, Cameron, Auden, Fuller and Orwell; it also takes in Robert Frost, one of the few American poets who (partly, one suspects, by virtue of his connections with Edward Thomas) has made an impression on Larkin. Frost's 'Directive' appeared in his 1947 collection *Steeple Bush,* and, like Auden's 'Not in Baedeker', makes its subject the revisiting of a place now fallen into disuse—a children's playhouse on 'a farm that is no more a farm'. The narrator invites the reader to follow his directive, suggesting that by doing so he will receive spiritual renewal. The assured tone of the conclusion; the play on the words 'whole' and 'hole'; the stately but also colloquial language; the use of the phrase 'your destination and your destiny's' (c.f. Betjeman's 'destined' and Larkin's 'destinies') at the poem's climax: these are indications that Frost's 'house in earnest' may have helped to build Larkin's 'serious house':

> Weep for what little things could make them glad.
> Then for the house that is no more a house,
> But only a belilaced cellar hole,
> Now slowly closing like a dent in dough.
> This was no playhouse but a house in earnest.
> Your destination and your destiny's
> A brook that was the water of the house,
> Cold as a spring as yet so near its source,
> Too lofty and original to rage . . .
> Here are your waters and your watering place.
> Drink and be whole again beyond confusion.
>
> (Frost)

> A serious house on serious earth it is,
> In whose blent air all our compulsions meet,
> Are recognised, and robed as destinies.
> And that much never can be obsolete,
> Since someone will forever be surprising
> A hunger in himself to be more serious,
> And gravitating with it to this ground,
> Which, he once heard, was proper to grow wise in,
> If only that so many dead lie round.
>
> (Larkin)

'I have no belief in "tradition"' Larkin declared. But as his colleague Wain has rightly said, Larkin's poems are 'superb examples of work with a tradition behind it, felt in the blood rather than held up as a banner'.[59] What Larkin means to reject, as Wain's comment and his own inverted commas hint, is Eliot's idea of a European tradition laboriously acquired and openly declared through textual notes and allusions.

'Church Going' underplays its dependence on previous literary texts, but is no less influenced than *The Waste Land* is by the pressure of a cultural heritage. The few living and many dead who 'lie round' it may not be writers of whom Eliot much approved, but he would have understood — having done so much himself to define the process — the adjustment of tradition which Larkin's poem signifies, the modification which gives a Hardyesque English line more prominence than an Imagist or Modernist one. Larkin's poem celebrates a building which contains tradition; it is itself such a building, upholding a tradition whose continuity has, like the church's, come under threat. The 'compulsions' of a heritage 'meet' in 'Church Going', are 'blent' and reordered there, and emerge 'robed' in testimony to the persistence of both the English Church and an English poetic tradition.

6

Divergent Lines:
The Movement after 1956

How often I have said
'This will never do',
Of ways of feeling that now
I trust in, and pursue.

Davie, 'Life Encompassed'

'. . . to hell with the Movement and with you too!'
   As he stormed the words he wondered why he was still
keeping up the pretence of ever having been interested in
the Movement. The only explanation seemed to be that he
had got involved so deeply in a false situation that there was
no time, now, to try to work his way back to the true one.

Wain, *Living in the Present*

It would be as difficult to give a precise date for the dispersal
of the Movement as it is to give a precise date for its inception.
The group had never been officially formed; nor was it ever
officially dissolved. It is arguable, however, that 1956 was
a crucial turning-point, and that after this date many of the
factors which had brought about the development of the
group ceased to operate. Hitherto-concealed differences of
approach became apparent; there were changes in the socio-
political climate which affected the group identity; and as
writers began to move in new directions, so they began to
question the validity of the original programme. At least one
member, Donald Davie, went so far as to repudiate the basic
aims of the Movement, and even the poets who remained
faithful to those aims began to find the group label restrictive.
Friendships and collaborations continued, but after 1956 it

was no longer possible to think of the Movement writers as being united in a common cause. Already by the beginning of the next year John Wain was writing that 'the revolt is now over, its work is done'.[1]

One reason why 1956 seems to have been a turning-point is that in this year the *New Lines* anthology of Movement poetry appeared. Public awareness of the Movement had been helped by Wain's *First Reading* broadcasts in 1953, and by the anonymous 'In the Movement' article of 1954, but it still remained for the group to be brought together in a single volume. D. J. Enright's anthology *Poets of the 1950's* (1955), which included all the Movement poets except Thom Gunn, might be said to have achieved this purpose, but the anthology did not appear in England. Enright was at that time teaching in Japan, and his anthology, published in Tokyo by the Kenyusha Press, was really intended for the Japanese. (Thus arose the curious situation whereby Japanese readers had a better opportunity to observe the Movement *in toto* than did British ones.) While preparing the anthology in 1954, Enright wrote to Conquest for advice on the choice of poets; it is not entirely a coincidence, therefore, that the choice of poets in the two anthologies should have been the same. Conquest felt that Enright should try to obtain an English publisher for *Poets of the 1950's*, but at the end of 1954 was himself commissioned by Macmillan to produce an anthology (the title, *New Lines,* was his own choice). In January 1955 he wrote to the poets whom he wanted to include requesting material, and by June of that year the selection of poems was complete, and the introduction to the book had been drafted. But copyright and other difficulties delayed publication for a further year, so that it was not until July 1956 that an anthology unmistakably representative of the Movement was available in England.

The publication of *New Lines* changed the status of the Movement. When they had written their introductions, Conquest and Enright had still felt it necessary to promote the Movement. By the standards of most literary manifestos, both introductions are surprisingly subdued (the strategy here is for the editors to practise the same 'moderation' and 'chastened common sense' which they detect in their contributors), but they nevertheless make concerted efforts to present the Movement poets as new and exciting: 'there is undoubtedly a new spirit stirring in English poetry,' Enright claims, and Conquest, in words very like those used by Edward Marsh in his first *Georgian Poetry* anthology, says that *New Lines* has been compiled in the belief 'that a genuine and healthy poetry of the new period has established itself'. Once *New Lines* appeared, however, the pressure to promote the Movement was lifted. The group now had the imprint of a reputable publisher; it was the object of much comment in literary periodicals; it had even begun to attract attention abroad.

The publication of *New Lines* thus meant something different to those connected with the group than it did to those on the outside. In a *New Statesman* review Stephen Spender described the anthology as 'promising',[2] the suggestion being that the Movement manner was still being formed, and that more and better along the same lines must be hoped for. But in the *Spectator,* Anthony Hartley, who had done so much to define and bring attention to the group over the previous two-and-a-half years, saw *New Lines* as the culmination of a literary programme. The Movement, he said, had succeeded in its effort to eradicate the 'cloudy obscurantism' of 1940s poetry; the victory achieved, it should now be prepared to risk some of the Romantic ambitions and postures which it had set out to oppose:

. . . the tougher attitude of the late Forties and early Fifties has produced a discipline which should keep poets from being mushy for sometime to come. Now they should let it rip. Some spade-work has been done, but poetry depends on a willingness on the writer's part to chance his arm, to risk making a fool of himself. . . . This is romanticism, if you like, but it is romanticism with the nonsense removed and has no connection with the incantatory rubbish of the Forties.[3]

Hartley's idea of 'risk' and 'chancing one's arm' anticipates Alvarez's Extremist thesis, and seems to repudiate much that was fundamental to the Movement. But Hartley's point is not that the Movement programme has been misdirected (on the contrary, he believes it to have been 'necessary'), but that it has fulfilled its aim: now it should be possible to attempt something more ambitious.

It is doubtful whether any of the Movement poets at this stage sympathized with Hartley's call for 'a reversion to dynamic romanticism', but they would probably have agreed that the publication of *New Lines* signalled a watershed. The Movement was now, in both senses of the word, 'established'. Until 1956, the poets had shared a sense of being up against 'the London Literary Racket', and had strenuously defended each other's work against those Establishment figures who seemed unreceptive to it. Once *New Lines* appeared, there was not the same pressure to protect each other, and the group became less exclusive. Previously it had felt bound to be highly critical of contemporaries who did not aspire to Movement standards, but when Conquest published a second anthology, *New Lines 2*, in 1963 he admitted that the attempt in *New Lines* to present a distinctive 'Poetry of the Fifties' had gone 'further than was strictly necessary in excluding some types of verse'. The second volume included all the Movement poets except John Holloway; but it also included sixteen additional poets, some of whom (Ted Hughes and Thomas Blackburn in particular) were antipathetic to the original Movement programme.

In the years 1954–5 the Movement had relied on particular literary magazines to make its work known to the public. Of these the most important was the *Spectator*, which had in Anthony Hartley a close ally of the group. Hartley did less reviewing for the *Spectator* after 1956, eventually leaving it for the *Guardian*, and the paper as a whole, though it continued to publish the work of some Movement poets, seemed less of a platform for the group. John Wain, who had reviewed regularly for the *Spectator* throughout 1954 and 1955, published his last piece there early in 1956, leaving to become fiction reviewer for the *Observer*. Wain was offended by an anonymous parody of the Movement which had appeared in the *Spectator* in December 1955.[4] Immediately after his departure, the *Spectator* printed an attack on Wain by Evelyn Waugh: this allowed Waugh the last word in a row which had originated in the *Observer* when Wain said of the ageing P. G. Wodehouse 'sooner or later the record will have to come off'; Waugh thought the remark 'caddish' and developed his views on Wain in the *Spectator*'s columns.[5] No reply from Wain was printed, but it is interesting that in a letter to the *London Magazine* in March 1957 Wain singled out a review by Iain Hamilton, who had been literary editor of the *Spectator* at the time of the Waugh row, as symptomatic of the appalling state of contemporary reviewing: relations between the *Spectator* and at least one Movement writer had undoubtedly gone sour.

In the early 1950s, a row between a Movement member like Wain and an older writer like Waugh would have been presented as part of the struggle between provincial academics and metropolitan amateurs. In the late 1950s it could no longer be seen in this light. Originally all the Movement writers had been closely associated with universities. But in 1955 Wain gave up his lectureship at Reading to devote himself to full-time writing; Amis later followed suit; and it became clearer that poets like Larkin and Jennings could not suitably be termed 'academic'. Moreover, the Movement could not as accurately be called 'provincial' as it could when—with Amis in Swansea, Enright in Birmingham, Wain in Reading and only Conquest of the others London-based—it first emerged. Gunn departed for California in 1954; Davie, Conquest and Amis also had spells in America; Enright lived in Japan, Germany and Thailand. Only Larkin, who has lived in Hull since 1955, has preserved the image of a provincial recluse.

The myth of the corrupt metropolis had been powerful in the early work of the Movement, but when he looked back on the 1950s in an essay called 'Lone Voices' (1960), Amis said that the 'London Literary world' had, in the event, 'proved benign'.[6] A striking instance of this was the changing relationship between Amis and Somerset Maugham, who in 1955 had described Jim Dixon and his type as 'scum'. When a panel of judges awarded Amis the prestigious Somerset Maugham travel award in 1956 (an award which resulted in the writing of *I Like It Here*), there might have been embarrassment on both sides. But in 1957 Maugham retracted his earlier criticism, and Amis, on receiving the award, wrote to his sponsor

saying what I'd been wanting to say for some years: that, though he might think he was out of favour with the then young, this was not so. I admired his works. I got a most courteous letter back. . . . I think he thought — wrongly on the whole, I would say — that this new hero and what he stood for represented a threat to the values by which he'd always lived . . . In fact, of course, later developments have seen to it that the non-gentleman and the gentleman would be standing together back to back, holding off the even more ungentlemanly people who have emerged since.[7]

The final idea of the former rebel defending the Establishment against later rebels is one that Amis explores again in his poem 'After Goliath', and points to his growing conservatism after 1956.

With the success of important Movement publications, then, the group no longer enjoyed the image of aspiration and rebellion. Increasingly, it was seen to represent the values against which future writers would have to react. Within a year of the publication of *New Lines*, Dannie Abse and Howard Sergeant had launched a counter-anthology called *Mavericks* (1957). Much of the introduction to *Mavericks*—which consisted, rather oddly, of letters from one editor to the other—was taken up with references to the limitations of the Movement, and Abse's call for a Dionysian revival was a calculatedly anti-Movement one. In practice only Abse himself seemed significantly different from the Movement, and poets like J. C. Hall and Anthony Cronin wrote orthodox, if undistinguished, *New Lines*-like verse. But the fact that *Mavericks* was offered as an anti-Movement anthology indicated the group's changed status. Since 1960 several other new ventures in English poetry have been careful to claim to be offering a departure from the Movement—among them the Hobsbaum/ Lucie-Smith 'Group', Ian Hamilton's *Review* school, and Michael Horovitz's 'Children of Albion'.

But the most celebrated departure from the Movement has come in the form of Ted Hughes, whose *The Hawk in the Rain* (1957) was immediately welcomed by some critics as a collection which displayed the Romantic energy and muscularity (Hughes was compared to Hopkins, Lawrence and Dylan Thomas) which the Movement had rejected. Hughes certainly saw himself as a poet in opposition to the Movement, as he has since explained:

One of the things those poets had in common I think was the post-war mood of having had enough . . .enough rhetoric, enough overweening push of any kind, enough of the dark gods, enough of the id, enough of the Angelic powers and the heroic efforts to make new worlds. They'd seen it all turn into death-camps and atomic bombs. All they wanted was to get back in civvies and get home to the wife and kids and for the rest of their lives not a thing was going to interfere with a nice cigarette and a nice view of the park . . . Now I came a bit later. I hadn't had enough. I was all for opening negotiations with whatever happened to be out there.[8]

In the late 1950s and early 1960s Hughes's work was linked with that of Sylvia Plath, Peter Redgrove and others, and there was talk of a new savagery and violence in contemporary poetry. A. Alvarez, developing the 'Extremist' thesis that would relegate the Movement to a 'negative feedback' and exalt the work of Plath, Hughes, Berryman, Lowell and Anne Sexton, announced in 1958 that 'the Movement has now ended. The convalescence after the breakdown, with its wanness and fear of exertion, is over'.[9] In similar vein, a 1960 TLS review suggested that new collections by Hughes and Redgrove 'could be taken to mark the dropping of the "Movement" as a pilot.'[10] Movement poetry might still be a point of orientation in critical discourse, but it was no longer felt to be new or fashionable.

In fiction, too, critics became aware of departures from the Comic Realism of Amis, Wain and their forerunner William Cooper. The work of William Golding, Muriel Spark, Lawrence Durrell, Doris Lessing, Anthony Burgess and Iris Murdoch prompted talk of a return to fiction of 'fantasy', 'exoticism' and 'experiment'. The development of Iris Murdoch was of special importance because her first novel, *Under the Net* (1954), had been seen at the time of its publication as a Movement work. Murdoch did, in some respects, belong to the Movement generation: she had been at Oxford as an undergraduate from 1939–42 and as a teacher there from 1948 onwards, and she was acquainted with Wain. The restless and rebellious hero of *Under the Net*, Jake Donoghue, and the novel's picaresque structure, invited comparisons with Amis's *Lucky Jim* and Wain's *Hurry on Down*; the author's interest in Existentialism invited comparisons with Thom Gunn. Murdoch's third novel, *The Sandcastle* (1957), also had its Movement elements: the central figure is a provincial schoolteacher, and several of the scenes would not have looked out of place in Cooper's *Scenes from Provincial Life* or Amis's *Take a Girl Like You*. But Murdoch's other novels from the 1950s, *The Flight from the Enchanter* (1955) and *The Bell* (1958), contained elements of mystery and allegory which were not compatible with the Movement programme, and which suggested that the brief Movement consensus in fiction had been dissolved. Although John Braine, David Storey, Alan Sillitoe, Stan Barstow, Malcolm Bradbury and others seemed to follow Movement precept, the most significant developments in English fiction of the late 1950s and early 1960s were generally felt to come from a rejection of the 'traditionalism' of Amis and Wain.

The Movement was not, however, entirely to be dissociated from new developments in writing. For a time, it remained at the centre of attention because of its connection with that other much-disputed English literary grouping of the 1950s, 'the Angry Young Men'. The theory, widely examined in newspapers and literary journals during the years 1956-8, that there had emerged in Britain a new 'angry' generation, had its origin in three events of May 1956: the opening of John Osborne's *Look Back in Anger* at the Royal Court Theatre on 8 May; the publication of Colin Wilson's *The Outsider*; and a *Times* leader for 26 May which linked Osborne and Kingsley Amis in the creation of a new anti-hero described as 'a thoroughly cross young man'. Leslie Paul's recently published *Angry Young Man,* despite being largely reminiscences of the 1920s and 1930s, provided a suitable catchphrase, and various rather bizarre connections were made: Harold Hobson in the *Sunday Times,* for example, suggested that '*Look Back in Anger* puts on the stage the outlook of *That Uncertain Feeling*'.[11] In 1957 Tom Maschler invited several of the supposed angries to expound their social views in a book called *Declaration.* There were contributions from Doris Lessing, Colin Wilson, John Osborne, John Wain, Kenneth Tynan, Bill Hopkins, Lindsay Anderson and Stuart Holroyd. By 1958 the Angry Young Man syndrome was already the subject of a critical work, Kenneth Allsop's *The Angry Decade,* which divided the participants into 'neutralists' (Amis and Wain), 'emotionalists' (Osborne) and 'law-givers' (Wilson, Holroyd and Hopkins).

It seems clear that the phenomenon was much more of a journalistic invention than was the Movement. Amis had always been happy to appear in Movement anthologies but refused to contribute to *Declaration*: 'I hate all this pharisaical twittering about the "state of our civilization", and I suspect anyone who wants to buttonhole me about my "role in society". This book is likely to prove a valuable addition to the cult of the Solemn Young Man'.[12] The last phrase may have been a dig at Colin Wilson, whose *The Outsider* Amis attacked in a 1956 review as 'a disturbing addition to the prevailing anti-rational mode.' Wilson's idea of the Romantic suffering artist was alien to the Movement, and Amis gave it typically brusque treatment: 'Admittedly to ask oneself: "How am I to live?" is to ask something real . . . But it would be hard to attach any meaning, except as an expression of lunacy or amnesia, to: "Who am I?"'.[13] The Movement writers were scarcely more sympathetic to Osborne. Jimmy Porter's talk of 'bears and squirrels' in *Look Back in Anger* seemed sentimental to them, and Osborne's Lawrentian stress on emotion—'I want to make people feel', he declared[14]—excessive and disquieting. In general they felt uneasy about the notion of rebellion which the 'Angry Young Man' slogan enshrined. Rather than lamenting a lack of 'good brave causes' for intellectuals to defend, they were inclined to welcome the absence of such causes as evidence that post-war British society was basically 'decent'. They regarded Porter's cry of frustration as that of a slightly younger generation than their own—the National Service generation, which included only Gunn of the Movement, and which had experienced less incentive to settle down and conform than they had.

There were also, however, some grounds for linking the Movement with the 'Angry Young Men' phenomenon. Osborne's Jimmy Porter is clearly in certain respects a hero in the Movement mould: 'tough', provincial, heterosexual, suspicious of pretension (one of his favourite words is 'phoney'), and resentful of class privilege while at the same time being drawn to women of a higher social class than his own. Equally, while anger, in the sense of righteous indignation against the social order, may not be a quality we associate with the Movement, there is clearly a rather undirected irritation in certain passages of Amis's and Wain's fiction. In the first chapter of Wain's *Living in the Present* (1955), for example, we are told: 'Maddened, Edgar seized an empty milk bottle and hammered on the floor'; 'savagely he pounded down the stairs'; 'worn out with rage and frustration, Edgar lifted his clenched fists above his head'; 'the cold rage in Edgar's heart forced him into action'; 'with a rush of blood to the head, Edgar jerked himself upright'—certainly anger of a kind. Again, not all the Movement would have shared Amis's impatience with *The Outsider*: Gunn was as interested as Wilson in Romantic heroes and Existentialism, and both he and Elizabeth Jennings wrote poems dissenting from Amis's view that to ask 'Who am I?' is not to ask a meaningful question:

> How much am I then what I think, how much what I feel?
> How much the eye that seems to keep stars straight?
> Do I control what I can contemplate
> Or is it my vision that's amenable?
>
> (Jennings, 'In the Night')
>
> Particular, I must
> Find out the limitation
> Of mind and universe,
> To pick thought and sensation . . .
> And thus I keep my guard
> On that which makes me man.
>
> (Gunn, 'Human Condition')

The Movement's various responses to writers like Osborne and Wilson brought into the open some previously concealed differences of approach and attitude.

The Angry Young Men phenomenon might have passed away fairly quietly had it not coincided with the Suez crisis of October 1956: here at last was a good brave cause and a chance for anger to be usefully directed. This crisis, too, had important consequences for the Movement. The political climate of the early 1950s had been quiet, with Butskellism and 'the End of Ideology' the dominant tenets. But the Suez crisis, and Soviet invasion of Hungary at the same time, aroused more political debate in Britain than there had been since the end of the Second World War: there was widespread condemnation of Eden's decision to send British troops to Egypt, and a feeling that the Suez fiasco had ended the British attempt to remain a world power by virtue of her 'moral leadership' (a much touted phrase of the time). In this climate the notion of political neutrality, to which the Movement had lent its support, began to come under attack. Reviewing Amis's pamphlet, *Socialism and the Intellectuals* in 1957, the then left-wing Paul Johnson announced that the apolitical age of Lucky Jim had passed with the events of Suez. Certain intellectuals, Johnson said, might 'have a vested interest in keeping him alive, in persuading people that he is dominating the political horizon with giant, uncommitted strides. But I suspect — in fact I am sure — that Lucky Jim, at least in his political context, is dead, killed in the afternoon of October 30, 1956, by Sir Anthony Eden; and that what Mr Amis has written in this pamphlet is merely Jim's last will and testament.'[15]

Johnson is not the most temperate of observers (he has since followed Amis's drift to the Right), but others were taking a similar view. The opening editorial of the newly founded *Universities and Left Review* (itself a manifestation of the changed intellectual atmosphere in Britain) said farewell to 'that comfortable womb world in which conservatives and socialists still held hands'. Its first issue contained articles by E. P. Thompson and David Marquand on Amis's Fabian pamphlet; its second featured a symposium on 'Socialism and the Intellectuals', all the contributors agreeing that it was important to move away from the negative character of Amis's (and by implication the Movement's) politics. Sartrean notions of commitment or *engagement* were much in evidence—and not only in the journals of the New Left. An editorial in the TLS on 1 February 1957 complained about the indifference towards politics shown by John Wain and others at a recent meeting in the Institute of Contemporary Arts: 'are there not some causes,' it asked, 'that might arouse even in young men committed very firmly to a sceptical and empirical attitude, a rational and positive enthusiasm?'

The Movement writers were not totally unresponsive to Suez. Amis, for instance, has said that he broke 'a habit of fifteen years' standing' by attending a Labour Party meeting on the subject, vowing to join the Party afterwards.[16] But for the most part they stood by their politics of neutrality, dismissing the new esteem for commitment as a fad. When a reviewer criticized the Movement for its 'uncommitment', Conquest replied that 'the writer does not seem to realize that this generation of poets is fully aware of his theses and has rejected them quite consciously,' explaining that 'we regard the acceptance of a set of prefabricated formulae as an intolerably frivolous reaction to serious and complicated issues.'[17] There may, however, have been another reason for the Movement's failure to intervene usefully in the debate over Suez: as Anthony Hartley suggests, they probably disapproved of Eden's policy, but the evidence of 'the dwindling of Britain's world power aroused in them not altogether surprising regrets and misgivings.'[18] Until 1956, the Movement's neutralist politics had been shared by many contemporaries; now the Movement's ambivalence over Suez, an issue on which most intellectuals felt able to take a stand, divided them from those contemporaries.

The Movement had rather more to say about the Soviet invasion of Hungary, which was seen as confirmation of the dangers of Soviet totalitarianism. As Amis said: 'This put paid for ever to my hopes that Communism might not be as bad as more and more voluminous and unignorable evidence kept suggesting to me it was'.[19] When, in February 1957, his Fabian pamphlet was favourably reviewed by Arnold Kettle in the *Daily Worker,* Amis hurriedly denied Kettle's odd suggestion that the pamphlet's political assumptions were 'nearer to Marxism than most Social-Democratic thinking'; Hungary, Amis suggested, had driven him away from the Left: 'I have had Marxism — in both senses of the word. I have experienced the ailment and so am immune. And I have also utterly rejected it . . . I used to be able to say that some of my best friends were Communists. I can't after Hungary.'[20] Amis's aversion to Soviet Communism grew in the late 1950s and early 1960s, partly as a result of his friendship with Conquest, who began to publish books critical of the Soviet Union. Two of these, *Back to Life: Poems from Behind the ron Curtain* (1958) and *Courage of Genius: The Pasternak Affair* (1961—dedicated to Larkin), paid tribute to dissidents n Eastern Europe; the others, including the most famous, *The Great Terror* (1968), were politico-historical works uncovering Soviet injustice and brutality of various kinds. The description in Amis's *Girl, 20* of 'an eminent Sovietologist' is almost certainly a reference to Conquest.) As their hostility to the Soviet Union grew, so the Movement writers became increasingly Conservative in their attitudes to domestic affairs, and increasingly pro-American in their attitude to international ones. A typical view is that put by Wain in 1963:

> The usual attitude taken by 'progressives' during the last fifteen years has been a blend of neutralism with sentimentality about the Soviet Union. The continuing state of international high tension has been consistently blamed on the United States for its 'provocative' attitude in standing firm against Soviet and Chinese threats. My opinion is exactly the opposite. Instead of quaking in my shoes every time the Americans refuse to retreat before Communist bluster, I quietly thank my stars that there is someone in the West who has the will and the power to show some firmness.[21]

Wain's 'progressive' intellectual looks very much like Amis's 'Lefty'—someone who 'says the East European satellites are really swinging places that have stopped bothering with politics' and 'who buys unexamined the abortion-divorce-homosexuality-censorship-racialism-marijuana package'.[22] The difficulty for the Movement was that up until 1956 they identified, or were identified, with 'progressive' attitudes; now they found themselves moving to the Right and becoming alienated from many fellow-intellectuals. A striking instance of this was the attitude of Amis and Conquest to the Vietnam war. In a published symposium of 1968, they were the only two out of twenty-three contributors to declare unequivocal support for American policy; Amis even recommended sending out British troops and 'stepping up rather than scaling down' the war effort.[23]

It is true that other Movement writers were not so extreme

in their views. In the same symposium, Gunn, Enright and Davie condemned American policy in Vietnam; and Davie later became embroiled in an argument with Amis in *Encounter* over the rights and wrongs of intervening in international affairs (Davie suggesting that non-intervention is the best foreign policy, Amis retorting that such pacifism plays into the hands of unscrupulous powers).[24] But fear of the Left seems to have been a dominant part of Movement ideology in the 1960s, with Amis, Conquest, Davie, Larkin and Wain in particular being affected by it. The result was that the neutralist consensus of the 1950s was dissolved, and the tone and attitude of Movement work underwent important changes. Until 1956, Movement texts had been divided between a desire for social reform and a desire to preserve the status quo; the tension was energetic and enriching. Now the conservative element in the Movement began to assume control.

Amis's shift from Left to Right is the best-known and most self-consciously documented of the Movement's political transitions. In *Lucky Jim* there is already one indication of a potentially 'reactionary' viewpoint: Dixon's reservations about the expansion of higher education expressed during a discussion with Beesley, anticipate Amis's much quoted slogan of the 1960s that 'MORE WILL MEAN WORSE'. However, the political philosophy of *Lucky Jim* is better represented by Dixon's assertion, in argument with Bertrand, that 'if one man's got ten buns, and another's got two, and a bun has got to be given up . . . then surely you take it from the man with ten buns': the perspective is Left-of-centre, and ties in with Amis's declaration, in *Socialism and the Intellectuals,* that unless something very surprising were to happen he would always vote for the Labour Party. In fact, Amis was announcing by 1960 that his 'love affair with it [the Labour Party] has got to the name-calling and walking-out stage',[25] and since 1967 he has voted Conservative. His change of allegiance was described in a *Sunday Telegraph* article of that year, 'Why Lucky Jim turned Right' (reprinted in *What Became of Jane*

Austen?), in which Amis suggested that 'experience is a Tory', and that the political consequence of a Movement-like loyalty to the 'real world' is Conservatism: 'I have seen how many of the evils of life — failure, loneliness, fear, boredom, inability to communicate — are ineradicable by political means, and that attempts so to eradicate them are disastrous. The ideal of the brotherhood of man, the building of the Just City, is one that cannot be discarded without lifelong feelings of disappointment and loss. But if we are to live in the real world, discard it we must'.

Amis's political transition is explored in two poems from his 1967 collection *A Look Round the Estate*. In the opening lines of 'After Goliath', David is seen to be (as, in the 1950s, the Movement was often seen to be) a destroyer of the established order. But when he faces for the first time those progressives who have given him their support, he begins to feel doubts:

> . . . who were they, anyhow?
> Academics, actors who lecture,
> Apostles of architecture,
> Ancient-gods-of-the-abdomen men,
> Angst-pushers, adherents of Zen,
> Alastors, Austenites, A-test
> Abolishers — even the straightest
> Of issues looks pretty oblique
> When a movement turns into a clique . . .

The final thought here is echoed in *Take a Girl Like You*, where Jenny Bunn sheds doubt on Jim Dixon's jauntily confident dictum, 'Nice things are nicer than nasty ones': 'things,' she discovers, 'were always less simple than they seemed at first'.

'After Goliath' is satirical about the hero's supporters, but sympathetic to the hero himself: his graduation in the social order, and probable future resistance to those who may threaten that order, are seen to be inevitable. 'Coming of Age' is a more self-accusing poem. It too features a rebel who 'moves up', a 'spiritual secret agent' who becomes one of the wealthy citizens whose behaviour he has set out to record, and (we presume) attack, in 'his black book'. But the imagery of the poem–the hero is seen as a 'stick-insect'—implies disapproval of his actions. We are told how, at first an outsider, but increasingly indistinguishable from insiders, he

> Mimicked their dress, their gestures as they sat
> Chaffering and chaffing in the Grand Hotel;
> Infiltrated their glass-and-plastic homes,
> Watched from the inside; then — his deadliest blow —
> Went and married one of them (what about that?);
> At the first christening played his part so well
> That he started living it from then on,
> His trick of camouflage no longer a trick.

This could well be read as an autobiographical poem, the 'black book', for instance, being *Lucky Jim*. As such, it can be correlated with changes in the patterns of Amis's fiction, which during the 1960s gradually became less preoccupied with social 'infiltration' and took on other subjects. Up until *One Fat Englishman* (1963) each of Amis's novels follows a similar development. The central figure is thrust into an unfamiliar world, usually materially better than that to which he or she is accustomed, and is observed struggling to 'adjust'. In three of these novels, *Lucky Jim, That Uncertain Feeling* and *Take a Girl Like You,* the adjustment is to a middle or upper-middle-class world; in the other two, *I Like It Here* and *One Fat Englishman,* it is adjustment to 'abroad' (Portugal and the USA); in all of the novels, sexual relations with a person from an unfamiliar world play an important role, and each central character must decide how much his or her moral scruples are to be compromised in order to 'get on'. All five novels have a basically comic resolution to the plot.

After 1963, new patterns emerge. Where the early fiction had drawn on Orwell's *Coming Up for Air, The Anti-Death League* (1966) draws on the nightmare atmosphere of *1984*. The military setting, the obsession with death, and the almost apocalyptic tone are a significant departure. The involvement of the characters in a complex operation against the Chinese reflects Amis's growing concern about totalitarianism (more recently explored again in his 1977 novel *The Alteration*). Amis is more outward-looking, less concerned with English social differences than with international politics. There is no central Amis male controlling the novel's point-of-view. Nor is there a comic resolution: the final fatalistic image is of a dog running out in front of a lorry, and of the driver's steering failing to respond.

Amis's next novel, *I Want It Now* (1968), is closer to the pattern of the early fiction since its main character, Ronnie Appleyard, seeks to secure wealth by marrying the daughter of a wealthy aristocrat, and thereby to move upward in society. But Appleyard, the host of a television programme, is significantly different from Amis's earlier protagonists—Dixon and Lewis—in having considerable power and status already. At the end of the novel he is able to attack, in front of millions of television viewers, some of the rich people at whose hands he has previously suffered indignity. The social milieu of this novel and of *Girl, 20* (1971) is sharply observed, but it is a well-to-do metropolitan milieu rather than the provincial milieu of the early work. It would be wrong to pretend that this development in Amis's fiction has been wholly damaging; in 1961 he was already being criticized by a fellow Movement poet, D. J. Enright, for perpetuating a 'Provincial Dream World'.[26] But in tackling more ambitious subjects Amis has sacrificed some of the interest and humour of his early fiction.

Changes in the socio-political perspective of Larkin's work have been less dramatic than the changes in Amis's, but follow a similar pattern. In the 1950s and 1960s, it was difficult to tell what political opinions Larkin held, but it was generally supposed that, just as he shared Amis's interest in lower-middle and even working-class settings, so, too, he shared Amis's support for Labour Party policies. Writing in 1958, A. Alvarez expressed the common image of Larkin as someone who, 'so far from being a snob, . . . is constantly blaming himself for his least wavering from a kind of enlightened middle class socialism. He writes as though he had been voluntarily nationalized.'[27] But in the late 1960s and early 1970s, Larkin published poems which suggested that he had changed from, or had never subscribed to, a socialist position. A couplet contributed to the second number of the Cox and Dyson *Black Papers on Education* shows disturbance at current student rebellion, and fear of Soviet expansion: 'When the Russian tanks roll westward, what defence for you and me?/Colonel Sloman's Essex rifles? The Light Horse of LSE?'. 'Homage to a Government', also published in 1969, makes explicit that regret for loss of Empire which was suppressed in the early work. What, Larkin asks, is to become of a country whose policies are determined only by economic motives? What of our former greatness and moral leadership?

> Next year we shall be living in a country
> That brought its soldiers home for lack of money.
> The statues will be standing in the same
> Tree-muffled squares, and look nearly the same.
> Our children will not know it's a different country.
> All we can hope to leave them now is money.

An obvious objection would be that financial motives are as involved in the posting of troops to colonies as they are in the withdrawal of them, but this is not an objection which Larkin's poem allows itself to face. The idea that modern-day England is too preoccupied with money also appears in another poem of about this time, 'Going, Going', where reverence for an older England—'The shadows, the meadows, the lanes,/The guildhalls, the carved choirs'—leads the poet to feel revulsion for the materialistic present:

> The crowd
> Is young in the M1 café;
> Their kids are screaming for more —
> More houses, more parking allowed,
> More caravan sites, more pay.
> On the Business Page, a score

> Of spectacled grins approve
> Some takeover bid that entails
> Five per cent profit (and ten
> Per cent more in the estuaries) . . .

In *Thomas Hardy and British Poetry,* Davie describes as 'thoroughly refreshing' Larkin's refusal to measure a depleted present against a richer past, and contrasts his admirable clearsightedness with Betjeman's 'nostalgia'. But in 'Going, Going', Larkin does sound nostalgic and Betjemanesque. A growing admiration for Betjeman has, indeed, been a feature of Larkin's development in the 1960s, and has not always proved deleterious: the concern with English continuities evident in poems like 'To the Sea' and 'Show Saturday' is far from disabling. Larkin also seems to have learnt from what, in a 1959 review, he called Betjeman's 'social expertise', his ability 'to hit off character and situation by . . . always insisting on the brand and the make and the actual expression and the details of clothes and furniture'.[28] Betjeman shared the Movement's belief in fidelity to the 'real' and 'ordinary', and his 'expertise' helped Larkin to develop as a writer in the late 1950s: the poems in *The Whitsun Weddings* are on the whole more precise in their social observation than are the poems in *The Less Deceived.* In 'Afternoons', for instance, the pity which the speaker feels for young mothers who are losing their physical attractiveness—

> Their beauty has thickened.
> Something is pushing them
> To the side of their own lives.

—is reinforced by his accuracy and attention. Carefulness becomes caring:

> Behind them, at intervals,
> Stand husbands in skilled trades,
> An estateful of washing,
> And the albums, lettered
> *Our Wedding,* lying
> Near the television.

But social accuracy of this kind is not always separable from condescension, and there are moments in *The Whitsun Weddings* when Larkin seems to patronize as well as to pity, to treat the working class as Betjeman does in a poem like 'The Dear Old Village'—'An eight-hour day for all, and more than three/Of these are occupied in making tea'. Davie has said that in 'Here', with its use of the phrase 'a cut-price crowd' to describe shoppers, 'the pity felt for the . . . "residents from raw estates" is more than a little contemptuous'; and David Holbrook reaches a similar conclusion about the following passage from 'The Whitsun Weddings' itself, describing it as 'an appeal to the reader to become enlisted in a particular denigratory attitude of the writer to his subject':[29]

> The fathers with broad belts under their suits
> And seamy foreheads; mothers loud and fat;
> An uncle shouting smut; and then the perms,
> The nylon gloves and jewellery-substitutes,
> The lemons, mauves and olive-ochres that
>
> Marked off the girls unreally from the rest.

It may seem harsh to call this a postcard-like caricature, especially since Larkin can be compared with Owen as well as with Betjeman: he has Owen's feeling of pity and responsibility for his subjects as well as Betjeman's affection and condescension. But it is clear, at least, that Larkin belongs to the tradition of the passive middle-class observer, and that over the years the distance between him and the 'cut-price crowd' has increased.

It is ironic that Davie should have criticized Larkin's 'condescending' reference to 'residents from raw estates', for Larkin's image probably derived from the description of a 'raw estate' in Davie's early poem, 'Hawkshead and Dachau in a Christmas Glass'. Moreover, Davie's political development since the early 1950s has followed much the same pattern as Larkin's and Amis's, with changes in the cultural climate pushing him to the Right. Davie dates his awareness of those changes from 1958: returning from a year in California, he 'found a changed climate of opinion and feeling. The younger intellectuals were turning Left once more, taking up populist attitudes which I had been glad to see discredited at the end of the '30s.'[30] There is a reference to 'enrolling in the party of the Right' in a 1960 poem, 'Right Wing Sympathies', but it was in the years 1965-8, when as a Professor of English and American Literature at Essex University he came into conflict with left-wing student opinion, that Davie moved decisively over to the Conservative Party. In 1969 he said in *Encounter*: 'I detect in myself much the same drift to the Right that Amis admits to, and I don't apologise for it any more than he does.'[31]

The nostalgic perspective of Davie's *The Shires* (1974) is not unlike that to be found in Larkin's poetry. The collection contains a poem for each of the English counties, exploring the notion of Englishness through personal anecdote, history and topography. But Davie's conservative vision has on the whole been less gentle than Larkin's: his patriotism, which seems to have increased since he has lived in America, leads him to express rancour and indignation at a 'depleted present' rather than to be merely wistful for the past. This spleen is particularly noticeable in his long and bitter poem 'England', written in 1969 shortly after he left Essex for America. Davie in this poem seems obsessed with the idea of declining moral standards; and his tone of address (the corporate 'we' now degraded and dissolved) becomes almost hysterical:

> The bluff stuff. Double bluff.
> Brutal manners, brutal
> simplifications as
> we drag it all down.
>
> And what is there left to be seen
> by Tom the butler now
> we couple like dogs in the yard?
>
> Gone, gone as the combo
> starts in digging the beat
> and the girls from the nearest College
> of Further Education
> spread their excited thighs.

Part of Davie's subject in 'England' is what is sometimes called the 1960s 'sexual revolution'. The approaches of Davie, Larkin and Amis to this phenomenon have differed. Davie has tended to feel an Eliot-like distaste for the relaxation of moral standards, equating freedom with libertinism. Larkin has been more wry, presenting himself as someone who—'just too late'—has missed out on the 'action'. Amis has found the 1960s rich in possibility for comedy: in *Girl, 20*, for example, he deals satirically with 'swinging London', promiscuity, drug-taking, left-wing politics and rock music. But common to all the approaches is the fact that Larkin, Amis and Davie are now to be seen at one remove from cultural and social change. They write as older men sometimes scornful about change, sometimes pained by it. The ironic treatment of the sexual revolution in Larkin's 'High Windows'—'I know this is paradise/ Everyone old has dreamed of all their lives'—closely resembles the closing irony of Amis's *Girl, 20*, where Penny Vandervane, hooked on heroin and with a life-expectancy of two years, announces: 'We're all free now'.

The essential fact about the Movement's socio-political identity since 1956, then, is that while there is still significant agreement amongst Movement writers—Amis, Conquest, Davie, Larkin and Wain have developed in broadly similar ways—the group has no longer been identifiable with new developments. The group posture had always been one of 'consolidation'; now it has become more overtly one of defence: defence of the English language against new idioms; defence of traditional jazz against modern jazz and rock music; defence of metrical laws and regular forms against free verse and 'pop poetry'; defence of 'humane' (conservative) values against 'totalitarian' (left-wing) ones.

The Movement has even begun to defend privilege and élitism, notions which in the 1950s, when emphasis fell upon the responsibility of individuals towards the community, it had largely opposed. In 1956, for example, Amis had attacked as 'unpleasant and damaging' D. H. Lawrence's 'recommendation, apparently as a practical measure, of the kind of theo-cracy, or hierocracy, in which the 'mass' (those who can't distinguish between property and life) bow down to the "elect"'.[32] But by 1968 Amis was reassuring a Conservative Party Summer School that 'there must be an élite, and there can't be equality'.[33] Wain and Davie have reached similar conclusions. In *Professing Poetry* (1977) Wain says that he 'can see nothing wrong with' an élite, and speaks of 'jelly-bellied democratisation (in a mass society, only the lowest level of finesse is acceptable)'.[34] Davie, in a 1977 essay, dis-parages the notion of 'community' to which, in the 1950s, the Movement had seemed to lend its support:

> . . . 'community' is an ignoble end to aim at, not just in religion but even in politics. Even if we did not know what it means in practice — that is to say, a central and swollen bureaucracy trying to impose equality at the level of the lowest common denominator, and even if we did not know from experience that it is inherently inefficient and cannot encompass the ends it aims at, what sort of an ideal is it anyway, for private and public life to be bent towards? An undiscriminating and unrestricted 'togetherness', as of cows huddled together in a byre to keep one another warm, one cosy and hearty *steam* enveloping the entire citizenry, a vocabulary in which 'ordinary' and 'common' are the terms of highest praise and greatest warmth, in which 'human' and 'social' are interchangeable — is that what the less than Utopian hopes of a Burke, a Montesquieu, or a John Adams have come down to, as the utmost to which a commonwealth may aspire?[35]

In this essay and elsewhere Davie redefines democracy to mean not that individuals ought to be responsible to the community, but that individuals have a right to be protected from com-munity pressure: the redefinition seems typical of the Move-ment shift after 1956.

The Movement's feelings about the notion of an academic élite have, however, been more ambivalent. As might have been expected—given that the group's largely 'Black Paper' stance has led it to resist measures to make education and culture more readily available for all—some of the Movement poets have sought to justify writing for an educated minority:

Davie in particular has defended the academic flavour of his verse by arguing that 'poetry is not a democratic institution, and it never was'.[36] But this development has not been constant throughout the group. On the contrary, writers like Amis, Conquest and Larkin have increasingly championed the cause of the Common Reader against that of the 'intellectual', and have lent their support to 'popular' writing. By 1958, A. Alvarez was already noting the uneasy co-existence in the group of, on the one hand, a 'rather esoteric university intellectualism' and, on the other, a 'deliberate philistinism'.[37]

This conflict in the group can be seen in the different attitudes to poetry taken by Larkin and Davie. Contributing, in 1959, to a symposium on the relationship between the poet and the university, Davie suggested that it was 'proper and natural that more and more of our poets should be connected with universities', and insisted on the professionalism of the poetic endeavour: 'What should be avoided at all costs is the impression that our writing of poems is a spare-time occupation or hobby, serving in our case as a substitute for the gardening of one colleague and the brass-rubbing of another.'[38] In 1964, Larkin expressed views directly in opposition to these, arguing that poetry 'should be a sideline . . . In what spare time I have poetry has to compete with letter writing, social life, reading, mending socks,' and expressing a dislike for academic audiences: 'I am never particularly pleased to be told that my work is being studied by some study group. But I am pleased when people who have read one of my poems write to tell me of similar experiences.'[39] This conflict of approaches—poetry as profession, poetry as hobby—was evident again when Larkin published his anthology, *The Oxford Book of Twentieth Century English Verse* in 1973, and was criticized by Davie for favouring amateur and light verse.

An element in the Movement has therefore consolidated that anti-intellectualism which was present but muted in the original programme. Larkin's hostility to the academics is shared by Amis, who announced in 1957, 'I am not, thank heaven, an expert',[40] and later went on to devalue academic research in a poem called 'Expert'. Amis's expert, using the term 'we' not to reach out to non-experts, but to cut himself off from them—'We have all known for a considerable time/ (Even some of you may know) . . .'--disputes the traditional version of the story of King Canute. Rather than admiring this scepticism, as in the 1950s the Movement might have done, Amis presents it as arrogant and destructive:

> Our rather more recent researches

> (Of which two or three of you may have possibly heard)
> Seemed to suggest that the old boy's real reason
> Was to discredit the banal superstition
> Of those who fancied he was some sort of god.

> Well, *now* we're largely convinced we were wrong there, too.
> Where's the right answer? You would ask that. Our brief
> Begins and ends with discouraging belief
> In what's funny or touching or grand and perhaps untrue.

Mockery of the academic expert, particularly the Eng.Lit. specialist, was also the basis for Robert Conquest's spoof article 'Christian Symbolism in *Lucky Jim*', written for *Critical Quarterly* in 1965 (reprinted in *The Abomination of Moab*, 1979). The joke was successful: a number of readers took Conquest's article seriously, and wrote in to dispute its interpretations.

That the Movement should have begun to disparage intellectuals and academics partly reflects the changes which the British literary intelligentsia has undergone since 1956. The dominance of Leavis and Empson in the early 1950s had not only shaped the kind of poetry which the Movement produced, but had provided them with an audience likely to appreciate ambiguity and irony. Increasingly, though, the methods of these two critics came under attack, and the homogeneous literary culture of the early 1950s was dissolved. The first signs of change came in the late-1950s, with the popularity of the work of Richard Hoggart and Raymond Williams. In the 1960s and 1970s a large number of British intellectuals turned their attention abroad, to figures such as Frye, McLuhan, Lukacs, Marcuse, Barthes, Benjamin and Lacan. The unified and insular literary culture of the 1950s had broken down.

This is not a change the Movement has welcomed. But nor has the group remained blindly partisan. The work of Leavis and Empson has been re-appraised, and in many cases rejected, from within the group as well as from without. Reservations about Empson's poetry had been felt from the beginning, and began to be expressed more openly from 1955 onwards. In his introduction to *Poets of the 1950's,* Enright criticized Empson's 'cold-bloodedly mathematical' approach, suggesting that 'the fallacy of "Empsonianism"' was its 'assumption that triviality or banality, if expressed ambiguously, changes into significant profundity'. *New Lines* was also critical of Empson's influence: 'Empsonianism has been almost as much a vehicle for unpleasant exhibitionism and sentimentality as the trends it was designed to correct'. As these comments suggest, it became common for the Movement to dismiss Empsonian intellectuality as a 'cover', as something which disguised rather than eliminated the sentimentality and banality associated with 1940s neo-Romantics. It was Amis, in Enright's anthology, who first made this point, conceding that 'the trouble with the newer poets, including myself, is that they are often lucid and nothing else—except arid and bald, and that, on the other hand, the strict forms seem to give some of them the idea that they can be as sentimental and trite as they please provided they do it in *terza rima*'. (Amis's reluctance to be thought a follower of Empson can be inferred from his decision not to include the most clearly Empsonian of his poems, 'Catch' and 'Better Sight Without Glasses', in his 1956 collection *A Case of Samples,* though both had previously been published.) Conquest and Enright later reiterated Amis's point: 'With most of his [Empson's] disciples,' Enright said, 'emotion only evinces itself in the form of an abrupt sentimentality—as if to say, "after so much intellectuality I have the right to gush like any Ella Wheeler Wilcox"'. Conquest put it more epigrammatically: 'the dryer the academicism, the wetter the sentimentalism it conceals.'[41]

Even the most clearly Empsonian of the Movement poets, John Wain, began to reject his master—a betrayal first made clear in September 1956. In that month a poem on Brecht appeared in the TLS: signed 'J. W.', it was Empsonian in manner, and looked like the work of Wain. But Wain, anxious to make his break with Empson official, wrote to explain that he was not the author: 'This poem, as it happens, bears an obvious stylistic resemblance to the poems I was writing four or five years ago; it was a manner my friends told me I ought to get out of, so I got out of it . . . I did not write the poem.'[42] Wain carefully placed at the front of his next collection, *Weep Before God* (1961), a poem called 'Time Was', which describes the emergence of a new poetic self. The opening phrase, 'A mind ago', suggests both that Wain has shed former thinking habits and that he is less reliant on 'mind' or reason in poetry. It also points to the influence of a poet previously arraigned by the Movement, Dylan Thomas, who has a poem called 'A Grief Ago'. Wain's description of his spiritual awakening reads like a pastiche of Thomas or Roethke; it would not look out of place in an anthology of the 1940s neo-Romantic poetry which the Movement had deposed:

> Time was I thought the world was thin and dry,
> A heap of shavings curled from heaven's blade.
> (Let fall a match, the flames would hit the sky.)
> I tried to hide, but shavings give no shade.
> The sunlight pierced my vitals like a knife.
> I writhed: I opened: suffering was life.

Another Peter-like denial of past allegiances came in *Sprightly Running* (1962), where Wain said that he would no more be numbered among Leavis's disciples than he would be 'a Baconian or Flat-Earther'. In the 1950s, Wain had helped to popularize the idea of commonsensical close readings of literary texts, taking his bearings partly from Leavis and partly from the American New Critical school. A review of

Pound's *Cantos* in 1960 signalled his departure from the critical procedures enshrined in *Interpretations*. Wain found the
Cantos to be 'verse which doesn't need — is actually better
without — close attention', and suggested that 'the best state
to get into before reading them is a state of trance. If one
simply goes ahead, understanding perhaps one line in ten . . .
and letting the succession of thoughts and images flow into
one's mind, the thing *works*.'[43] Wain did not really adopt this
critical method as a general principle, but the fact that he
can recommend it at all suggests a relaxation of Movement
standards.

Amis, too, has moved away from Leavis. The 'provincial'
tendencies of his early work were such that he might reasonably have expected Leavis to have found it to some degree
congenial. But this was not so. When Amis was in Cambridge from 1961 to 1963, he believed that he was being
snubbed by Leavis, an impression subsequently confirmed
when he learnt that Leavis had denounced him as a 'pornographer'.[44] Later, Leavis began to cite Amis as an example of
the kind of false reputation that is created by a corrupt metropolis and debased culture: 'the spectacle of an academic critic
going out of his way to pronounce a Kingsley Amis novel a
"serious study in amorality" would have been possible only
in a period marked by a collapse of standards.'[45] Amis, for
his part, has revised the high estimate of Leavis and *Scrutiny*
which he had held as late as 1960: 'My present view,' he said
in 1970, 'is that he and it have, on balance, done more harm
than good to literature and its study'.[46]

Enright, though a former pupil of Leavis's and on the whole
more loyal to him than the rest of the Movement, has also
come to feel doubts about his work. Several of the poems in
his 1956 collection express scepticism about the idea that to
preserve high literary standards is, as Leavis and Lawrence held,
a humanizing force. In 'Standards', for example, Enright attacks
if not Leavis himself then certainly a Scrutineer. The bar-girl
heroine of the poem 'reads/The shoddiest of she-girl maga-

zines', yet is tender and humane, 'keeps/By her dirty work an invalid mother'. Enright reflects on this apparent confutation of Leavis:

> I once knew, in England, a man of impeccable taste,
> Who wrote stern books about education.
>> He was much concerned with standards.
> He was not easily to be deceived, he saw through me,
>> found me unbraced,
> And left me floundering. Remembering him here —
> As this girl pulls to his feet a prostrate drunkard
> Who she knows will never tip her — I am appalled to recall
>> his cold and silent and derivative sneer.

In a more recent poem, 'The Cure', which recalls his undergraduate days, Enright implies criticism not only of Leavis's stress on standards, but his notion of the 'organic community':

> When I went to Cambridge
> I found the ills had been diagnosed,
> And correctly too.
>
> But I wasn't too sure of the cure,
> And couldn't quite believe
> Things had once been so much better.

The Movement poet who has best faced the implications of a rejection of Leavis is Donald Davie. By 1967, Davie was arguing that Leavis's 'concern for literature is excessive . . . He expects too much of literature'. By this Davie meant to question Leavis's belief that to 'conserve' English literature was also to hold on to certain continuities of English life. Davie could not accept this, and so to him, Leavis's criticism was useless– 'useless because it takes its bearings from a state of culture such as, in the English-speaking world, no reader and no writer will experience henceforward'.[47] In a 1976 review, Davie expressed his disillusionment with Leavis more strongly still: 'for me, as for many of my generation, Leavis is the god that failed.'[48]

Davie's recognition that the intellectual consensus which in the 1950s Leavis's influence had helped to provide now no longer existed, or existed only in an unworthy form, also had important consequences for his attitude to a poet's audience. The early work of the Movement had been confident in its addresses to the reader, and had made much use of sociable asides. But already by the late-1950s Davie was reassessing the Movement's attempt to solicit the reader's attention, no longer feeling it to have been valuable. The attempt to address work to 'the readers of *Essays in Criticism* and the ex-readers of *Scrutiny*' had, Davie said, 'crippled "the Movement" from the start':

What we all shared to begin with was a hatred of writing considered as self-expression; but all we put in its place was writing as self-adjustment, a getting on right terms with the reader (that is, with our society), a hitting on the right tone and attitude towards him . . . Hardly ever did we seem to write our poems out of an idea of poetry as a way of knowing the world we were in, apprehending it, learning it . . . The most obvious register of this is the striking absence from 'Movement' poetry of outward and non-human things apprehended crisply for their own sakes. I'm not asking for 'nature poetry', but simply for an end to attitudinising.[49]

This repudiation of the Movement owes much to Charles Tomlinson's earlier attack on the *New Lines* poets for their 'singular want of vital awareness of the continuum outside themselves, of the mystery bodied over against them in the created universe, which they fail to experience with any degree of sharpness or to embody with any instress or sensuous depth.'[50] Though Davie had, in 1957, disputed these criticisms, his doubts about the Movement quickly grew. By November of that year he was already beginning to express sentiments very close to Tomlinson's, asking that the contemporary poet 'regain his faith in a world outside man, bodied against him as something other with its own structure and its own modes of being open to him to discover'.[51] Their use of the phrases 'bodied against' and 'bodied over against' suggests that both Davie and Tomlinson were familiar with the philosophy of Martin Buber, who in the 'I consider a tree' section of *I and Thou* uses the phrase *Er leibt mir gegenüber* ('it is bodied over against me and has to do with me'). Tomlinson uses this phrase in one of his poems from *The Necklace* (1955), 'Observation of Facts'—

> The house encloses: or fails to signify
> As being bodied over against one,
> As something one has to do with.

—and Davie also picks it up in his introduction to that collection when he suggests that Tomlinson's poems 'appeal outside themselves only to the world perpetually bodied against our senses'.[52]

Davie's friendship with Tomlinson undoubtedly played some part in his disenchantment with the Movement. They had been in contact since 1947, when Davie had been Tomlinson's supervisor at Cambridge, and Davie came increasingly to feel that the exclusion of Tomlinson from *New Lines* (he had submitted Tomlinson's work to Conquest, but Conquest had rejected it) was confirmation of the group's limitations: in a letter to the TLS on 30 November 1956 he admitted that 'there are indeed whole areas of poetry undreamed of in the philosophy of 'the movement'; Charles Tomlinson . . . is a case in point.' Tomlinson, for his part, largely excluded Davie from his strictures against *New Lines*, arguing that his latest work 'promises a real development away from his earlier manner'.[53] And Davie, from the publication of Tomlinson's *Seeing Is Believing* in 1959 onwards, has continued to press his former student's case and to pronounce the comparative neglect of him in England to be 'a national disgrace'.

Davie explored his relationship with Tomlinson in a 1957 poem, 'To a Brother in Mystery', which depicts the poets as two thirteenth-century stonemasons. Their approaches have previously been very different, the speaker's (Davie's) a Movement-like one, concerned 'to frame some small and human incident/Domestic or of venery', his companion's (Tomlinson's) more severe: 'A sort of coldness is the core of it,/A sort of cruelty'. Now, however, they are beginning to 'change places' and to 'infect/Each other': Davie's work is becoming more 'refined' while Tomlinson's has developed Davie's 'cordial knack'. It is a mark of his disenchantment with the Movement that Davie warns Tomlinson against this development:

> You, I fear,
> Will find you bought humanity too dear
> At the price of some light leaves, if you begin
> To find your handling of them growing thin,
> Insensitive, brittle. For the common touch,
> Though it warms, coarsens. Never care so much
> For leaves or people, but you care for stone
> A little more. The medium is its own
> Thing, and not all a medium, but the stuff
> Of mountains: cruel, obdurate, and rough.

Davie's feeling that the common touch associated with the Movement can 'coarsen' is evident in 'Common-Mannerism', a 1957 review in which he attacks D. J. Enright's 'verse-journalism', dissociating himself from the 'ugly' philistinism of the Movement and suggesting that 'there seems to be a genuine danger that impatience with cultural pretentiousness is turning into impatience with culture'.[54] This was also a theme in his 1957 'The Poet in the Imaginary Museum' broadcasts, where he developed Malraux's idea that what distinguishes the modern artist from his predecessors is a freedom, created by technological advance, to have at his disposal the art of all cultures and ages. For Davie, this means that poetry must be pluralistic, and even parodistic, as *The Waste Land* and *Ulysses* were. He now sees the Movement as anti-modernist and retrogressive, and, while admitting that his spontaneous sympathies are still with it, is forced by his historical analysis to adjudge it a provincial and limited achievement:

These poets are my friends and I think I know perfectly well what makes them, being finely civilized men, pretend to be barbarians; why, though they are humane persons and responsible citizens, they pretend sometimes to be cultural teddy-boys. They are putting the house of English poetry in order: not before time, too. Or rather they're trying to build it afresh, an altogether humbler structure on a far narrower basis. On all sides, our good poets are 'pulling in their horns'. They are getting rid of pretentiousness and cultural window-dressing and arrogant self-expression, by creating an English poetry which is severely limited in its aims, painfully modest in its pretensions, deliberately provincial in its scope. I do not think they would be very offended or even make demur if one added: 'inevitably marginal in importance'.[55]

There were, in fact, several demurs from other Movement poets. John Holloway objected to the idea that poets merely rearrange older styles, and found Davie's thesis impregnated with 'that Alexandrianism, that stultifying substitution of the word for the thing, the library for the reality, which we now see much too often'; Conquest also found Davie's aestheticism unpalatable, concluding 'the Imaginary Museum should either be closed down or extended across Exhibition Road to include the National History and Science Museums'.[56] But Davie's broadcasts made clear that he now wished to break with the Movement, and to broaden out in several ways: by taking a greater interest in foreign cultures and translation; by being more sympathetic to Modernism; and by reconsidering the possible merits of the position of art for art's sake. On the last page of *Articulate Energy* (1955) he had made a humanist case against what he then saw as the artistic self-enclosure of Symbolism: 'It is my case against the symbolist theorists that, in trying to remove the human smell from poetry, they are doing harm. For poetry to be great, it must reek of the human . . .' One of his poems of the early 1960s expresses an opposite view:

> The practice of an art
> is to convert all terms
> into the terms of art.
> By the end of the third stanza
> death is a smell no longer;
> it is a problem of style.   ('July 1964')

Davie's gradual break with the Movement can be followed in the poems he wrote during the late 1950s and early 1960s. Much of the work in *A Winter Talent* (1957) was composed

in accordance with *New Lines* precept, but there is already
one hint of defection: 'Time Passing, Beloved' has an emotional freedom reminiscent at times of Lawrence's poem
'Piano', and its use of alliteration, repetition and assonance
seems surprising in an author who shared the Movement's
belief that 'sound' in poetry had been overvalued at the
expense of 'sense':

> Time passing, and the memories of love
> Coming back to me, carissima, nor more mockingly
> Than ever before; time passing, unslackening,
> Unhastening, steadily; and no more
> Bitterly, beloved, the memories of love
> Coming into the shore.

In 1959, Davie published *The Forests of Lithuania,* a long
narrative poem based on Mickiewicz's *Pan Tadeusz.* Though
he used G. R. Noyes's English prose version of the poem rather
than translating directly, Davie's growing interest in foreign
literature was now apparent, and was to be consolidated in
subsequent years with his translations of Pasternak, his essays
on the problems of translation, and his appointment as the
Head of a University department, at Essex, which was committed to a Comparative Literature programme. By the time
of *Events and Wisdoms* (1964), Davie had also developed a
lyrical freedom which, though not alien to the Movement
manner *per se* (Larkin achieves it while adhering to the
Movement programme), is alien to the wit and self-consciousness which had been Davie's main contribution to the Movement:

> I see the low black wherry
> Under the alders rock,
> As the ferryman strides from his ferry
> And his child in its black frock
>
> Into his powerful shadow
> And out of it, skirmishing, passes
> Time and again as they go
> Up through the tall lush grasses.   ('House-Martin')

The new baby is fed.
I stumble back to bed.
I hear the owls for a long time

Hunting. Or are they never
In the winter grey of before the dawn,
Those pure long quavers,

Cries of love? . . .

('A Christening')

'The metaphysicality/Of poetry, how I need it!' Davie
exclaims in 'Or, Solitude', but adds: 'it was for years/What I
refused to credit'. Davie is surely right in supposing that his
break with the Movement liberated him, and enabled him to
write some of his best work. But despite his repudiation of
parts of the Movement aesthetic, he has continued to defend
many of the values for which the Movement stood (rationalism,
scepticism, fair-mindedness, moderation), and echoes of other
Movement poets continue to appear in his work.[57]

Perhaps the most important aspect of Davie's break with
the Movement was his greater respect for Modernism. This
respect did not turn Davie into a regular practitioner of free
verse (his occasional experiments in open forms have not been
very successful), but it led him to an increasing appreciation
of Pound, and of various poets (Charles Olson, Edward Dorn,
Basil Bunting, J. H. Prynne) seemingly indebted to Pound.
Larkin, on the other hand, has hardened his attitude against
Pound. In a 1957 review of Pound's 'Rock-Drill' Cantos, his
feelings were still mixed; he described the *Cantos* as a 'curiosity, the ultimate (and immediate) value of which I personally
think very small', but conceded that 'the sardonic asides and
the evocative images of this historical kaleidoscope are sufficiently fascinating to suggest that those who think otherwise
may well be right'.[58] By the time he came to write the introduction to *All What Jazz* (1970), Larkin was less diffident,
and placed Pound alongside Picasso and the jazz musician
Charlie Parker in order to attack Modernist artefacts as 'irresponsible exploitations of technique in contradiction of

human life as we know it. This is my essential criticism of modernism, whether perpetrated by Parker, Pound or Picasso: it helps us neither to enjoy nor endure. It will divert us as long as we are prepared to be mystified or outraged, but maintains its hold only by being more mystifying and more outrageous: it has no lasting power.'[59]

In the early 1950s, disagreement about Modernism did not arise, partly because there was ambivalence on the part of poets like Larkin and Davie, and partly because the Movement slogan 'consolidation' disguised important differences of opinion. It was not until 1958 that Wain explained, in a letter to the TLS on 2 May, that what he meant by 'consolidation' was 'the critical and imaginative effort of assimilating the discoveries of those giants who dominated English literature in the first half of this century'. Wain's failure to explain before 1958 exactly what 'consolidation' meant was convenient: it enabled the term to be taken as having a quite different implication, notably that the thing to be consolidated was not Modernism, but rather the 'English tradition' which had been interrupted by Modernism. Thus while Davie and Gunn, and to a lesser extent Wain and Enright, were sympathetic to Modernism, they did not come into conflict with Amis, Larkin and Conquest, who were anti-Modernist. By 1959 Davie had realized that there was among his contemporaries a 'conspiracy to pretend that Eliot and Pound never happened',[60] but for a time before this discovery the slogan 'consolidation' served conflicting purposes.

Davie enjoys playing the part of defiant defector from the Movement, but it would be wrong to suppose that he travelled alone. In the 1960s D. J. Enright, whose poems had from the beginning differed from the rest of the Movement's in having many subjects and settings from 'abroad', joined him in haranguing former colleagues for being 'little-Englanders'.[61] And in moving towards a greater appreciation of Modernist poetry, Davie had an ally in Thom Gunn, whose second collection, *The Sense of Movement* (1957), contained two poems pointing to his development away from the Movement. The poems were 'Market at Turk' and 'Vox Humana', Gunn's first experiment in syllabics. Possibly Gunn's interest in syllabics derived from his Stanford tutor Yvor Winters, who had a high regard for an early exponent of the syllabic form, Elizabeth Daryush; but the interest also suggests Gunn's engagement with an American tradition—one presided over by William Carlos Williams, whom Gunn described as 'somebody from whom it is time we started taking lessons'[62]—in which alternatives to conventional metrical patterns were being explored. In *My Sad Captains* (1961) Gunn blatantly drew attention to his development away from the Movement by dividing the collection into two halves: sixteen poems using standard metrical forms in Part One, thirteen syllabic poems (appropriately beginning with 'Waking in a Newly-Built House') in Part Two. Gunn saw syllabics as a step towards writing free verse and as a means of achieving a more relaxed tone-of-voice. Perhaps his most successful syllabic experiment at this stage was 'Considering the Snail', which though Movement-like in its attempt to dignify a small object, shows a greater responsiveness to the natural world than most Movement poems:

> The snail pushes through a green
> night, for the grass is heavy
> with water and meets over
> the bright path he makes, where rain
> has darkened the earth's dark. He
> moves in a wood of desire,
>
> pale antlers barely stirring
> as he hunts. I cannot tell
> what power is at work, drenched there
> with purpose.

Despite its concern with a non-human world (a concern which Davie and Tomlinson were at that time demanding of their contemporaries), Gunn might legitimately see this as a more 'humane' poem than his early ones. The patient and attentive observation suggests a poet quite different from the restless Existentialist of the early work, and it is possible that in the final lines of the poem—'I would never have/imagined the slow passion'—Gunn is drawing attention to this development: the former Gunn, they hint, would not have been capable of such insight. This poem and 'The Feel of Hands' promised a gentler manner which was finally realized in the title poem of *Touch* (1967). 'Touch' is a free verse poem, though its 'seeping from line to line'[63] owes a good deal to the experiments in syllabics. The process which it describes is exactly that breaking down of the 'resilient chilly hardness' of the ego which Gunn's overall poetic development has followed:

> What I, now loosened,
> sink into is an old
> big place, it is
> there already, for
> you are already
> there, and the cat
> got there before you, yet
> it is hard to locate.
> What is more, the place is
> not found but seeps
> from our touch in
> continuous creation, dark
> enclosing cocoon round
> ourselves alone, dark
> wide realm where we
> walk with everyone.

Partly as a result of his residence in San Francisco, where he was exposed to radical populist ideas, Gunn is the one Movement poet to have moved not from the communal towards the individual, but from the individual towards the communal. For younger readers, he has also been more readily identifiable than other Movement poets with the spirit of the times: in *Moly* (1971) are poems about drug-taking, surfing, open-air rock concerts. This development should not be oversimplified: Gunn has not abandoned his interest in the controlling individual 'will', and there is in *Moly* and *Jack Straw's*

Castle (1976) a fear of self-immolation which counterbalances the urge to 'transcend' (through drugs) or 'merge' (through communal experience) the 'chilly hardness' of selfhood. But, particularly in its exploration of sexuality, Gunn's work now has a range of feeling which was absent from the early *Fighting Terms* poems, where the determination to present himself as *l'homme moyen sensuel* (and thus to deny a range of feeling outside Movement-like heterosexuality) produced serious flaws. (Gunn's suppression of 'A Village Edmund' in later editions of *Fighting Terms,* and his moving of 'Carnal Knowledge', originally the opening poem, to the middle of that volume, suggest recognition of these flaws.)

While the question of Modernism is one that has divided the Movement poets, the question of Romanticism is one on which they have still been largely in agreement, even though their original position has undergone a significant alteration. In the early 1950s, the group agreed on an anti-Romantic programme, despite the fact that (especially in the cases of Larkin and Gunn) this to some extent meant going against instinctive inclinations. Since then the Movement writers have been more willing to acknowledge the strengths of Romantic poetry, and to concede that their attempt to 'oust' Romanticism was the result of a historically foreshortened view. As Davie put it in 1966:

. . . we must be glad to be compelled to recognize that we are all, like it or not, post-Romantic people; that the historical developments which we label 'Romanticism' were not a series of aberrations which we can and should disown, but rather a sort of landslide which permanently transformed the mental landscape which in the twentieth century we inhabit, however reluctantly. It seems to me now that this was a recognition which I came to absurdly late in life; that my teachers when I was young encouraged me to think that I could expunge Romanticism from my historical past by a mere act of will or stroke of the pen, and that by doing this I could climb back into the lost garden of the seventeenth century. It is not a question of what we want or like; it is what we are stuck with -- post-Romantic is what we are.[64]

One example of Davie's increased tolerance of formerly

unacceptable Romantic tenets is his changed view of the composition of poetry. Several times in the early 1960s he quotes
Pasternak to the effect that, at certain moments during composition, language is in the 'ascendancy' and 'begins to think
and speak' for the poet. This may not be a strictly 'inspira-
tional' view of poetry, but it is one which recognizes that in
the poetic process something other than the conscious intention of the poet is a determining factor. It is much closer to
a Romantic view of composition than the Movement would
have allowed, but it is a view which Davie finds he can 'partially
confirm from [his] own experience in writing poems'.[65] Wain
has also changed his common sense Movement view of composition, reverting to a Romantic view of poetry as a raid on
the subconscious: 'We are powered by deep instinctual and
archetypal forces . . . They hide like great fish in an opaque
sea . . . The mind, however, can get away from its limited
nature if it rises on the wing-beats of art.'[66] As the Movement poets have begun to recognize the existence of forces
unencompassed by a rational or empirical world-view, so
they have shown greater sympathy to Romanticism.

One Romantic tenet which the Movement has continued
to resist, however, is the idea that poetry and madness are
closely allied. This was an idea which occasioned new interest
in the early 1960s as a result of poems written by Lowell,
Berryman, Plath, Hughes and others—poems about mental
breakdown, suicide and violence. Thom Gunn was also occasionally linked with them—a mistaken connection, but one
which led Davie, in 1962, to deplore the fact that 'a poetic
programme less than ten years old, which called for a return
to rational order and control, has been overturned from
within its own ranks, by writers like Gunn and Alvarez who
dwell instead upon the pain and violence of psychic disturbance'.[67] Davie was cynical about Alvarez's Extremist thesis:
'Poets nowadays know that it helps their reputations and sales
if they can manage a spell in the psychiatric ward.'[68] Larkin
made an identical point some years later, when he described

the present as 'an age when almost any poet who can produce evidence of medical mental care is automatically ranked higher than one who has stayed sane: "very mad, very holy" as the natives say in one of Evelyn Waugh's novels, and we must take care not to copy their way of thinking. Poetry is an affair of sanity, of seeing things as they are.'[69] In his poem 'Out-Patient' Amis is typically brisk in deciding whether it is better to be 'cured' or mad: 'Right then, mine's a lobotomy'.

Despite these declarations, the Movement had less success in the 1960s in upholding reason and commonsense. This was particularly noticeable in the case of Elizabeth Jennings, who, notwithstanding the occasional reflection that her Movement stance might be too cosy and evasive ('Big questions bruised my mind but still I let/Small answers be a bulwark to my fear' as she self-accusingly puts it in the 1955 poem 'Answers'), had for much of the 1950s fitted neatly into a programme for order, lucidity and reason. The opening, title poem of *Song for a Birth or a Death* (1961) made clear that she had changed, and was now about to allow violent and disturbing visions into her works:

> Last night I saw the savage world
> And heard the blood beat up the stair;
> The fox's bark, the owl's shrewd pounce,
> The crying creatures — all were there,
> And men in bed with love and fear.
>
> The slit moon only emphasized
> How blood must flow and teeth must grip . . .

It was personal experience, as well as susceptibility to the work of Hughes, Plath and even American Beat poets like Ginsberg, which brought about the changes in Jennings's work in the 1960s. Many of the poems in *Recoveries* (1964) and *The Mind Has Mountains* (1966) describe the ordeal of a nervous breakdown in the early 1960s. 'Pain', the first poem from a 'Sequence in Hospital', is typical of the confessional mode in which Jennings relates this experience:

> At my wits' end,
> And all resources gone, I lie here,

> All of my body tense to the touch of fear,
> And my mind,
>
> Muffled now as if the nerves
> Refused any longer to let thoughts form,
> Is no longer a safe retreat, a tidy home.

Other Movement poets have also found that the mind is not 'a safe retreat, a tidy home', and that reason lacks the power to deal with the full range of human experience. In the title poem of his collection, *In the Stopping Train and Other Poems* (1977), Davie refers to 'the man going mad inside me': the earlier, Movement Davie would have erased this line, feeling it to be too melodramatic, but he now challenges those readers who might be surprised to 'Catch our clean-shaven hero/tied up in such a knot'. A similarly disturbed central figure inhabits Amis's *The Green Man* (1969): Maurice Allington is an alcoholic who is subject to hallucinations and inexplicable fears. It is true that the ghost story motif in the novel provides a rational basis for Maurice's disturbance, but he seems a more disturbed and frightened figure than any of Amis's pragmatic heroes of the 1950s. Enright's poem 'Doctor, Doctor' seems to sum up the Movement dilemma:

> (You think it is easy, all this sanity?
> Try it. It will send you mad.)

Another feature of Amis's work of the 1960s and 1970s is its increasing preoccupation with death: even when his heroes are most fully engaged in 'life', that is in sexual intercourse, death is never very far away. This co-existence of sex and death can be found, for example, in the poem, 'Fforestfawr', where Evans, immediately after his father's funeral, arranges to meet his mistress in a pub; in *The Green Man,* where Maurice Allington, immediately after his father's death, makes love to his wife; and in 'Nothing to Fear', where—just as had happened with Patrick Standish in *Take a Girl Like You*—the male protagonist finds his pleasant anticipation of a sexual encounter being interrupted by thoughts of death:

> Why this slight trembling,
> Dry mouth, quick pulse-rate, sweaty hands,
> As though she were the first? No, not impatience,
> Nor fear of failure, thank you, Jack.
> Beauty, they tell me, is a dangerous thing,
> Whose touch will burn, but I'm asbestos, see?
> All worth while — it's a dead coincidence
> That sitting here, a bag of glands
> Tuned up to concert pitch, I seem to sense
> A different style of caller at my back,
> As cold as ice, but just as set on me.

Amis's heroes are not sad or stoical about death; they find the prospect of it dreadful, and consider wild schemes for avoiding it. In *The Anti-Death League* an organization is formed to abolish death, and in *Take a Girl Like You* Patrick Standish reflects that there is 'quite a good chance of his never actually being called upon to die at all. Those medicos would probably come up with something in the next decade or so'. But thoughts of death cannot be abolished, and in *The Green Man* Maurice Allington wonders 'why everybody who isn't a child, everybody who's theoretically old enough to have understood what death means doesn't spend all his time thinking about it'. A similar idea is voiced in Amis's *Ending Up* (1973), when there is a discussion between two younger relatives who are visiting a household of geriatrics: '"Do you think, er," said Keith, "do you think they spend *all* their time thinking about it, or merely nearly all their time?" "Quite possibly not as much time as all that," answered Trevor . . . "If you live with something you may end up with it not meaning as much to you as if it only turned up now and then. You know, like background noise"'.

Larkin's 'The Old Fools' has interesting similarities to Amis's *Ending Up*. Both texts are concerned with elderly people; both begin with a show of tough-mindedness towards their subjects which makes the gradual unfolding of sympathy towards them more convincing; and both provide a metaphorical solution to the problem of how old people deal with the prospect of imminent death. Amis uses the image of death as habitual 'background noise'; Larkin pictures it as a mountain peak which ceases to be distinguishable as one approaches it:

> For the rooms grow farther, leaving
> Incompetent cold, the constant wear and tear
> Of taken breath, and them crouching below
> Extinction's alp, the old fools, never perceiving
> How near it is. This must be what keeps them quiet:
> The peak that stays in view wherever we go
> For them is rising ground. Can they never tell
> What is dragging them back, and how it will end? Not at night?
> Not when the strangers come? Never, throughout
> The whole hideous inverted childhood? Well,
>   We shall find out.

The characteristic persona in the early work of Larkin and Amis is a young person who is trapped by his elders (Catherine in *A Girl in Winter* by Anstey, Dixon in *Lucky Jim* by Welch). As they have grown older, the Movement have begun to observe how such elders may themselves be trapped. There is not, of course, anything intrinsically 'anti-Movement' in a concern with old age and death: even in the 1950s, Larkin was treating these subjects interestingly, notably in the poem 'Wants', with its Romantic death-wish 'Beneath it all, desire of oblivion runs'. But the fact that the Movement has become increasingly preoccupied with these subjects, is a reminder that the outlook of the group has inevitably changed as the poets have grown older. What is of deepest concern to the Movement writers now was of somewhat less concern to them when, as young men in the 1950s, they first emerged.

It is little wonder, then, that the poets should have retrospectively denied or impugned the original confederacy: the movement which had once served to bring them valuable attention became, in the 1960s, a burdensome label, one that tied them to ideas and feelings and preoccupations which, in some cases at least, they no longer had. After 1956 the work of Gunn and Davie in particular underwent considerable change; and even writers like Amis and Larkin, who have

remained largely faithful to the Movement's aims, have developed to a point where they feel strongly that their work
should be judged on individual merit rather than as part of
a now defunct collective. The Movement, they would say, is
no longer in motion; its members have moved out, moved on,
moved away.

The group's dispersal makes it easier for us to assess it.
Anyone trying to reach conclusions about the Movement
is, however, likely to come up against the problem faced by
Garnet Bowen in Amis's *I Like It Here*. Bowen is writing
a book about the still very active Graham Greene: 'He had
nothing against that author either personally or aesthetically,
but wished he would die soon so that his lecture on him would
not keep on having to have things added to it every eighteen
months or so'. As I write all the Movement poets are still
alive and writing—with the exception of Philip Larkin, who
published only one major poem, 'Aubade', between *High
Windows* and his death in 1985, and whose premature silence
is a great sadness. All eight continue to publish work which,
though not always or even very often in the spirit of the
Movement, modifies the picture of what it stood for. To take
just a few examples: Enright's *Paradise Illustrated* (1978)
jokily reworks the myth of Creation and Fall, and his *A
Faust Book* (1979) the Faust legend: both collections show
that concern with God, Christianity, the flesh and the Devil
which seemed likely to develop as the Movement poets grew
older. Amis's novel *Jake's Thing* (1978) features a hero who
has difficulties with his libido and who exhibits a growing
dislike of women: such themes were implicit and waiting to be
developed in Amis's earlier fiction, and have been explored
again more recently in *Stanley and the Women* (1984), which
addresses itself to the question of whether 'all women are
mad' and concludes, no less misogynistically, 'No. They're
not mad, They're all too monstrously, sickeningly, *terrify-
ingly* sane. That's the *whole trouble*.' In between these two
Amis published *Russian Hide-and-Seek* (1980), a novel which

imagines a twenty-first century Britain ruled by Russia but which refuses to become the anti-communist satire which such a setting and Amis's public statements would lead one to suppose. Sexual reassessment of another kind is present in Thom Gunn's *The Passages of Joy* (1982), the first collection in which he unambiguously 'comes out' as a homosexual, declaring his attraction to men and boys ('I could eat you whole') and hymning the pleasures of male companionship—a male companionship very different from the Movement's, however. Gunn's book neatly highlights the kind of movements in our society—from feminism to Gay Liberation—which have made the Movement seem reactionary, moribund, antique.

This study has been concerned primarily with the Movement's 'spokesmanship', its articulation of ideas and feelings widely prevalent in Britain in the 1950s. The emphasis has had its drawbacks: I am conscious of an injustice to the idiosyncrasy of Enright and of a failure to account for large areas in Thom Gunn's work which have nothing to do with his somewhat peripheral connection with the Movement. I have also for the most part withheld judgement on the relative merits of the Movement writers, though I happen to believe (as may be apparent) that Larkin is by far and away the group's finest poet, Amis its best (and an underrated) novelist, and Davie its outstanding critic. As to the group's overall achievement, I think it undeniable that much of the writing seems in retrospect dry, academic, insular, repressed, lacking in scope. But Larkin, Amis, Davie, Gunn and Enright all at their best proved capable of transcending these limitations and ensured that the group would have a lasting importance. And even the minor figures deserve a footnote in literary history for helping to swell that common voice which—with nostalgia and fascination—we recognize as the voice of the 1950s.

Notes

Full bibliographical details found in the Select Bibliography are not repeated here. Page references refer to the latest edition of a work.

Introduction

1. See J. D. Scott, 'A Chip of Literary History', *Spectator*, 16 April 1977. p. 20, which put an end to over twenty years' speculation about the identity of the anonymous author.
2. Nuttall, *Bomb Culture*, MacGibbon and Kee (London), 1968, p. 58; Sergeant and Abse (eds.), *Mavericks*, p. 12; Logue, 'Jazz and Poetry', *Twentieth Century*, Aug. 1959, p. 85.
3. Hamilton, 'The Making of the Movement', *New Statesman*, 23 April 1971, p. 570. The essay is reprinted in Hamilton's *A Poetry Chronicle*, pp. 128-33.
4. Davie, *Pound*, p. 35.
5. Larkin, 'Four Conversations' (interview with Ian Hamilton), *London Magazine*, Nov. 1964, p. 69; Amis, *What Became of Jane Austen? And Other Questions*, p. 176; Gunn, 'A Sense of Movements', *Spectator*, 23 May 1958, p. 661; Enright, letter to William Van O'Connor, 8 May 1958; Jennings, (ed.) *An Anthology of Modern Verse, 1940-1960*, p. 11; Conquest in *The Poet Speaks*, ed. Peter Orr, Routledge and Kegan Paul (London), 1966, p. 49; Davie, *The Poet in the Imaginary Museum: Essays of Two Decades*, pp. 72-5.
6. Tomlinson, 'The Middlebrow Muse', *Essays in Criticism*, 7 (1957), 208-17.
7. Alvarez, *The New Poetry*, pp. 21-32.
8. Bedient, *Eight Contemporary Poets*, p.ix.
9. Thurley, *The Ironic Harvest*, see esp. pp. 137-62.
10. Longley, 'Larkin, Edward Thomas and The Tradition', *Phoenix*, Nos. 11-12 (1973-4), p. 64.

Chapter 1

1. Larkin, letter to O'Connor, 2 April 1958. Cf. this from 'Not the Place's Fault', *Umbrella*, 1 (Summer 1959), p. 111, which almost certainly has Amis in mind: 'when friends of mine have promoted

to paper things I have said or written to them privately, I have not felt that my jokes sounded unworthy of their reputations'.

2. This is reported to be Larkin's joke to Philip Oakes, 'The Unsung Gold Medallist', *Sunday Times Magazine*, 27 March 1966, p. 65.

3. Wain, *Preliminary Essays*, p. 189.

4. Amis, 'Anglo-Saxon Platitudes', *Spectator*, 5 April 1957, p.445. This seeks to discover 'the most boring long poem in English', and considers as candidates *Troilus and Criseyde* ('that footling rigmarole'), *Piers Plowman*, *Sir Gawain and the Green Knight*, *Havelock the Dane* and *The Owl and the Nightingale* ('nobody in full possession of their faculties could enjoy them'). See also *I Like It Here*, p. 72, which describes *The Dream of the Rood* as 'some piece of orang-utan's toilet-requisite from the dawn of England's literary heritage'.

5. Larkin, 'Four Conversations', p. 76.

6. Edmund Crispin, 'An Oxford Group', *Spectator*, 17 April 1964, p. 525.

7. Morgan, quoted by Philip Oakes, 'The Unsung Gold Medallist', p. 65.

8. Wain, *A House for the Truth*, p. 67.

9. Wain, *Sprightly Running*, p. 204. Amis, in *What Became of Jane Austen?*, p. 175 also refers to this undergraduate novel, which was never published and which was more serious in tone than *Lucky Jim*.

10. See Amis in *The Poetry of War, 1939–45*, ed. Ian Hamilton, New English Library (London), 1972, p. 155.

11. *Oxford Poetry 1949*, eds. Amis and Michie, p. 3.

12. Jennings, 'New Novels', *Listener*, 9 April 1964, p. 601.

13. Amis, letter to O'Connor, 21 Jan. 1958.

14. Conquest, letter to O'Connor, 12 May 1958.

15. Jennings in *Poetry Review*, Aug–Sept. 1949, p. 252. Not collected.

16. Jennings, 'Black and White', *Listener*, 14 April 1955, p. 654. Not collected.

17. Amis and Michie, *Oxford Poetry 1949*, p. 4; Wain, *Preliminary Essays*, p. 174.

18. Larkin, quoted in John Horder, 'Poet on the 8.15', *Guardian*, 20 May 1965, p. 9.

19. Amis, quoted in Clive James, 'Kingsley Amis — A Profile', p. 22. For a similar comment, see Amis, 'Real and Made-up People', *Times Literary Supplement*, 27 July 1973, p. 847.

20. Amis, quoted in 'The Art of Fiction — LIX: Interview with Kingsley Amis', *Paris Review*, 16 (Winter 1975), 45.

21. Davie, 'The Varsity Match', *Poetry Nation*, No. 2 (1973), p.73.

22. Gunn in *My Cambridge*, ed. Ronald Hayman, p. 145.

23. Ibid, p. 140.

24. Coleman in *Granta*, 15 Nov. 1952, p. 81. The same issue contained Gunn's 'Carnal Knowledge', His 'A Village Edmund', 'The Beach Head' and 'A Mirror for Poets' also appeared in *Granta* around this time.
25. Enright, *Conspirators and Poets*, p. 31; Davie in *My Cambridge*, ed. Hayman, p. 86; Gunn, ibid., pp. 138-9.
26. Gunn quoted in Ronald Hayman, *Leavis*, Heinemann (London), 1976, p. 50.
27. Davie in *Poetry from Cambridge in Wartime*, ed. Geoffrey Moore, Fortune Press (London), 1946, p. 27.
28. Enright in *Scrutiny*, II (1942-3), 78-9.
29. Enright, 'The Significance of Poetry London', *The Critic*, I (Spring 1947), 3-10.
30. Conquest, 'Rhyme-Lag', *Spectator*, 24 Jan. 1958, p. 111.
31. Tambimuttu, *Poetry London–New York*, No. 1 (March-April 1956), p. 2.
32. Davie, *The Poet in the Imaginary Museum*, pp. 3-5.
33. Wain, (ed.) *Anthology of Modern Poetry*, p. 33.
34. Davie, 'Towards a New Poetic Diction', *Prospect*, 2 (Summer 1949), 5.
35. Saunders, *The Profession of English Letters*, Routledge (London), 1964, p. 235.
36. Wain, in *Mandrake*, No. 9 (1953), p. 266; Enright, in *Nimbus*, 2 (Autumn 1953), 3-6.
37. Empson, 'Monks and Commissars', *New Statesman*, 13 Dec. 1952, p. 724; Fraser, 'The New Smoothness', *New Statesman*, 15 Nov. 1952, p. 582.
38. Amis, letter to *Listener*, 6 Nov. 1952, p. 771.
39. Enright, 'Signs of the Times', *The Month*, Aug. 1952, p. 107.
40. Conquest, letter to *New Statesman*, 26 Dec. 1953, p. 822.
41. Enright, 'Verse: New, Old and Second-Hand', *The Month*, Nov. 1951, p. 309.
42. Gunn, 'Four Conversations', pp. 69-70.
43. Davie, *Purity of Diction in English Verse*, p. 198.
44. Larkin, 'Four Conversations', p. 72; Wain, *Sprightly Running*, p. 168; Wain 'The "Third" Man', *Twentieth Century*, Dec. 1956, p. 504.
45. Davie, 'Augustans New and Old', *Twentieth Century*, Nov. 1955, p.465.
46. In *Springtime*, ed. G. S. Fraser, for instance, we are told that 'Irish poets, like Mr Larkin, though writing in standard English, reflect another regional value, that of rootedness' (p. 12); and in the 'Notes on Contributors' section of Alan Brownjohn's magazine *Departure*, 3 (Spring 1955), 20, we are told that Larkin was 'born in Northern Ireland'.

47. Massingham, 'Watch and Listen', *New Statesman,* 18 July 1953, p. 72.
48. Fraser, letter to *New Statesman,* 1 Aug. 1953, p. 132.
49. Larkin, 'Four Conversations', p. 72.
50. Davie, letter to O'Connor, 31 Dec. 1957.
51. Ibid.
52. Conquest, letter to O'Connor, 19 May 1958.
53. Davie, 'The Varsity Match', p. 74.
54. Amis criticized Sitwell's lack of interest in 'communication' in 'The Critical Forum', *Essays in Criticism,* 2 (1952), 342–5. Davie's attack came in 'Is there a London Literary Racket?', p. 544. Amis later suggested—in 'Connolly in Court', *New Statesman,* 6 Dec. 1963, p. 836—that 'in this country we take the gravest possible view of people who go round saying that Edith Sitwell is a great poet'.
55. Scott, 'A Chip of Literary History', p. 20.
56. Allen, 'New Novels', *New Statesman,* 30 Jan. 1954, p. 136. See also Snow, 'New Trends in First Novels', *Sunday Times,* 27 Dec. 1953, p. 3, and Priestley, 'Thoughts in the Wilderness: The Newest Novels', *New Statesman,* 26 June 1954, p. 824.
57. Anon, 'London Diary', *New Statesman,* 22 Aug. 1953, p. 197. Cf. V. S. Pritchett in 'First Stop Reading', ibid. 3 Oct. 1953, p. 379: 'If Mr G. S. Fraser is right in speaking of contributors [to *First Reading*] as people who live in the provinces, they could have tried starting new literary movements in the regions as well as on the Third'.
58. Davie, 'The Varsity Match', p. 77.

Chapter 2

1. Green, *A Mirror for Anglo-Saxons,* p. 53; Alvarez, *The New Poetry,* pp. 24–5; Oakes, 'A New Style in Heroes', *Observer,* 1 Jan. 1956, p. 8.
2. Davie, for instance, writes in 'Remembering the Movement' (1959): 'I remember nothing so distastefully as the maidenly shudders with which I wished to know nothing of the machinery of publicity, even as I liked publicity and profited by it'.
3. Davie, letter to O'Connor, 31 Dec. 1957.
4. Spender, 'On Literary Movements', *Encounter,* Nov. 1953, p. 66; Sitwell, in *Mightier Than The Sword: The P.E.N. Hermon Ould Memorial Lectures, 1953–61,* Macmillan (London) 1964, p. 60; Waugh, 'An Open Letter to the Honourable Mrs Peter Rodd (Nancy Mitford) . . .', *Encounter,* Dec. 1955, p. 11; Maugham, 'Books of the Year', *Sunday Times,* 25 Dec. 1955, p. 4.

5. Wain, 'Orwell', *Spectator*, 19 Nov. 1954, pp. 630-4; Larkin, 'Four Conversations', p. 77.

6. Hartley, *A State of England*, p. 48. Cf. Davie, 'Pleasures of Ruins', *New Statesman*, 19 May, 1956, p. 571: 'The new provincialism is showing its fangs . . . There's a sort of snobbery about pretending that the really interesting things are in Basingstoke or Hull.'

7. Holloway, *London Magazine*, June 1957, p. 64.

8. Amis, 'My Kind of Comedy', *Twentieth Century*, July 1961, p. 50. Cf. his letter to the *Spectator*, July 8 1955: 'I'm not grumpy about furrin (sic) parts only about people being silly about them' (p. 47). Bowen's attitude, and his author's, are well explained by Orwell in 'The English People', CEJL, Vol. 3, p. 18: 'Travelling abroad, speaking foreign tongues, enjoying foreign food, are vaguely felt to be upper-class habits, so that xenophobia is reinforced by class jealousy.'

9. Amis, 'That Certain Revulsion', *Encore*, 3 (June–July 1957), 11.

10. Davie, *The Late Augustans*, Heinemann (London), 1958, p. xii. See also *Purity of Diction*, pp. 198-9.

11. Wain, *A House for the Truth*, p. 27.

12. Davie, 'Academicism and Jonathan Swift', *Twentieth Century*, Sept. 1953, p. 217. See also his 'The Reader Vanishes', *Spectator*, 11 Sept. 1953, pp. 274-5; 'The Earnest and the Smart: Provincialism in Letters', *Twentieth Century*, Nov. 1953, pp. 387-94; and 'Is there a London Literary Racket?', ibid, June 1954, pp. 540-6.

13. Hartley, *A State of England*, p. 43.

14. Quoted from an Oxford Magazine by David Marquand to support his claim that 'Lucky Jim's attitudes are shared by the overwhelming majority of those who think at all', 'Lucky Jim and the Labour Party', *Universities and Left Review*, I (Spring 1957), 57.

15. Amis, 'My Kind of Comedy', *Twentieth Century*, July 1961, p. 50.

16. Amis, *What Became of Jane Austen?*, p.145; Gunn in *My Cambridge*, ed. Hayman, p. 136; Wain, 'Engagement or Withdrawal? Some Notes on the Work of Philip Larkin', *Critical Quarterly*, 6 (Summer 1964), 177. See also Davie in *My Cambridge*, ed. Hayman, p. 90.

17. Wain, letter to *Encounter*, June 1955, p. 69.

18. Wain, 'Along the Tightrope', *Declaration*, ed. Tom Maschler, p. 101. cf. Amis on Dixon in his *Paris Review* interview, 'The Art of Fiction . . .', p. 45: 'He didn't want to change the system. He certainly did not want to *destroy* the system.'

19. Amis, *What Became of Jane Austen?*, p. 192.

20. Laslett, 'The Changing Face of English Education', *Texas Quarterly* (Winter 1960), p. 19.

21. Amis, 'My Kind of Comedy', *Twentieth Century*, July 1961, p. 50.

22. Amis, 'That Certain Revulsion', *Encore*, 3 (June–July 1957), 10.
23. Amis, 'Editor's Notes', *Spectator*, 7 Oct. 1955, p. 459.
24. Davie, *Thomas Hardy and British Poetry*, p. 100.
25. Lodge, 'The Modern, the Contemporary and the Importance of Being Amis', *Critical Quarterly*, 5 (1963), 340. The essay is reprinted in Lodge, *The Language of Fiction*, Routledge (London), 1966, pp. 243-67.
26. Amis, 'The Art of Fiction . . .', p. 44. Cf. Wain who describes himself as 'believing passionately in the great liberating wave of social justice that my generation expected to result from the 1945 Labour Victory' (*Sprightly Running*, p. 180).
27. Davie in *My Cambridge*, ed. Hayman, pp. 83-4.
28. Larkin's *The Oxford Book of Twentieth Century English Verse* contains several poems which might have acted as models: Andrew Young's 'Wiltshire Downs'—'The stable boys thud by/Their horses slinging divots at the sky'; F. R. Higgins's 'The Old Jockey'—'His last days linger in that low attic/That barely lets out the night'; and Dorothy Wellesley's 'Horses'—'A horse's ears bob on the distant hill/ . . . Remembering adventures of his kin . . .'.
29. The unspoken rejoinder—where a frustrated Movement protagonist picks up a word spoken by someone he dislikes, does silent destruction to it, but maintains politeness—is also a feature of Orwell's *Keep the Aspidistra Flying*. In the following exchange, for example, Comstock must defer to a customer at his bookshop:
'Good afternoon. Can I do anything for you? Are you looking for any particular book?'
'Oh, no, not weally.' An R-less Nancy voice. 'May I just bwowse? I simply couldn't wesist your fwont window. I have such a tewwible weakness for bookshops! So I just floated in — tee-hee!'
Float out again, then, Nancy. Gordon smiled a cultured smile, as booklover to booklover.
30. Hartley, *A State of England*, pp. 148-9. For a similar comment on the plight of the post-war intelligentsia, see Wain, 'Thirties Together', *Spectator*, 19 March 1945, p. 333.
31. Davie, *Thomas Hardy and British Poetry*, p. 86.
32. In 'Life and Letters' D. J. Enright admits that, like Davie, he is 'loth to face the fashionable terrors,/Or venture among sinister symbols'; but he insists on the need 'to write lucidly'—'Poems, at least,/Ought not to be phantoms'.
33. Wain, *Anthology of Modern Poetry*, pp. 34-5.
34. Davie, *Ezra Pound: Poet as Sculptor*, p. 244. Cf. Conquest, 'Ezra Pound', *London Magazine*, April 1963, p. 41: 'Pound's theme is, his apologists would say, Civilization. Yet seeing how much he has

misunderstood the one in which he is actually situated, one fails to be adequately impressed by the confidence with which he tackles ancient China and ancient Egypt.' In his book on Pound (above), Davie took Conquest to task for his 'boyish petulance' and 'scandalous' dismissal of Pound (p. 86), yet their views on this particular point are remarkably similar.

35. Amis, *Socialism and the Intellectuals*, pp. 3–4.
36. Spender attacked the poem in *Encounter*, Sept. 1956, p. 52, and brought this reply from Davie in the Nov. issue, p. 70: 'it [the poem] is about the pathos of the fact that no generation, however brilliantly resourceful and persuasive, can convey wholly to any other generation its sense of the urgency of the issues which confront it. The poem says that this is nobody's fault, but is in the scheme of things.' Davie's comment seems borne out by Elizabeth Jennings in her review, 'And Remembering the Thirties', *Spectator*, Nov. 20, 1964, p. 683: 'the poetry of the 1930s seems even more remote from us than that of the Victorians and the Romantics'.
37. Wain, 'Thirties Together', p. 332. Cf. his Lumley in *Hurry on Down*, who finds himself despising 'the expensive young men of the thirties' and their 'desire to enter, and be at one with, a vaguely conceived People' (pp. 38–9).
38. Davie in *My Cambridge*, ed. Hayman, p. 89. Cf. his 'Eliot in One Poet's Life', *Mosaic*, 6 (Fall 1972), 232: 'The break between the generations was very sharp; for men and women who had gone up to University only eighteen months before me had had time to invest something in the ideology of the Popular Front . . .' Cf. also Wain, *Professing Poetry*, p. 257.
39. Amis, *Socialism and the Intellectuals*, p. 8.
40. Hartley, *A State of England*, pp. 47–8.
41. Gunn, letter to *London Magazine*, June 1957, pp. 65–6. Gunn adds that, in any case, 'political engagement has nothing to do with literary merit'. This view was also put by Larkin and Enright in their contributions to the symposium in May: Larkin said that 'a writer's only "necessary engagement" is with his subject-matter, which is not primarily a conscious choice at all' (p. 47), and Enright that 'the writer's only artistic duty is to find a subject suited to his talent' (pp. 41–2).
42. Amis, *Socialism and the Intellectuals*, p. 7; Enright, *Poets of the 1950's*, p. 12. Cf. also, the complacency in Wain's admission that 'we tended to assume that the actual engineering of social change, by legislation and so forth, could best be left to professionals' (*A House for the Truth*, p. 26).
43. Holloway, *The Charted Mirror*, p. 137.

Chapter 3

1. Davie, *The Poet in the Imaginary Museum*, p. 72.
2. Davie, 'The Toneless Voice of Robert Graves', *Listener*, 2 July 1959, p. 12.
3. Gaskell, 'The Critical Forum', *Essays in Criticism*, 7 (1957), 462; Tomlinson, 'The Middlebrow Muse', 209; Press, *Rule and Energy*, p. 47. See also Patrick Swinden's essay 'English Poetry' in *The Twentieth Century Mind: Vol. 3, 1945-65*, eds. C. B. Cox and A. F. Dyson, pp. 386-413.
4. Seymour-Smith, 'The Literary Situation', *Departure*, 3 (Spring 1955), 16.
5. Tomlinson, 'The Critical Forum', *Essays in Criticism*, 7 (1957), 460.
6. Davie, *Purity of Diction*, pp. 23 and 138-9.
7. Amis, 'Communication and the Victorian Poet', *Essays in Criticism*, 4 (1954), 398-9.
8. Wain, 'The Strategy of Victorian Poetry', *Twentieth Century*, May 1953, pp. 388-9.
9. Q. D. Leavis, *Fiction and the Reading Public*, Chatto and Windus (London), 1932; 1965, pp. 229-31.
10. F. R. Leavis, *Education and the University*, Chatto and Windus (London), 1943; new ed. 1948, pp. 106-7.
11. Ibid., p. 106.
12. Ibid (Appendix 3), p. 143; p. 144.
13. Leavis, *New Bearings in English Poetry* (1932; reprinted with 'Retrospect 1950', Penguin (Harmondsworth) 1972), p. 16; p. 73.
14. Leavis, *How to Teach Reading*, Gordon Fraser — The Minority Press (London) 1932, p. 26.
15. Wain, *Preliminary Essays*, p. 95.
16. Bateson, *English Poetry*, Longmans (London), 1950; 2nd ed., 1966, pp. 268-9.
17. Ibid., preface, p. ix.
18. Ibid., p. 66. Bateson also made the familiar Movement point that such knowledge had been possible in the eighteenth century: 'the Augustan poets knew exactly whom they were writing for' (pp. 68-9), whereas the Romantics were unable 'to identify that ghostly "gentle reader" they are so fond of addressing' (p. 67).
19. Timms, *Philip Larkin*, pp. 15-16.
20. Amis in Peter Firchow, ed. *The Writer's Place*, University of Minnesota Press (Minneapolis), 1974, pp. 22-3.
21. Davie, letter to *Delta*, No. 9 (Summer 1955), p. 28; Conquest, *New Lines*, p. xvi.

22. Davie, 'Academicism and Jonathan Swift', *Twentieth Century*, Sept. 1953, p. 217.
23. Davie, *The Poet in the Imaginary Museum*, p. 77.
24. Gunn, 'Four Conversations', p. 69. For further discussion of Gunn and riddles see Neil Powell's 'The Abstract Joy: Thom Gunn's Early Poetry', *Critical Quarterly*, 13 (1971), 219-27, and John Fuller in Hamilton, ed. *The Modern Poet: Essays from the Review*, pp. 17-22.
25. Rosenthal, *The New Poets*, p. 238.
26. Larkin on *The Poet Speaks* (Argo Record Company, mono RG 518, Arg 2843, record no 8, 1967).
27. Larkin, 'The Pleasure Principle', *Listen*, 2 (Summer-Autumn 1957), 28-9.
28. Enright, 'The Poet, the Professor and the Public',*Nimbus*, 2 (Autumn 1953), 4.
29. Enright, *The Apothecary's Shop*, p. 236.
30. Conquest, interview with Hilary Morish in *The Poet Speaks*, ed. Peter Orr, Routledge (London), 1966, pp. 48-9.
31. Orwell, 'Writers and Leviathan' (1948) in CEJL, Vol. 4, p. 463.
32. Orwell, 'Poetry and the Microphone' (1943) in CEJL, Vol. 2, p. 378.
33. Amis, 'That Certain Revulsion', p. 10.
34. Conquest, letter to *London Magazine*, Sept. 1963, p. 83.
35. Amis, *What Became of Jane Austen?*, p. 93.
36. Ibid, p. 55.
37. Larkin, quoted by Douglas Dunn, 'Larkin at 50', BBC Third Programme, 9 Aug. 1972, and by Frances Hill, 'A Sharp Edged View', TES, 19 May, 1972, p. 19; 'Speaking of Writing: XIII — Philip Larkin', *Times*, 20 Feb. 1964, p. 16; 'Four Young Poets: I, Philip Larkin', TES, 13 July 1956, p. 933; ibid., p. 933.
38. Wain in *Declaration*, ed. Maschler, p. 102; 'A Writer's Prospect', *London Magazine* (Nov. 1956), p. 60.
39. Davie, *Articulate Energy*, pp. 128-9.
40. Enright, *Man Is an Onion*, p. 162.
41. Larkin, 'No Fun Any More', *Guardian*, 18 Nov. 1958, p. 4.
42. Wain in *The Writer's Place*, ed. Peter Firchow, p. 315.
43. Larkin, 'Betjeman en Bloc', *Listen*, 3 (Spring 1959), 14.
44. *Arts Council Tenth Annual Report* (1955), p. 7; '*The First Ten Years*': *Arts Council Eleventh Annual Report* (1956), pp. 59-60; P.E.N., *The Author and the Public: Problems of Communication*, Hutchinson (London), 1957, p. 24.
45. Pinto, *Crisis in English Poetry*, Hutchinson (London), 1951, p. 208.
46. Karl Miller in *William Empson: The Man and His Work*, ed. Roma Gill, Routledge (London), 1974, pp. 44-5.

47. Wain, ed. *Interpretations*, p. vii.
48. Bergonzi, 'Critical Situations: From the Fifties to the Seventies', *Critical Quarterly*, 15 (1973), 59–73.
49. Hoggart, *Speaking to Each Other*, Chatto and Windus (London), 1970, p. 44.
50. Davie, 'Entering into the Sixteenth Century', *Essays in Criticism*, 5 (1955), 162–3.
51. Davie in *Poet's Choice*, ed. Joseph Langland and Paul Engle. Dial Press (New York), 1962, p. 198.
52. Anderson in *Declaration*, ed. Maschler, p. 166.
53. Raban, *The Society of the Poem*, p. 67, on what he calls the 'English liberal style' of Auden and Larkin.

Chapter 4

1. Herman Peschmann, *The Voice of Poetry*, Evans Brothers (London), 1969, p. 16.
2. Davie, letter to *London Magazine*, March 1954, p. 74; Wain, 'The Last Time', *Mandrake*, No. 10 (Autumn–Winter 1954–5), p. 354.
3. Enright, *Conspirators and Poets*, p. 46.
4. Reprinted in *Preliminary Essays*, pp. 180–5.
5. *What Became of Jane Austen?*, pp. 55–9.
6. Bateson, *English Poetry*, p. 35.
7. Amis, 'That Certain Revulsion', p. 10.
8. Davie, *Articulate Energy*, pp. 127–8. Cf. Davie's rather similar criticisms of the 'muscle-bound monstrosity' of Hopkins's verse—'word is piled on word, and stress on stress' (*Purity of Diction*, p. 175).
9. Bloom, *The Anxiety of Influence*, Oxford University Press (London), 1973, p. 5.
10. Orwell, *Coming Up for Air*, p. 73. For a similar opinion, see Larkin's review 'The Savage Seventh', *Spectator*, 20 Nov. 1959, p. 713.
11. Davie, 'Eliot in One Poet's Life', *Mosaic*, 6 (Fall 1972), 231.
12. Holloway, 'New Lines in English Poetry', p. 592.
13. Fraser in *The White Horseman*, ed. J. F. Hendry and Henry Treece, Routledge (London), 1941, p. 14.
14. Amis, 'The Day of the Moron', *Spectator*, 1 Oct. 1954, p. 408.
15. Wain, 'Poetic Virtues', *Observer*, 15 June 1952, p. 7.
16. Amis, 'Ulster Bull . . .', *Essays in Criticism*, 3 (1955), 473.
17. Davie, 'Syntax in Poetry and Music', *Twentieth Century*, Feb. 1953, pp. 131–2. The passage reappears slightly altered in *Articulate Energy*, pp. 18–19.
18. Ayer, *Language, Truth and Logic*, Gollancz (London), 1936; 2nd ed. 1946, pp. 34, 51, 118. For an account of the relationship

between the Movement and Logical Positivism see Derek Stanford's 'Thoughts on Contemporary Literature', *Contemporary Review*, 191 (April 1957), 234–8.

19. Ayer, p. 44.
20. Davie, *The Poet in the Imaginary Museum*, p. 28.
21. Press, *Rule and Energy*, p. 92.
22. Bateson, *English Poetry*, p. ix. For further comment on the relationship between Amis's poem and Bateson's see Patrick Swinden, 'English Poetry' in *The Twentieth Century Mind: Vol. 3, 1945–65*, ed. C. B. Cox and A. E. Dyson, pp. 386–90.
23. Amis, *What Became of Jane Austen?*, p. 21. See also his essay 'The Curious Elf: A Note on Rhyme in Keats', *Essays in Criticism*, 1, (1951), 189–192.
24. Bradbury, introduction to *Eating People is Wrong*, p. 5.
25. Amis, 'A Man on Rockall', *Spectator*, 9 Nov. 1956, p. 656.
26. Wain, *Preliminary Essays*, p. 155.
27. As well as 'Hall's-Distemper boards', there are the phrases 'Kodak-instant' in 'Whatever Happened?' and the (probably imaginary) 'Granny Gravesclothes' Tea' in 'Essential Beauty', cf. Amis, who criticizes T. S. Eliot for his omission of brand names: 'I think a few mentions of (say) Nestle's condensed milk, Woodbines, Spink's plum-and-apple jam, and Scotch and Apollonians would have done *The Waste Land* a world of good. As it is, the poem, by setting out not to be limited to or by its immediate period, has no social-temporal context either, and has become just one more of the featureless lumps of cultural lumber it purports to be superior to.' (*The James Bond Dossier*, Cape (London), 1965, p. 104.)
28. Davie, *Thomas Hardy and British Poetry*, p. 66.
29. Holloway, *The Lion Hunt*, p. 42.
30. For a fuller account of this poem, see Donald Davie, 'Augustans New and Old', pp. 471–2. Davie reads the poem as an attack on Imagist 'particularity'; it seems to me more probably an attack on nineteenth-century 'nature poetry'.
31. As well as Davie's 'An English Revenant' and 'The Garden Party', see George Scott's autobiography *Time and Place*, Staples Press (London), 1956, which contrasts 'the blackness and the hardness and the harsh taciturn grandeur' of his native Northern landscape with the 'lazy, conventional prettiness' of the 'home counties' (pp. 42–3). Scott was a contemporary of the Movement, and this autobiography was felt at the time of its publication to be a typical Movement product.
32. Leavis, *Revaluation: Tradition and Development in English Poetry*, 1936; Penguin (Harmondsworth), 1972, p. 201.

33. Ibid, p. 194.
34. Davie, *Thomas Hardy and British Poetry*, p. 66. Cf. what he says in *Poets of the 1950's*: 'I have been influenced by Wordsworth, in those places where he is more interested in the relationship of man with man than in the relationship of man with natural scenery'.
35. Enright, *Academic Year*, p. 44; cf. the game of 'Detestable Characters' played in Edmund Crispin's *The Moving Toyshop*.
36. Amis, *What Became of Jane Austen?*, p. 95.
37. Rabinovitz, *The Reaction Against Experiment in the English Novel, 1950–60*, p. 32.
38. Viereck, *Metropolitics*, Knopf (New York), 1941, p. 315. Denis Donoghue noted the connection between Viereck's ideas and Donald Davie's in his 'Poetry and the New Conservatism', *London Magazine*, April 1956, pp. 54–63. A contemporary of the Movement's (he was born in 1916), Viereck defended both political and poetic conservatism, wishing to restore clarity, discipline and traditional form to poetry. He was hostile both to Modernism and to the academic esteem for it:

> Here's the eighth form of ambiguity,
> The *new* philistia loves 'obscurity',
> And only we still dare to hate it
> Because a *texte* without a Muse in
> Is but a snore and an allusion.
> Well then, let's turn the tables hard:
> The snubs all snubbed, the baiters baited,
> The explicators explicated,
> The avant-garde the new rearguard.

(*The First Morning*, Charles Scribner (New York), 1952, p. 86.)

A poem such as this would have appealed to the Movement, and one can see now where a piece of word-play for which John Wain has been given credit—his statement that 'by the middle of the '50's one thing had begun to emerge about the avant-garde of English poetry: that it was a rearguard' ('English Poetry: The Immediate Situation', *Sewanee Review*, 1957, p. 353)—had its origins.

39. Wain in *Declaration*, ed. Maschler, p. 99.
40. Gindin, *Postwar British Fiction*, Cambridge University Press (London), 1962, p. 91.
41. Alvarez, *The New Poetry*, p. 25.
42. Wain, *Sprightly Running*, p. 190.
43. Treece, *How I See Apocalypse*, Lindsay Drummond (London), 1946, p. 35. Or again, in a passage which outdoes even an Amis

parody, 'artists are a minority force who are able to see further than their brothers. They are the spearheads of sensibility . . . who, one day, will be instrumental in elevating the non-artists to a higher plane of perception' (p. 25).

44. Conquest, 'Poetry in Britain', *Litterair Paspoort*, Oct.–Nov. 1956, p. 191.

45. Davie, *Purity of Diction*, p. 199. Cf. the introduction to his anthology *The Late Augustans*, which deplores the 'still common conviction (Romantic in origin) that the poet's vocation is necessarily at odds with all disciplines other than its own, and can flower only in rebellion and excess . . . To crown the case it was convenient to suppose that the best poetry — in fact the only true poetry — came out of the madhouse' (p. xxvii).

46. Wain, 'New Novels', *Observer*, 29 Jan. 1956, p. 9.

47. Amis, letter to *London Magazine*, Sept. 1954, p. 76.

48. Larkin, quoted in Philip Oakes, 'The Unsung Gold Medallist', p. 65.

49. Amis in *Poets' Choice*, ed. Langland and Engle, p. 196.

50. Amis, letter to *London Magazine*, Sept. 1954, p. 76.

51. Jennings, *Let's Have Some Poetry!*, Museum Press (London), 1960, pp. 20–1.

52. Amis, 'Hock and Soda-Water', *Spectator*, 31 Dec. 1954, p. 832.

53. Gunn, 'Energy Control', *Spectator*, 2 Aug. 1957, p. 167.

54. Gunn in the *Cambridge Review*, 22 Nov. 1952; reprinted in *The Cambridge Mind*, ed. Eric Homberger, Jonathan Cape (London), 1970, pp. 285–7.

55. Gunn, 'Yes and No', *Granta*, 1 Nov. 1952, p. 26.

56. Timms, *Philip Larkin*, p. 43.

57. Larkin, 'The Life with a Hole in It' in *Poetry Supplement Christmas 1974*, Poetry Book Society (London), 1974, no pagination.

58. Winters, *In Defence of Reason*, Routledge (London), 1960, p. 9.

59. Hulme in *Twentieth Century Poetry: Critical Essays and Documents*, ed. Graham Martin and R. N. Furbank, Open University Press, (Milton Keynes), 1975, p. 68.

Chapter 5

1. Larkin, letter to *Agenda*, 15 (Summer–Autumn 1977), 11.

2. Martin, *T. S. Eliot: Criticism*, Open University Twentieth Century Poetry Course, Unit 9, Open University Press (Milton Keynes), 1976, p. 12.

3. Timms, *Philip Larkin*, p. 113.

4. Allsop, *The Angry Decade*, p. 18.

5. Larkin, *The Whitsun Weddings*, quoted by Roger Day, *Phili*,
   Larkin, Open University Twentieth Century Poetry Course, Uni
   28, p. 32.

6. Wain, *Spectator*, 29 April 1955, p. 553. Cf. Wain's 'How It Strike
   a Contemporary', *Twentieth Century*, March 1957, p. 231, on th
   possibility of a classless society: 'the answer of the English peop
   has always been quite unambiguous. They *don't* want a classles
   society. Only a few people here and there, mainly among th
   intelligentsia, certainly not 'normal' English folk, have ever wante
   such a thing.'

7. Sassoon, *Memoirs of a Fox-Hunting Man*, Faber and Gruyer (Lor
   don), 1928, p. 307.

8. Larkin, 'Wanted: Good Hardy Critic', *Critical Quarterly*, 8 (1966)
   177.

9. Larkin, 'A Great Parade of Single Poems: Interview with Anthon
   Thwaite', *Listener*, 12 April 1973, p. 473.

10. Larkin, 'Four Conversations', p. 71.

11. Davie, 'In the Pity', *New Statesman*, 28 Aug. 1964, p. 282.

12. Davie, *Thomas Hardy and British Poetry*, pp. 11–12.

13. Wain, *Twentieth Century*, March 1957, pp. 229–30. The essa
    prompted Lindsay Anderson to comment—in 'Get Out and Push
    Declaration, ed. Maschler, p. 168—that 'Wain is talking already lik
    an empty-headed avuncular Tory'.

14. Davie in *My Cambridge*, ed. Hayman, p. 80.

15. Leavis, *Anna Karenina and Other Essays*, Chatto and Windus (Lor
    don), 1967, p. 223. Cf. Leavis and Denys Thompson, *Culture an*
    Environment, Chatto and Windus (London), 1933, p. 1: 'it is o
    literary tradition that the office of maintaining continuity must rest.

16. Wain, letter to *New Statesman*, 1 Aug. 1953, p. 132.

17. Wain, *London Magazine*, Nov. 1956, p. 61.

18. Enright, letter to *London Magazine*, Jan. 1957; expanded to becom
    'The Brain-Washed Muse: Some Second Thoughts on Tradition
    The Apothecary's Shop, pp. 225–30.

19. Davie, *The Poet in the Imaginary Museum*, p. 51.

20. Wain, *Preliminary Essays*, pp. 158–9.

21. Holloway, 'The Writer's Prospect', *London Magazine*, June 1957
    reprinted as 'The Prospect for a Poet' in *The Colours of Clarity*
    pp. 124–33. See also his *The Lion Hunt*, p. 46: 'Poetic tradition
    To rollingstock a little further along the line laid by William Empson
    To "go back to Eliot, Pound and Yeats (any more?) and to g
    forward from there". "Berryman and Lowell . . . the thing is to g
    on from there." Aweary, aweary . . . it is an image, that of the rail
    way, that of the on-from, out of not Spenser and the commo

tongue, but the dreary staple of our time: steady expansion of the firm, progress of the Plan, extrapolation of the curve. It is the staple of the organizer; and must therefore, in the realm of the arts, be not development but un-development.'

2. Larkin, 'Four Conversations', p. 71. The theory Larkin had in mind here was also put by Davie in his 'Imaginary Museum' talks: 'The modern style in poetry is the arrangement in new patterns of the styles of the past.' Larkin attacked this theory again in 'Context', *London Magazine*, Feb. 1962, p. 31: 'There is a theory that every new poem like an engineer's drawing should sum up all that has gone before and take it a step further, which means that before anything worthwhile can be written everything worthwhile must be read. This seems to me a classroom conception.'

3. Larkin, 'Context', pp. 31-2.

4. Amis, 'Fresh Winds from the West', *Spectator*, 2 May 1958, p. 565. Cf. his description of his own novels in *Contemporary Novelists*, ed James Vinson, St James Press (London), 1972, p. 46: 'believable stories about understandable characters in a reasonably straight-forward style: no tricks, no experimental foolery.'

5. Wain, 'Lost Horizons?', *Encounter*, Jan. 1961, pp. 69-70.

6. Davie, letter to *Delta*, no. 9 (Summer 1956), p. 27.

7. Davie, *Articulate Energy*, p. 129.

8. Davie, *Purity of Diction*, p. 99.

9. Davie, *Thomas Hardy and British Poetry*, p.6.

0. See, for example, Larkin's 'The War Poet', *Listener*, 10 Oct. 1963, pp. 561-2, which claims that Owen is 'the only twentieth-century poet who can be read after Hardy without a sense of bathos'.

1. Conquest, Review, *London Magazine*, June 1967, p. 111; Larkin, 'Down Among the Dead Men', *Spectator*, 18 Dec. 1959, p. 912.

2. Corke, 'The Bad Old Style', *Encounter*, June 1955, pp. 23-6.

3. Davie, 'Modernist Precursors', *New Statesman*, 3 Oct. 1953, p. 382.

4. Davie, 'In the Pity', p. 282. Cf. *Thomas Hardy and British Poetry*, p. 75: 'Hardy and Larkin may have sold poetry short; but at least neither of them has sold it so short as to make the poet less of a human being.'

5. Amis, 'Art and Craft', *Spectator*, 13 July 1956, pp. 68-9. Cf. his 'Grave and Gay', *Encounter*, April 1955, p. 78: '. . . only a genius can be completely grave, can ignore all the promptings of humour and irony and gaiety, without rolling over the slippery margin that divides the grave from the glum. And these days — not that it worries me at all — geniuses are thin on the ground.'

6. Amis, 'Anglo-Saxon Platitudes', *Spectator*, 5 April 1957, p. 445. Cf. Davie, in a 1954 essay 'Professor Heller and the Boots'; 'while

Dante is no doubt a classic in the strict sense of a permanent mode
from whom all poets at all times have something to learn, he i
doing us no good if he teaches to reach after what can no longer b
grasped, if in fact he teaches us to be too — well, too big for ou
boots' (*The Poet in the Imaginary Museum*. p. 24).

37. Graves, *The Crowning Privilege*, Cassell (London), 1955, pp. 114
    p. 21.

38. Enright, *Conspirators and Poets*, p. 52. For other Movement discus
    sions of Graves, see Gunn, 'The Well Turned Poet', *Spectator*, ‹
    Sept. 1957, p. 311; Larkin, 'Graves Superior', *Guardian*, 2 Dec
    1958, p. 4; and Davie, 'Eliot in One Poet's Life', *Mosaic*, 6 (Fal
    1972), 240.

39. Conquest, *New Lines 2*, p. xxiv; Wain, *Anthology of Modern Poetry*
    p.17.

40. See Gunn on his euphoric undergraduate days in *My Cambridge*
    ed. Hayman, p. 138: 'One windy Autumn night I was walkin₁
    along Jesus Lane . . . Coming to the corner of Sidney Sussex Stree‹
    I could see my own window above. Friends would shout up at m‹
    from this street corner . . . I noticed that I had left my light on an‹
    found myself imagining that I had called my name aloud and coul‹
    now see my own head stick out of the window above. There wer‹
    times when anything seemed possible.'

41. Holloway, *The Colours of Clarity*, p. 86.

42. 'Four Conversations', p. 77.

43. Davie, *Thomas Hardy and British Poetry*, p. 61; p. 4.

44. 'Philip Larkin Praises the Poetry of Thomas Hardy', *Listener*, 25
    July 1968, p. 111.

45. Peter Ferguson, 'Philip Larkin's *XX Poems*: The Missing Link'‚
    Agenda, 14 (Autumn 1976), 63.

46. Wain uses this phrase in his introduction to *Selected Shorter Poems*
    of Thomas Hardy, Macmillan (London), 1966, p. xiii. Leavis had
    said, in *New Bearings in English Poetry*, p. 49, that Hardy's 'rustic
    stiffness serves as a kind of guarantee of integrity', and one can see
    the influence of this view throughout Wain's introduction, pp. ix–
    xix: 'a village craftsman', 'a certain stiff deliberation', 'the patience
    and silent strength of an animal', 'peasant's realism', 'a plain man
    struggling to speak awkward truths'. It is a crude and patronizing
    view of Hardy—but the last effect Larkin tries to incorporate into
    his poetry.

47. Graves, quoted approvingly by Enright, *Conspirators and Poets*,
    p. 61.

48. Timms, *Philip Larkin*, p. 82; Anon, 'The State of Poetry', TLS,
    7 March 1958, p. 127.

49. Davie, *A Gathered Church: The Literature of the English Dissenting Interest, 1700–1930*, Routledge and Kegan Paul (London), 1978.
50. Wain *Sprightly Running*. p. 8, and in *Declaration*, ed. Maschler, pp. 91–2.
51. Davie, 'Eliot in One Poet's Life', p. 238; Amis, *What Became of Jane Austen?*, pp. 226–7.
52. Larkin, 'Four Conversations', p.73.
53. Anon, *Listener*, 15 Nov. 1956, p. 809.
54. Wain, letter to *London Magazine*, March 1957, p. 56.
55. Tomlinson, 'The Middlebrow Muse', p. 214.
56. Included in *The Penguin Book of Everyday Verse*, ed. David Wright, Allen Lane (London), 1976, p. 485. Mr Wright's notes suggest the following translation: 'Unsuited to the cloister, I cower with worry; /I look like a fool and — listen to my tale — /Singing high C makes me sigh grievously/And I sit stuttering over a song for a month or more.'
57. Fuller, *A Reader's Guide to W. H. Auden,* Thames and Hudson (London), 1970, p. 217. Had Fuller been concerned with 'Church Going' rather than with 'Not in Baedeker', he might have pointed out that another possible source for it is his father's 'Youth Revisited'. Published in Roy Fuller's 1954 collection, *Counterparts,* this poem describes the poet revisiting with his son a 'tiny church set on the parkland's edge', and noticing its decay:

> I am glad to find the place has marked
> Dramatically my absence. All the roof
> · Has gone, grass flutters on the broken stone,
> A notice says *These walls are dangerous.*
> Through unglazed windows marble monuments
> Are glimpsed like modest spinsters in their baths.
> Bombs or neglect, informants are not sure.
> In any case the church will now decay
> With other luxuries.

cf. Larkin's poem:

> Grass, weedy pavement, brambles, buttress, sky,
>
> A shape less recognizable each week,
> A purpose more obscure.

58. See Timms, *Philip Larkin,* p. 67.
59. Wain, 'A Writer's Prospect', p. 62.

Chapter 6

1. Wain, 'English Poetry: The Immediate Situation', *Sewanee Review*, LXV (1957), 359.
2. Spender, 'New and Healthy', *New Statesman*, 7 July 1956, p. 20.
3. Hartley, 'Poets of the Fifties', *Spectator*, 20 July 1956, p. 101.
4. The offending article was the pseudonymous Dr Aloysius C. Pepper's 'At the Poetry Reading', *Spectator*, 30 Dec. 1955, pp. 887-8. Wain was suspected of writing the article, and, as he explains in a prefatory note to the reprint of 'Samuel Deronda' in *Shenandoah*, 8 (Spring 1957), 3, this added to the affront.
5. Wain, 'New Novels', *Observer*, 29 Jan 1956, p. 9; Waugh, 'Dr Wodehouse and Mr Wain', *Spectator*, 24 Feb. 1956, pp. 243-4.
6. Amis, *What Became of Jane Austen?*, p. 175.
7. Amis, 'The Faces of Maugham', *Listener*, 7 Feb. 1974, p. 168. Maugham's retraction of his earlier view of Amis can be found in the *Sunday Times*, 6 Oct. 1957, p. 26.
8. 'Ted Hughes and *Crow*' (interview with Egbert Fass), *London Magazine*, Jan. 1971, pp. 10-11.
9. A. Alvarez, 'Poetry of the Fifties in England', *International Literary Annual*, ed. Wain, John Calder (London), 1958, p. 99.
10. Anon, 'The Renewing Voice', TLS, 15 April 1960, p. 238.
11. Hobson, 'Two Worlds', *Sunday Times*, 24 June 1956, p. 6.
12. Amis, quoted in *Declaration*, ed. Maschler, pp. 8-9.
13. Amis, *What Became of Jane Austen?*, p. 96. See also Davie's criticism of Wilson, letter to *London Magazine*, Feb. 1957, p. 61.
14. Osborne in *Declaration*, ed. Maschler, p. 65.
15. Johnson, 'Lucky Jim's Political Testament', *New Statesman*, 12 Jan. 1957, p. 36.
16. Amis, *Socialism and the Intellectuals*, p. 11. Significantly, however, Amis did not do so: he recounts how he was soon disillusioned by the speeches at the meeting.
17. Conquest, letters to TLS, 22 March 1957, p. 177, and 5 April 1957, p. 209.
18. Hartley, *A State of England*, p. 69.
19. Amis, *What Became of Jane Austen?*, p. 213.
20. Kettle, 'Some of My Best Friends Are Intellectuals', *Daily Worker*, 12 Feb. 1957, p. 2; 'Amis Replies to Kettle: Capitalism Hasn't "Had" It', ibid., 14 Feb., p. 2.
21. Wain, 'Our Situation', *Encounter*, May 1963, p. 8.
22. Amis, *What Became of Jane Austen?*, p. 217.
23. Amis, 'Poets on Vietnam War', *Review*, No. 18 (April 1968), p. 29; Conquest's contribution, p. 31. They express similar views in

Authors Take Sides on Vietnam, eds. Cecil Woolf and John Bagguley, Peter Owen (London), 1967, pp. 48-9.

24. Davie, 'On Hobbits and Intellectuals', *Encounter,* Oct. 1969, pp. 87-92; Amis, 'A Reply', ibid., Dec. 1969, pp. 94-6; Davie and Amis letters, ibid., March 1970, pp. 95-6.

25. Amis, 'You That Love England', *New World Writing,* No. 16 (Jan.-June 1960), p. 13.

26. Enright, 'The New Pastoral-Comical', *Spectator,* 3 Feb. 1961, pp. 154-5.

27. A. Alvarez, 'Poetry of the Fifties in England', pp. 100-101.

28. Larkin, 'Betjeman en Bloc', *Listen,* 3 (Spring 1959), 19-20. cf. Betjeman's tribute to Larkin's 'deadly and memorable accuracy', 'Common Experiences', *Listener,* 19 March 1964, p. 483.

29. Davie, *Thomas Hardy and British Poetry,* p. 81; Holbrook, *Lost Bearings in English Poetry,* Vision Press (London), 1977, p. 167.

30. Davie, 'Eliot in One Poet's Life', p. 236.

31. Davie, 'On Hobbits and Intellectuals', p. 87.

32. Amis, *What Became of Jane Austen?,* pp. 53-4.

33. Amis, *Lucky Jim's Politics,* Conservative Political Centre Summer School Series no. 410, 1968, p. 17.

34. Wain, *Professing Poetry,* p. 155.

35. Davie, 'Dissent and Individualism', *Proteus,* No. 1 (Nov. 1977), p. 29. Cf. the anti-community bias of his 'Eliot in One Poet's Life', p. 240: 'democracy as it used to be understood in this country more perhaps than in any other, consisted precisely in the right of the householder to slam the door in the face of the Nosey Parker, to tear up the questionnaire and put it in the waste-paper basket, the right *not* to join the Union or the club if he didn't want to . . .'.

36. Davie, 'Views', *Listener,* 10 May 1973, p. 611.

37. Alvarez, 'Poetry of the Fifties in England', p. 97.

38. Davie, Untitled Statement, *Universities Quarterly* 13 (1959), 341-2.

39. 'Speaking of Writing: XIII — Philip Larkin', *Times,* 20 Feb. 1964, p. 16.

40. Amis, 'Anglo-Saxon Platitudes', *Spectator,* 5 April 1957, p. 445.

41. Enright, 'The Sons of Spiders', *The Month,* 8, March 1956, p. 178; Conquest, 'The Critical Forum', *Essays in Criticism,* 8 (1958), 226.

42. Wain, letter to TLS, 28 Sept. 1956, p. 569. Cf. G. S. Fraser, *New World Writing,* Vol. 7, April 1955, p. 106: 'John Wain spends a lot of time these days telling me he is no longer in any real sense a disciple of Empson.' The author 'J. W.' was almost certainly John Willett, who later published a book on Brecht.

43. Wain, 'The Shadow of an Epic', *Spectator,* 11 March 1960, p. 360.

44. Amis uses this phrase in his memoir of Cambridge, 'No More Parades',

What Became of Jane Austen?, p. 197, without saying that it was Leavis who had used it. But Davie in *My Cambridge*, ed. Hayman, p. 92, confirms that he and Holloway were at the Faculty meeting during which Leavis had called Amis a pornographer.

45. Leavis, *English Literature in Our Time and the University*, Chatto and Windus (London), 1969, p. 56.
46. Amis, *What Became of Jane Austen?*, p. 181.
47. Davie, *The Poet in the Imaginary Museum*, p. 152.
48. Davie, 'A Voice in the Desert', TLS, 1 Oct. 1976, p. 1233.
49. Davie, *The Poet in the Imaginary Museum*, p. 74.
50. Tomlinson, 'The Middlebrow Muse', 215.
51. Davie, 'Common and Uncommon Muses', *Twentieth Century*, Nov. 1957, p. 468.
52. Davie, introduction to Tomlinson, *The Necklace*, Fantasy Press (Oxford), 1955; reprinted Oxford University Press (London), 1966, p.xii.
53. Tomlinson, 'The Middlebrow Muse', 213.
54. Davie, *The Poet in the Imaginary Museum*, pp. 43-4.
55. Davie, ibid, p. 48.
56. Holloway, letter to TLS, 27 Sept. 1957, p. 577; Conquest, 'Science Fiction and Literature', *Critical Quarterly*, 5 (1963), 366.
57. See, for example, 'Magdalene', from Davie's 1965 translations of Pasternak, which has a debunking tone towards Christian myth distinctly reminiscent of Amis:

> People spruce themselves for a party.
> Keeping clear of this lot,
> I wash down with balm from a bucket,
> Your feet without spot.

58. Larkin, Notice of 'Rock-Drill', *Guardian*, 26 March 1957, p. 4.
59. Larkin, *All What Jazz*, p. 17. For another strong Movement attack on Pound, see Conquest's 'Ezra Pound', *London Magazine*, April 1963, pp. 33-49.
60. Davie, *The Poet in the Imaginary Museum*, p. 67.
61. See, for example, *Memoirs of a Mendicant Professor*, pp. 23-4 and p. 38.
62. Gunn, 'William Carlos Williams', *Encounter*, July 1965, p. 73.
63. A phrase used in the excellent account of this poem by Martin Dodsworth in his collection of essays *The Survival of Poetry*, pp. 193-215.
64. Davie, *The Poet in the Imaginary Museum*, p. 144.
65. Davie in *The Modern Poet*, ed. Hamilton, p. 174. See also *The Poet in the Imaginary Museum*, p. 109.

66. Wain, 'Dark Forces', *Listener*, 22 Jan. 1976, p. 77.
67. Davie, 'Reason Reversed', *New Statesman*, 4 May 1962, p. 640.
68. Davie, 'John Clare', *New Statesman*, 19 June 1964, p. 964.
69. Larkin, 'Big Victims: Emily Dickinson and Walter de la Mare', *New Statesman*, 13 March 1970, p. 368.

Select Bibliography

Poetry and Fiction

Kingsley Amis

Bright November, Fortune Press (London), 1947.

A Frame of Mind, University of Reading School of Fine Art (Reading), 1953.

Lucky Jim, Gollancz (London), 1954; Penguin (Harmondsworth), 1961.

That Uncertain Feeling, Gollancz (London), 1955; Panther (London), 1975.

A Case of Samples, Gollancz (London), 1956.

I Like It Here, Gollancz (London), 1958; Panther (London), 1975.

Take a Girl Like You, Gollancz (London), 1960; Penguin (Harmondsworth), 1962.

My Enemy's Enemy, Gollancz (London), 1962.

One Fat Englishman, Gollancz (London), 1963; Penguin (Harmondsworth), 1966.

The Anti-Death League, Gollancz (London), 1966; Penguin (Harmondsworth), 1968.

A Look Round the Estate: Poems 1957–1967, Jonathan Cape (London), 1967.

I Want It Now, Jonathan Cape (London), 1968; Panther (London), 1970.

The Green Man, Jonathan Cape (London), 1969; Panther (London), 1971.

Girl, 20, Jonathan Cape (London), 1971; Panther (London), 1973.

Ending Up, Jonathan Cape (London), 1974; Panther (London), 1976.

The Alteration, Jonathan Cape (London), 1977.

Jake's Thing, Hutchinson (London), 1978.

Collected Poems 1944–1979, Hutchinson (London), 1979.

Russian Hide-and-Seek, Hutchinson (London), 1980.

Stanley and the Women, Hutchinson (London), 1984.

Robert Conquest

A World of Difference: A Modern Novel of Science and Imagination, Ward, Lock and Co. (London), 1955.

Poems, Macmillan (London), 1955.
Between Mars and Venus, Hutchinson (London), 1962.
Co-author with Kingsley Amis, *The Egyptologists,* Jonathan Cape (London), 1965.
Arias from a Love Opera and Other Poems, Macmillan (London), 1969.
Forays, Chatto and Windus (London), 1979.

Donald Davie

Brides of Reason, Fantasy Press (Oxford), 1955.
A Winter Talent and Other Poems, Routledge and Kegan Paul (London), 1957.
The Forests of Lithuania, Marvell Press (Hessle), 1959.
A Sequence for Francis Parkman, Marvell Press (Hessle), 1961.
Events and Wisdom: Poems 1957-1963, Routledge and Kegan Paul (London), 1964.
Essex Poems: 1963-1967, Routledge and Kegan Paul (London), 1969.
Six Epistles to Eva Hesse, London Magazine Editions (London), 1970.
Collected Poems 1950-1970, Routledge and Kegan Paul (London), 1972.
The Shires, Routledge and Kegan Paul (London), 1974.
In the Stopping Train and Other Poems, Carcanet (Manchester), 1977.
Three for Water-Music, Carcanet (Manchester), 1981.
Collected Poems 1970-1983, Carcanet (Manchester), 1983.

D. J. Enright

The Laughing Hyena, Routledge and Kegan Paul (London), 1953.
Academic Year, Secker and Warburg (London), 1955.
Bread Rather than Blossoms, Secker and Warburg (London), 1956.
Heaven Knows Where, Secker and Warburg (London), 1957.
Insufficient Poppy, Chatto and Windus (London), 1960.
Some Men Are Brothers, Chatto and Windus (London), 1960.
Addictions, Chatto and Windus (London), 1962.
Figures of Speech, Heinemann (London), 1965.
The Old Adam, Chatto and Windus (London), 1965.
Selected Poems, Chatto and Windus (London), 1968.
Unlawful Assembly, Chatto and Windus (London), 1968.
Daughters of Earth, Chatto and Windus (London), 1972.
The Terrible Shears: Scenes from a Twenties Childhood, Chatto and Windus (London), 1973.
Sad Ires, Chatto and Windus (London), 1975.
Paradise Illustrated, Chatto and Windus (London), 1978.
A Faust Book, Oxford University Press (Oxford), 1979.
Collected Poems, Oxford University Press (Oxford), 1981.
Instant Chronicles: A Life, Oxford University Press (Oxford), 1985.

Thom Gunn

Fighting Terms, Fantasy Press (Oxford), 1954; Faber and Faber (revised ed.) (London), 1962; 1970.
The Sense of Movement, Faber and Faber (London), 1957; 1968.
My Sad Captains, Faber and Faber (London), 1961; 1974.
Positives: Verses by Thom Gunn, Photographs by Ander Gunn, Faber and Faber (London), 1966; 1973.
Touch, Faber and Faber (London), 1967; 1974.
Moly, Faber and Faber (London), 1971.
Jack Straw's Castle, Faber and Faber (London), 1976.
Selected Poems 1950–1975, Faber and Faber (London), 1979.
The Passages of Joy, Faber and Faber (London), 1982.

John Holloway

The Minute and Longer Poems, Marvell Press (Hessle), 1956.
The Fugue and Shorter Pieces, Routledge and Kegan Paul (London), 1960.
The Landfallers, Routledge and Kegan Paul (London), 1962.
Wood and Windfall, Routledge and Kegan Paul (London), 1965.
Planet of Winds, Routledge and Kegan Paul (London), 1977.

Elizabeth Jennings

Poems, Fantasy Press (Oxford), 1953.
A Way of Looking, André Deutsch (London), 1955.
A Sense of the World, André Deutsch (London), 1958.
Song for a Birth or a Death, André Deutsch (London), 1961.
Recoveries, André Deutsch (London), 1964.
The Mind Has Mountains, Macmillan (London), 1966.
Collected Poems, 1967, Macmillan (London), 1967.
The Animals' Arrival, Macmillan (London), 1969.
Lucidities, Macmillan (London), 1970.
Relationships, Macmillan (London), 1972.
Growing-Points, Carcanet (Manchester), 1975.
Consequently I Rejoice, Carcanet (Manchester), 1977.
Moments of Grace, Carcanet (Manchester), 1979.
Selected Poems, Carcanet (Manchester), 1979.
Celebration and Elegies, Carcanet (Manchester), 1982.

Philip Larkin

The North Ship, Fortune Press (London), 1945; 2nd ed. with introduction, Faber and Faber (London), 1966; 1973.
Jill, Fortune Press (London), 1946; 2nd ed. with introduction, Faber and Faber (London), 1964; 1975.

A Girl in Winter, Faber and Faber (London), 1947; 1975.
XX Poems, privately printed in limited edition of 100 (Belfast), 1951.
The Less Deceived, Marvell Press (Hessle), 1955; 1973.
The Whitsun Weddings, Faber and Faber (London), 1964; 1971.
High Windows, Faber and Faber (London), 1974.

John Wain

Mixed Feelings, University of Reading School of Fine Art (Reading), 1951.
Hurry on Down, Secker and Warburg (London), 1953; reissue with new introduction, 1978.
Living in the Present, Secker and Warburg (London), 1955.
A Word Carved on a Sill, Routledge and Kegan Paul (London), 1956.
The Contenders, Macmillan (London) 1958; Penguin (Harmondsworth), 1962.
A Travelling Woman, Macmillan (London), 1959.
Nuncle and Other Stories, Macmillan (London), 1960.
Weep Before God, Macmillan (London), 1961.
Strike the Father Dead, Macmillan (London), 1962.
Wildtrack, Macmillan (London), 1965.
Letters to Five Artists, Macmillan (London), 1969.
A Winter in the Hills, Macmillan (London), 1970.
Feng, Macmillan (London), 1975.
Poems 1949–1979, Macmillan (London), 1981.

Criticism (including Movement essays, reviews, autobiography, anthologies, and political statements)

Kingsley Amis

(Co-editor with James Michie) *Oxford Poetry 1949,* Basil Blackwell (Oxford), 1949.
'The Critical Forum' Emily-Coloured Primulas', *Essays in Criticism,* 2 (1952), 342–5.
'Ulster Bull: The Case of W. R. Rodgers', *Essays in Criticism,* 3 (1953), 470–5.
Socialism and the Intellectuals, Fabian Tract No. 304, Fabian Society (London), 1957.
'That Certain Revulsion', *Encore,* 3 (June–July 1957), 10–12.
Lucky Jim's Politics, Conservative Political Centre Summer School Studies Series, No. 410 (London), 1968.
What Became of Jane Austen? And Other Questions, Jonathan Cape (London), 1970; Panther (London), 1972.

Robert Conquest

(ed.) *New Lines*, Macmillan (London), 1956.

'The Critical Forum: New Critics and New Lines', *Essays in Criticism*, 8 (1958), 225–7.

(ed.) *New Lines 2*, Macmillan (London), 1963.

'Profile: Robert Conquest Discusses Kingsley Amis . . .', *Listener*, 9 Oct. 1969, pp. 485–6.

The Abomination of Moab, Maurice Temple Smith (London), 1979.

Donald Davie

Purity of Diction in English Verse, Chatto and Windus (London), 1952; reissue with postscript, Routledge and Kegan Paul (London), 1967.

'Is There a London Literary Racket?', *Twentieth Century*, June 1954, pp. 540–6.

Articulate Energy: An Enquiry into the Syntax of English Poetry, Routledge and Kegan Paul (London), 1955.

'Augustans New and Old', *Twentieth Century*, Nov. 1955, pp. 464–75.

'A. Alvarez and Donald Davie: A Discussion', *The Review*, No. 1 (April–May 1962), pp. 10–25.

Ezra Pound: Poet as Sculptor, Routledge and Kegan Paul (London), 1965.

'Eliot in One Poet's Life', *Mosaic*, 6 (Fall 1972), 229–41.

Thomas Hardy and British Poetry, Routledge and Kegan Paul (London), 1973.

'Larkin's Choice', *Listener*, 29 March 1973, pp. 420–1.

'The Varsity Match', Poetry Nation, No. 2 1974, pp. 72–80.

Pound, Fontana (London), 1975.

The Poet in the Imaginary Museum: Essays of Two Decades, ed. Barry Alpert, Carcanet (Manchester), 1977. (This contains an invaluable bibliography.)

A Gathered Church: The Literature of the English Dissenting Interest 1700–1930, Routledge and Kegan Paul (London), 1978.

Trying to Explain, Carcanet (Manchester), 1980.

These the Companions: Recollections, Cambridge University Press (London), 1982.

D. J. Enright

The World of Dew: Aspects of Living Japan, Secker and Warburg (London), 1955.

(ed.) *Poets of the 1950's*, The Kenyusha Press (Tokyo), 1955.

The Apothecary's Shop: Essays on Literature, Secker and Warburg (London), 1957.

Conspirators and Poets, Chatto and Windus (London), 1966.
Memoirs of a Mendicant Professor, Chatto and Windus (London), 1969.
Man Is an Onion, Chatto and Windus (London), 1972.
(ed.) *The Oxford Book of Contemporary Verse 1945-1980*, Oxford University Press (Oxford), 1980.
A Mania for Sentences, Chatto and Windus (London), 1983.
(ed.) *The Oxford Book of Death*, Oxford University Press (Oxford), 1983.
Fair of Speech: The Uses of Euphemism, Oxford University Press (Oxford), 1983.

Thom Gunn

(ed.) *Poetry from Cambridge 1951-52*, Fortune Press (London), 1952.
'A Sense of Movements', *Spectator*, 23 May 1958, p. 661.
'My Suburban Muse', *Worlds: Seven Modern Poets*, ed. Geoffrey Summerfield, Penguin (Harmondsworth), 1974, pp. 58-62.
The Occasions of Poetry: Essays in Criticism and Autobiography, Faber and Faber (London), 1982.

John Holloway

'New Lines in English Poetry', *Hudson Review*, 9 (1956-7), 592-7.
(ed.) *Poems of the Mid-Century*, Harrap and Co. (London), 1957.
The Charted Mirror: Essays, Routledge and Kegan Paul (London), 1960.
The Colours of Clarity: Essays, Routledge and Kegan Paul (London), 1964.
The Lion Hunt: A Pursuit of Poetry and Reality, Routledge and Kegan Paul (London), 1964.
A London Childhood, Routledge and Kegan Paul (London), 1966.
The Establishment of English, Cambridge University Press (London), 1972.
The Proud Knowledge: Poetry, Insight and the Self 1620-1920, Routledge and Kegan Paul (London), 1977.
Narrative and Structure: Explanatory Essays, Cambridge University Press (London), 1979.
The Slumber of Apollo, Cambridge University Press (London), 1983.

Elizabeth Jennings

(ed.) *An Anthology of Modern Verse*, Methuen & Co. (London), 1961.
Poetry Today, 1957-60, Longmans, Green and Co. (London), 1961.
'The Making of a Movement', *Spectator*, 2 Oct. 1964, pp. 446-8.

Philip Larkin

'Not the Place's Fault', *Umbrella*, 1 (Summer 1959), 107–12.
All What Jazz: A Record Diary, 1961–68, Faber and Faber (London),
    1970.
(ed.) *The Oxford Book of Twentieth Century English Verse*, Oxford
    University Press (London), 1973; reprinted with corrections, 1974.
Required Writing: Miscellaneous Pieces 1955–1982, Faber and Faber
    (London), 1983.

John Wain

(ed.) *Interpretations: Essays on Twelve English Poems*, Routledge and
    Kegan Paul (London), 1955; 2nd ed. with additional introduction,
    1972.
Preliminary Essays, Macmillan (London), 1957.
'English Poetry: The Immediate Situation', *Sewanee Review*, 65 (1957),
    353–74.
(ed.) *International Literary Annual Nos. 1 and 2*, John Calder (London),
    1958, 1959.
Sprightly Running: Part of an Autobiography, Macmillan (London),
    1962; reprinted with alterations, 1963; 1965.
Essays on Literature and Ideas, Macmillan (London), 1963.
(ed.) *Anthology of Modern Poetry*, Hutchinson (London), 1963.
'Engagement or Withdrawal: Some Notes on the Work of Philip Larkin',
    Critical Quarterly, 7 (1964), 167–78.
A House for the Truth, Macmillan (London), 1972.
Professing Poetry, Macmillan (London), 1977.

Books referring to the Movement (*contains useful bibliography)

Allsop, Kenneth, *The Angry Decade,* Peter Owen (London), 1958.
Bedient, Calvin, *Eight Contemporary Poets*, Oxford University Press
    (London), 1974.
Bergonzi, Bernard, *The Situation of the Novel*, Macmillan (London),
    1970: Pelican (Harmondsworth), 1972.
Dekker, George (ed.), *Donald Davie and the Responsibilities of Litera-
    ture*, Carcanet (Manchester), 1983.
Dodsworth, Martin (ed.), *The Survival of Poetry,* Faber and Faber
    (London), 1970*
Fraser, G. S., *The Modern Writer and His World,* Derek Verschoyle
    (London), 1963; revised ed. Pelican (Harmondsworth), 1964;
    reprinted with epilogue, 1970.

Green, Martin, *A Mirror for Anglo-Saxons,* Longmans and Co. (London), 1961.

Hamilton, Ian, *A Poetry Chronicle: Essays and Reviews,* Faber and Faber (London), 1973.

— (ed.) *The Modern Poet: Essays from the Review,* Macdonald (London), 1968.

Hartley, Anthony, *A State of England,* Hutchinson (London), 1963.

Hewison, Robert, *In Anger: Culture in the Cold War 1945-60,* Weidenfeld (London), 1981.

Homberger, Eric, *The Art of the Real: Poetry in England and America Since 1939,* Dent (London), 1977.*

Lodge, David, *The Modes of Modern Writing: Metaphor, Metonymy, and the Typology of Modern Literature,* Edward Arnold (London), 1977.

Mander, John, *The Writer and Commitment,* Secker and Warburg (London), 1961.

Motion, Andrew, *Philip Larkin,* Methuen & Co. (London), 1982.

O'Connor, William Van, *The New University Wits and the End of Modernism,* Carbondale: Southern Illinois University Press, 1963.

Press, John, *A Map of Modern English Verse,* Oxford University Press (London), 1969; reprinted with corrections, 1971.*

— *Rule and Energy: Trends in British Poetry Since the Second World War,* Oxford University Press (London), 1963.

Raban, Jonathan, *The Society of the Poem,* Harrap (London), 1971.

Rabinovitz, Rubin, *The Reaction Against Experiment in the English Novel, 1950-60,* Columbia University Press (New York), 1967.*

Rosenthal, M. L., *The New Poets: American and British Poetry Since World War II,* Oxford University Press (London), 1967.

Thurley, Geoffrey, *The Ironic Harvest: English Poetry in the Twentieth Century,* Edward Arnold (London), 1974.

Thwaite, Anthony (ed.), *Larkin at Sixty,* Faber and Faber (London), 1982.

Timms, David, *Philip Larkin,* Oliver and Boyd (Edinburgh), 1973.*

Walsh, William, *D. J. Enright: Poet of Humanism,* Cambridge University Press (London), 1974.*

Contemporary Comment on the Movement, 1950-9

Allen, Walter, 'New Novels', *New Statesman,* 30 Jan. 1954, p. 136.

Anon, 'Four Young Poets', *Times Educational Supplement,* 3 July-3 August 1956, pp. 933, 957, 995. (Larkin, Wain, Gunn).

Bateson, F. W., 'Auden's (and Empson's) Heirs', *Essays in Criticism,* 6 (1957), 79-80.

Delta, No. 8 (Spring 1956) and No. 10 (Autumn 1956), special issue on the Movement.

Fiedler, Leslie, 'The Un-Angry Young Men', *Encounter*, Jan. 1958, pp. 3–12.

Gorer, Geoffrey, 'The Perils of Hypergamy', *New Statesman*, 4 May 1957, pp. 566–8.

Hartley, Anthony, 'Critic Between the Lines', *Spectator*, 8 Jan. 1954, p. 47.

— 'Poets of the Fifties', *Spectator*, 27 Aug. 1954, pp. 260–1.

Hurrell, John D., 'Class and Conscience in John Braine and Kingsley Amis', *Critique*, 2 (Spring–Summer 1958), 39–53;

Lehmann, John, 'The Wain-Larkin Myth: A Reply to John Wain', *Sewanee Review*, 1958, pp. 578–87.

Shils, Edward, 'The Intellectuals — I: Great Britain', *Encounter*, April 1955, pp. 5–16.

Spender, Stephen, 'On Literary Movements', *Encounter*, Nov. 1953, pp. 66–8.

Tomlinson, Charles, 'The Middlebrow Muse', *Essays in Criticism*, 7 (1957), 208–17.

Essays, Reviews, Interviews from 1960 onwards

Anon, 'Speaking of Writing XIII: Philip Larkin', *Times*, 20 Feb. 1964, p. 16.

— 'The Art of Fiction — LIX: Interview with Kingsley Amis', *Paris Review*, 6 (Winter 1975), 39–72.

Bergonzi, Bernard, 'After the "Movement": English Poetry Today', *Listener*, 24 Aug. 1961, pp. 284–5.

— 'Critical Situations: From the Fifties to the Seventies', *Critical Quarterly*, 15 (1973), 59–73.

Bragg, Melvyn, 'Kingsley Amis Looks Back', *Listener*, 20 Feb. 1975, pp. 240–1.

Dekker, George, 'Donald Davie: New and Divergent Lines in English Poetry', *Agenda*, 14 (Summer 1976), 45–57.

Dodsworth, Martin, 'Donald Davie', Agenda, 14 (Summer 1976), 15–32. Reprinted in Unit 31 of Open University Twentieth Century Poetry Course, Open University Course (Milton Keynes), 1976, pp. 5–23.

Falck, Colin, 'Essential Beauty', (Larkin), *Review*, No. 14 (Dec. 1964), pp. 3–11.

— 'Opinion: Poetry and Ordinariness', *New Review*, April 1974, pp. 37–42.

Haffenden, John, *Viewpoints: Poets in Conversation* (Larkin and Gunn), Faber and Faber (London), 1981.

Hamilton, Ian, 'Four Conversations: Thom Gunn', *London Magazine*,

Nov. 1964, pp. 64–70.
—— 'Four Conversations: Philip Larkin', *London Magazine*, Nov. 1964, pp. 71–7.
Hobsbaum, Philip, 'The Road Not Taken', *Listener*, 23 Nov. 1961, 860–3.
James, Clive, 'Kingsley Amis: A Profile', *New Review*, July 1974, pp. 21–8.
Phoenix, 11–12, Special 'Philip Larkin Issue', Autumn–Winter, 1973–4.
Scobie, W.I., 'Gunn in America', *London Magazine*, Dec. 1977, pp. 5–15.
Scott, J. D., 'A Chip of Literary History', *Spectator*, 16 April 1977, p. 20.
Swigg, Richard, 'Descending to the Commonplace', *P. N. Review*, No. 2 (1977), pp. 3–13.
Swinden, Patrick, 'English Poetry', *The Twentieth Century Mind: Vol. 3, 1945-65*, ed. C. B. Cox and A. E. Dyson, Oxford University Press (London), 1972, pp. 386–413.
—— 'Old Lines, New Lines: The Movement Ten Years After', *Critical Quarterly*, 9 (1967), 347–59.
Thwaite, Anthony, 'A Great Parade of Single Poems: Philip Larkin . . . Discusses His Oxford Book of Twentieth Century English Verse', *Listener*, 12 April 1973, pp. 472–4.

Other relevant works

Abse, Dannie and Sergeant, Howard, *Mavericks*, Poetry and Poverty (London), 1957.
Alvarez, A., (ed.) *The New Poetry*, Penguin (Harmondsworth), 1962; revised, 1966.
Bradbury, Malcolm, *Eating People Is Wrong*, Secker and Warburg (London), 1959; reissue with new introduction, 1978.
Braine, John, *Room at the Top*, Eyre and Spottiswoode (London), 1957; Penguin (Harmondsworth), 1959.
Cooper, William, *Scenes from Provincial Life*, Jonathan Cape (London), 1950; Penguin (Harmondsworth), 1961.
Fraser, G. S. and Fletcher, Ian (ed.) *Springtime*, Peter Owen (London), 1953.
Hayman, Ronald (ed.) *My Cambridge*, Robson Books (London), 1977.
Maschler, Tom (ed.) *Declaration*, MacGibbon and Kee (London), 1957.
Miller, Karl (ed.) *Writing in England Today: The Last Fifteen Years*, Penguin (Harmondsworth), 1968.
Murdoch, Iris, *Under the Net*, Chatto and Windus (London), 1954.
Osborne, John, *Look Back in Anger*, Faber and Faber (London), 1957; 1960.
—— *The Entertainer*, Faber and Faber (London), 1957; 1961.
Scott, George, *Time and Place*, Staples Press (London), 1956.

Index